89601

381.81

Beat the Competition!

Beat the Competition!

How to Use Competitive Intelligence to Develop Winning Business Strategies

Ian Gordon

Basil Blackwell

First published 1989

Basil Blackwell Ltd
108 Cowley Road, Oxford, OX4 1JF, UK

Basil Blackwell Inc.
3 Cambridge Center
Cambridge, Massachusetts 02142, USA

British Library Cataloguing in Publication Data

A CIP catalogue record for this book is available
from the British Library.

Library of Congress Cataloging in Publication Data

Gordon, Ian.
    Beat the competition! How to use competitive
intelligence to develop winning business strategies / Ian Gordon.
        p.   cm.
    Bibliography: p.
    ISBN 0-631-15991-6
    1. Business intelligence.   2. Competition.   I. Title.
HD38.7.G67   1989
658.4'7--dc19
                                                        89-92
                                                        CIP

Typeset in 10 on 12 pt Palatino by P & R Typesetters Ltd, Salisbury, Wiltshire
Printed in Great Britain by T.J. Press Ltd, Padstow, Cornwall

For Louis and Gladys Gordon

Contents

Preface

Many companies report that coping with increasingly intense competition is their number-one concern. This book is about how to beat the competition. Ethically. Intelligently.

In a few decades, the orientation of the global economy has shifted its focus from production to selling, then to marketing and, today, to a marketplace where competition is the predominant factor. Companies can now no longer rely on market growth to propel their sales and profits to higher levels. They must gain market share at the expense of competitors and prevent their enemies from raiding their own positions. Competition thus should be the central focus of business strategy in today's environment. The informal, ad hoc approach to competition in general, and information gathering in particular, is no longer adequate for success in today's crowded and aggressive marketplace. This book presents the approach required now: systematized and organized for winning at the expense of competitors in the 'zero sum game', in which someone must lose if another is to win. Issues covered include:

- determining current and future competitors, and which ones to analyze

- developing a competitive intelligence system

- understanding which data sources are available for ethical and legitimate use

- establishing who should gather what information and how it should be analyzed

- examining competitors' strategies

- anticipating competitors' activities, initiating competitive thrusts and finding new ways to achieve a competitive advantage

- focusing resources so that minimal additional manpower or effort is required to undertake these tasks.

This book will assist those managers and executives who wish to:

- penetrate their existing markets profitably by understanding the nature of competitive activity and the strategies of specific market participants

- assess competition in new markets into which they are considering entry

- examine acquisition candidates prior to formally approaching them.

The principles described can be applied not only by goods and service producers, but by not-for-profit organizations (such as charities competing for donators), by national, regional and local governments (for example, in attracting business), by educational institutions competing for students and grants, by hospitals seeking more patients and doctors – essentially by any organization competing to attract scarce resources.

Until now, there has been a shortfall in the business literature. Academics have provided frameworks for understanding the factors that drive business profitability in competitive markets. Librarians and researchers have identified information sources. There has not been a sufficiently workable, comprehensive, integrated approach to gathering and analyzing competitive information and using it for strategic and tactical advantage. This book is written by a consultant who has employed several practical techniques to assist clients in achieving competitively superior profits and market positions. He details how data can be assembled, piece by piece, from publicly available sources – which makes the intelligence operation quite ethical – and provides insight about the best information sources, how to use them and how to organize the information obtained for the most strategic impact. The book concludes by discussing approaches to achieving a lasting competitive edge.

About the Author

Ian Gordon is a management consultant with over 14 years of strategic planning and marketing experience. He pioneered the discipline of competitive intelligence and has conducted numerous strategic competitive intelligence assignments for world-scale clients in diverse industries. His work includes assisting companies in increasing their market penetration by analyzing competitors' strategies, examining competitors' positioning with customers and middlemen, gathering the information necessary to help win competitive bids, assessing acquisition candidates, implementing competitive intelligence systems and conducting other assignments which are based on the material presented in this book.

His client list includes four of the ten largest firms in North America. He has instructed over half the Fortune 500 firms in the use of competitive intelligence in the course of conducting executive briefings on behalf of Business Week Executive Programs and has assisted several hundred companies in Europe and Japan.

He has documented his views in over 20 articles published in leading North American magazines. He is a Professional Electrical Engineer, has an MBA, is Past-President of the Industrial Marketing and Research Association of Canada, and lectures marketing to undergraduate and MBA students at York University in Toronto, Canada.

Ian Gordon is a Partner with the Marketing and Economics Group in the Toronto office of Woods Gordon Management Consultants, one of the largest and longest established consulting organizations in North America. Woods Gordon is a sister firm of Canada's leading accounting firm, Clarkson Gordon, and a member of the 30,800-employee Arthur Young International network, with audit and consulting offices in 409 cities and 74 countries.

Acknowledgements

The author would like to thank the clients who worked with him to achieve competitive superiority by employing the principles upon which this book is based. Your investment of time, money and effort has ultimately made this book possible. Your friendship has provided even more return.

He also wishes to acknowledge the contributions of the management consultants at Woods Gordon whose guidance and insight make this firm a great environment for achievement.

He appreciates his wonderful wife, Joanne, for her warm support and encouragement.

1 Introduction

- The evolution of the competitive era

- Characteristics of today's competitive markets

- Needed: a new way of thinking about competition

- Definitions

- The relationship between market share and profitability

- The relationship between competitive intelligence and marketing and strategic planning

- Customers' needs – the key battleground

- Information for a competitive advantage

- Shadow marketing

- Keeping practices ethical – competitive intelligence vs industrial espionage

Managers usually consider competition to be an uncontrollable element of their business environment, like social, legal, economic, cultural and regulatory issues. Intense competitive pressure is now causing many to challenge this basic assumption. Companies are finding that, although they have always had an informal eye on the competition, a formal approach to gathering and analyzing competitive information can improve strategy development and even yield short-term benefits, such as advance knowledge of new product introductions and price changes. Executives, once wary of the legal or ethical implications of obtaining such information, now appreciate that competitive intelligence indeed can be conducted in a forthright manner.

This, then, is the reason behind this book – to make the reader aware of perfectly legitimate ways to enhance the long-term value of a company by focusing on competition. Although the orientation of this book is towards competition among businesses, the approaches which are described could equally well apply to all forms of competition, such as partnerships, not-for-profit institutions, trade associations, unions and even countries. For example, I am aware of one Canadian province using the ideas presented here to attract businesses from other regions of North America. Concepts such as these are used by countries to compete for funds in a global marketplace. Increasingly charities, art galleries, theaters and unions are competing for various forms of 'market share'. The principles thus have general applicability, but the primary focus will be on helping increase the net present value of a for-profit business enterprise. (Net present value is the discounted value of projected cash flows, less current investment and other expenditures that must be made to realize the potential cash flows.)

For firms trying to grow in hostile industries, the main challenge is how to gain market share at the expense of competitors. Because most markets are maturing, companies must increase the size of their slice of the pie if they want to grow. Market growth alone may not propel them to the level of sales and profit growth for which their business plans call. Certainly there are some growth markets, but the competition there is usually no less intense than elsewhere because of the large numbers of firms that are often attracted. The outlook for the business environment presents the prospect of even more intense competition, so it is vital that those firms seeking a long-term market presence appreciate the significance of transferring market share from their competitors. Those that do not could become tomorrow's casualties.

The challenge to increase market share implies that companies should have a competitor orientation as well as a customer focus – perhaps it should be given even greater emphasis, for reasons that will be discussed. However, many companies are still trying to reorient from a production or selling orientation to a market driven one. These firms would do well to accelerate their progress in order to be ready sooner for the next stage of evolution for their firms – from being an exclusively market driven company to becoming a competitor oriented *and* market driven company. Those executives whose firms are already largely directed by their primary stakeholders – their customers – should be planning a transition to a more competitive enterprise. The principal focus of this reorientation will be the competitive intelligence and strategy development functions, which –

particularly in the case of competitive intelligence – will need to be formalized and systematized in accordance with clearly defined responsibilities, timing and outputs.

Executives beginning to adopt a more organized approach to competitor analysis need not be concerned that this approach will be just another 'flavour of the month', like so many of the grids, graphs, matrices and other theoretical approaches with limited practical application that are introduced with much fanfare, only to be discarded when they are shown to have modest value in the real world. Unlike some of these approaches, competitive intelligence is grounded in reality – in what is going on in the marketplace, what will be happening in the marketplace, and what needs to be done to ensure that the aggressive company increases the percentage of transactions directed in its favour.

A survey of senior executives in 1,000 large companies conducted by Woods Gordon Management Consultants in Canada has found that their major problem is coping with competitors. Many executives feel that their businesses are now more competitive than they have ever been, and they are seeking an ethical, legitimate and structured way to understand competitors' strategic direction. Two-thirds of them said they were currently unhappy with the ways in which they improve their competitiveness. Woods Gordon's client experience with firms of different sizes in countries around the world suggests that companies in most major industrialized countries are facing the same problem: how to improve profitability in the face of competitive forces that work against profit growth. This book presents a formal, structured, strategic approach to competitor examination that can lead to the development of a sustainable, profitable competitive edge.

1.1 The Evolution of the Competitive Era

Industrialized economies are facing declining population growth and a slowing rate of GNP expansion. Examining long-term real rates of growth in GNP over the past three decades reveals a similar downward trend in virtually all Western countries – although there have been short-term departures from this, as with the commercialization of North Sea oil in the UK, and economic growth in the US, Canada and elsewhere stemming from large budgetary deficits.

Even though long-term trends in GNP indicate a slowing of industrial growth, some decades have seen market expansion more consistently than have others. In the 1960s, many companies benefited from fairly consistent GNP growth which enabled sales and profitability to soar in tandem with market growth. The 1960s witnessed the emergence of the conglomerate and diversified portfolio of business units as companies sought to participate in many markets, anticipating that their mere presence would enable them to benefit from widespread growth. In the 1970s, the oil-induced recession led companies to challenge the wisdom of a strategy that relied solely on market expansion. They now recognized that the game was not simply a matter of gaining a slice of a market pie and watching the overall growth of all pies increase their sales and profits. Their focus changed to improving gross margins, often through the focusing that comes with the rationing and efficient allocation of scarce resources. This led some firms to return to the basic core of their businesses, a trend that has accelerated in the 1980s.

Today, the goal of business should be to transfer market share profitability from competitors. A company can accomplish this by improving its position in the minds of its key stakeholders – including customers intermediaries, employees, bankers, suppliers and stockholders. This is the territory from which the company – like a country at war – should be seeking to rid the competitor.

1.2   Characteristics of Today's Competitive Markets

Competition in today's markets is characterized by the ten trends discussed in the following subsections.

Maturing Markets

Weak GNP expansion in many countries, as noted above, has led to slowing rates of market growth. This maturing has led to intensified competition for the sales that remain. While there are obvious exceptions, such as in electronic technologies and biotechnology, these areas tend rapidly to attract new market entrants eager to find greener pastures, making it difficult for such companies to achieve profit targets even in the growth phase of the industry life cycle, which is usually the most profitable.

Supplier Proliferation

Companies participating in large markets are also experiencing market share pressures as new entrants from abroad and new start-ups attempt to seize their market positions. Deregulation of some industries is also increasing the number of market participants. Proliferation of suppliers and their investment brings associated overcapacity in the industry – a major restriction on long-term profit growth. Companies seeking to improve their own and overall industry profitability should do their utmost to discourage competitors from investing in their industries.

Mature Infrastructure

Because Western countries already have much of the infrastructure in place to provide for the basic requirements of industrialized societies, future projects either will be on a very grand scale (such as the Eurotunnel) or will address specialized requirements (such as the infrastructure necessary for cellular telephones). The outlook is for less building of new establishments or sites of various kinds, and more refurbishing of what already exists. This will shift emphasis away from new installations to retro-fit and replacement of the present installed base of equipment and infrastructure. This is an altogether more competitive proposition, because the competition is not only the competitive vendor, but the currently existing equipment. Often this still has considerable useful life left, may not be fully depreciated, and may not yet have paid out its investment – all of which serve as competitive barriers to adoption.

Globalization of Investments and Markets

World trade and cross-border investment are increasing dramatically, and both are now often coming from non-traditional sources – such as vehicles from Taiwan and Korea, and investment dollars from countries without a promising economic, market or political outlook (such as Hong Kong) or where success has raised the value of their currencies to uncompetitive levels (as is the case in Japan). For instance, US investment in Canada has long been a part of the Canadian economy and psyche, but Canadian investment in the US has grown sevenfold in the last ten years, and is now over half the cumulative US investment in Canada.

The main competitive implication is that firms must frequently compete on a global or international scale to survive. Multiple market participation through diversified production operations means that currency exchange rate changes may no longer serve to weaken aggressive international competitors and should not be relied upon to restore the competitiveness of individual firms. Globalization of markets and investments may bring with it economies of scale, scope and knowledge that are not available to firms competing on a more modest scale. The outlook for many firms will be to discover or rediscover their international markets, or risk erosion of their sales volume both abroad *and in domestic markets*. There thus may be no alternative to supplying global, or at least international, markets –

particularly for mass market participation, but increasingly for maintaining market niches.

Market Fragmentation

Those firms unable to compete in mass markets are looking to smaller and smaller niches to find profitable, tenable market positions. Some companies are finding that, no matter how small their targeted market segments, competitors are able to serve yet smaller opportunities. Technology is assisting them; intelligent production, assembly and distribution operations enable them to supply niches at close to the same cost as mass markets. Indeed, some major firms have begun to address the ultimate market niche – the individual – by offering customized products and services. Examples include General Electric's electric meter business, and the farm equipment made by John Deere.

Market fragmentation has been aided by media fragmentation: now messages can be economically tailored to smaller markets. But the large number of advertisers makes it more and more difficult to 'cut through the clutter' of competitive advertising, even with more channels available for advertising.

Mobile Production

For firms seeking cost leadership positions, production is becoming increasingly mobile as companies search for the right balance of cost structure and management lines of communication. Some firms that went to developing countries in a quest for lower labor assembly costs are now repatriating production to domestic markets as new technology has become available to provide an equivalent delivered cost without incurring the aggravation entailed by lengthy plane journeys, misplaced or delayed shipments, and communication across multiple time zones. One example is the adoption of surface mount device technology which automatically populates printed circuit boards with electronic components and limits the need for off-shore suppliers to provide the more labor-intensive services usually required for leaded, through-the-board technology.

With lower cost positions comes the temptation for many firms to compete on price, which undermines the very benefit that going abroad sought to achieve.

Adoption of Advanced Technologies

By seeking improved competitive positions through adoption of advanced technologies, companies are increasing the fixed costs of their operations. As a result, they need a higher minimum level of plant throughput to cover the fixed investment, and this is leading to intense price competition in many markets. If advanced technologies do not bring with them an associated improvement in product or market differentiation, and the possibility that this can be sustained, then their adoption should be considered primarily because there is little alternative to remain at parity with competitors. This was the case when AT & T and GTE followed Northern Telecom in making their central office switches fully digital.

Short Life of Technological Monopolies

The 'window of opportunity' available to companies producing novel products is now shorter than ever, even in industries where technological leadership used to guarantee some respite from competition. Now companies must make back their investment rapidly before their monopoly position is eliminated by new market entrants. Differentiation on the basis of a single new technology is often useless — duplication of the benefits delivered by innovation usually follows the gathering of detailed information on 70 per cent of new products within a year of their development.*

The short life of technological monopolies poses pricing problems. Is one to skim the market at the outset, looking for the fastest payback, only to risk long-term market participation when a new entrant launches a lower priced entry? — as was the case when Hewlett Packart lost its early lead in the calculator market. Is penetration pricing more appropriate to deter competitive product introductions? But what of the forgone profits if a new entry arrives nevertheless, which has occurred in numerous segments of the consumer electronics industry? Pricing in an intensely competitive environment, as for all other aspects of strategy, requires thorough application of the principles in this book.

Vendors with Significant Resources

A company may well have talented, hard-working and capable management and staff, good morale, productive and new equipment, advanced technology, access to 'deep pockets' and a well-conceived marketing mix. Unfortunately, this may not cause a company to differ much from its competitors. Many companies now enjoy these attributes, making competitive success harder to achieve. Only by understanding where to apply the resources that will

---

* E. Mansfield, 'How Rapidly Does New Industrial Technology Leak Out?', *Journal of Industrial Economics*, December 1985, p. 217.

make a difference in the minds of both customers and intermediaries can effort be translated into reward.

Differentiation Reduction

The copying of innovation and the application of similarly significant financial, human and technological resources often lead to reduction of differentiation. This has happened in a wide variety of industrial and consumer markets, from numerically controlled machine tools to laundry detergents. Considerable price competition is symptomatic of reduced differentiation – it may even help to create the impression that there are indeed limited competitive differences. A key challenge is efficiently and effectively to restore the perception of differences among alternative choices available to the customer and ensure that one product alone is perceived to be better – yours, of course!

1.3   Needed – a New Way of Thinking about Competition

Executives have been guided by the marketing concept 'identify and satisfy customer needs at a profit' since the 1960s. Among other activities this has led them to research product and market opportunities, reorganize and restructure their firms, acquire and divest companies, enter new markets, introduce new products and modify or enhance their channels of distribution. Although this helped companies achieve respectable growth in the economic environment of that time, now executives are finding that the growth they seek cannot be achieved without a more meaningful recognition of the role of competitors. This means that the informal, casual approaches to analysis and action that have previously characterized competitor assessments must become more structured and analytical.

Many companies have monitored their competitors informally for a long time. They may know something about their competitors' management, their plant locations, products and services. However, executives very infrequently apply their knowledge in an *organized, systematic and formal* manner to achieve a competitive advantage. Instead, they focus their attention on market issues, changing things a little, attending to internal pressures and customers' requirements. In so doing, many are fighting today's wars with yesterday's thinking.

Executives would be better served by guiding themselves according to the 'competitive concept', which may be defined as 'identifying customers' needs that either are not served by competitors, or are inadequately or insufficiently addressed, and then satisfying these needs at a profit or consistently with the organization's objective'. This concept requires that firms explore the competitive battleground – the customer's mind – for relevant needs and the degree to which competitors are satisfying them; that they understand competitors' strategies; and that they develop appropriate winning strategies to counter competitive thrusts and transfer market share profitably from the competitors to their own firms.

This, then, is the principal objective of competitive intelligence and competitor analysis – to develop strategies to transfer market share profitably. All data gathering should be geared to this end. If it is not, such competitive information as is generated will fall into the category of 'nice to know' without having much strategic impact.

The second implication is that examination of competitors should take place principally at the business unit and product line levels, because these are where market share is won or lost; not at the corporate level, which serves primarily as a banking and directional board for the business unit. To this end, corporate examination is, of course, required. In addition, corporate assessments are required to establish the expectations and support of business units and product lines and thus the level of resources available to, and return expected from, the business unit and product line. More about this in chapter 5.6.

1.4 Definitions

Before competitive intelligence is discussed in depth, it is appropriate to review what competitive intelligence means, not only so that the reader and the writer of this book have a common understanding of it, but so that everybody undertaking an aspect of competitive assessment in their organization will be considering their activities from the same perspective. Otherwise, the lack of a common understanding could result in competitive issues being reviewed from a basis of confusion.

- **Competitive data** are uncollated, unorganized and unevaluated input which requires consideration and assessment by individuals working on the competitive intelligence program.

- **Competitive information** is data that have been collated, organized and evaluated to derive insight about the competition.

- **Competitive intelligence** is the work involved in gathering this information. It is the process of obtaining and analyzing publicly available data to develop the information necessary to serve as input to competitive strategy development. When used as a noun, competitive intelligence is the output of the intelligence process, including the development of competitor profiles and analysis of competitors' strategic direction. Why not call this activity *competitor* intelligence, given the focus on competitors? Because the feature of undertaking this activity in the competitor orientation; the benefit is to make the corporation more competitive.

- **Competitive strategy** is the direction, approach and momentum of resource allocation, commitment and deployment, to enhance the net present value of the enterprise – typically by seeking to transfer market share for specific products from competitors to a given firm.

- A **competitor profile** is the report that presents a 'photograph' of the competitor at a particular point in time. It provides an overview of the company, its important product lines, key executives, financial performance and conformance to customers' requirements. It incorporates competitor analysis, analyzing issues such as the company's strengths and weaknesses, areas of vulnerability, strategic direction and resource availability and deployment, for its impact on the firm doing the analysis.

- **Competitive advantage** is the reason the competitive intelligence is undertaken in the first place: to transfer market share consistently and irrevocably, trending towards monopoly.

1.5   The Relationship between Market Share and Profitability

The reader may question the assumption that the objective of competitive intelligence is to transfer market share. Could it not be to improve profitability or return on investment, or to achieve other objectives? Certainly some firms will have their own reasons for conducting competitive intelligence: when acquiring a company, for example. For many, however, market share transfer will be the primary goal. The Profit Impact of Market Strategy (PIMS) has shown that there is a relationship between high market share in a served market and return on investment (ROI). Business units with market share over 50 per cent enjoy a return on investment over three times that of businesses with less than 10 per cent market share.*
Clearly, high market share may be indirectly rather than directly linked to high ROI. Reasons could include the high quality of many products that

---

*R. Buzzell and B. Gale, *The PIMS Principles*, The Free Press, 1987.

have significant market shares, and quality and profitability have been shown to be closely linked. In addition, the economies of scale that high-share businesses enjoy, and the high levels of customer awareness that the number-one brand in a market has, may both serve partially to explain the linkage of share to profitability. Whatever the reason, it is clear that the higher the market share, the greater the likelihood of increased profitability. This is particularly true if market share growth has been accomplished via non-price means – the situation at Ford, where record earnings were achieved after Ford focused on product design and quality in all aspects of its operations and communications ('Quality is Job 1').

High market share is a good thing, but higher market share is even better! When *monopoly* market power is achieved then unregulated organizations could be expected to have dramatic profitability levels. Monopoly power is virtually impossible to achieve in production or indeed in distribution, although some companies have come close to achieving it in both categories. US examples might include Searle's Aspartame brand enzyme sweetener, Hartz pet foods in the supermarket channel and American Hospital Supply's computer linkages to hospitals which give the firm strong distribution for consumables and disposables. Because of the difficulty of achieving a monopoly of production and distribution (partly because of regulatory or anti-trust action), many firms should shift their attention still further downstream – to establishing a monopoly position in the mind of the customer where dominant levels of product awareness, trial and satisfaction could be expected to achieve the market share transfer objective.

1.6   The Relationship between Competitive Intelligence and Marketing and Strategic Planning

Competitive intelligence and market and strategic planning must be co-ordinated. They are not separate activities with different objectives. Competitive intelligence must feed into the market and strategic planning cycles and result in modification to, or confirmation of, an organization's thrust. Thus competitive intelligence should not be regarded as a disjointed, ad hoc activity, but should receive the active support of, and co-operation from, the same individuals conducting product and business planning – typically the line management. Competitive intelligence should not be conducted in response to one apparent competitive threat or opportunity, but on an ongoing basis to achieve a sustainable advantage. Many marketing and strategic plans already pay some attention to competition. Usually this is an afterthought – to show that competition was indeed considered in the generation of the plan. The consideration is often weak, based on informally gathered information which may have been available at the time of document preparation and updates of the previously existing plan. Competitive intelligence should be a *central* component of business planning – ranking on a par with customer knowledge and desired profitability. Business plans should thus be structured to incorporate this insight at an early point of the planning cycle.

The planning cycle in a highly competitive firm might resemble that described in figure 1.1, but should, in particular, involve the development of competitor profiles, market and competitor situation assessments. The process should also allow an organization to anticipate what a competitor might do, both on its own initiative and in response to those of the investigating company. This could be accomplished using 'war games', discussed in chapter 1.9.

The development of competitive profiles, a detailed consideration of competition in the situation analysis, and the undertaking of 'war games' before developing or refining strategy constitute a major departure from typical business planning. A competitor orientation must be incorporated into the planning cycle if business plans are to accord with reality and not simply remain at the level of wishful thinking.

■   To illustrate what happens when competition is overlooked in business planning, consider the case of Texas Instrument's home computer fiasco. Texas Instruments (TI) lost a monumental amount of money because of competitive oversight, or perhaps poor advice, when they slashed prices on their home computer in an attempt to gain market share. They wanted to move down their experience curve to gain a competitive cost advantage. Competitors would not let TI gain market share without a fight, and a price war ensued. This resulted in massive deterioration of industry profitability – including that of TI, who have since exited the business of home computers. This example is not unique to TI. (Indeed, this assessment of TI probably would not hold true today – the firm now has an active competitor orientation.) Virtually every firm that initiates innovation of a price or non-price nature fails to conduct adequate competitive contingency planning.

Competitor orientation involves understanding how competitors are reacting to the issues of the time, including their competition. Much of this insight will come from competitive intelligence, but, as important as this intelligence is, it cannot be regarded as a substitute for all the many aspects of business planning in which organizations are engaged. As shown in figure 1.1, competitive intelligence and other activities feed into competitor analysis, which is one element of several in the development of a relevant business plan. An understanding of competition, customers' and intermediaries' needs, an audit of the industry, firm and environment and an assessment of the expectations of all stakeholders, should guide the required analysis of opportunities, strengths and weaknesses, barriers and threats for the company to address.

1.7 Customers' Needs – the Key Battleground

As noted in chapter 1.1, the goal of business should be to transfer market share profitability from competitors to the firm. This can be accomplished by improving the company's position in the minds of all its key stakeholders –

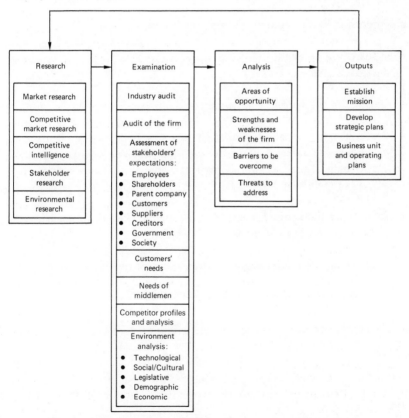

Figure 1.1 Business planning for a competitive edge

including customers, distributors and other intermediaries, employees and suppliers. Of these, customers are by far the most important category. When they vote their money to a particular product or service, they determine which firms will win and which will fail. The central objective of any organization must therefore be the capture and retention of a profitable customer base.

The transfer of market share from competitors to your firm requires a superior understanding of customers' current and emerging needs, and the development of strategies to satisfy customers better than competitors do (their customers) or could (your customers). All the efforts of the company should be directed towards ensuring that customer satisfaction receives the highest possible priority – competitively superior customer satisfaction is king! These efforts should be directed by the sequence of events depicted in figure 1.2.

Customer satisfaction stems from:

- understanding customers' current and emerging needs

- researching competitors' positioning in the minds of customers and intermediaries

- examining the barriers which impede gaining market share

- assessing current and potential threats and opportunities (including technological advances, tariff changes, capital, labor, energy and other input costs, anti-pollution requirements, and other issues which could affect competitiveness)

- identifying the competitors that represent the real enemy from which market share will be gained

- establishing what needs to be known about competitors

- gathering, organizing and analyzing the information

- developing strategies based on your findings

- implementing these strategies in the field to achieve competitively superior customer satisfaction, then tracking your performance in the minds of customers – and so the wheel turns as the process continues.

These issues are discussed in more detail in chapter 2.3.

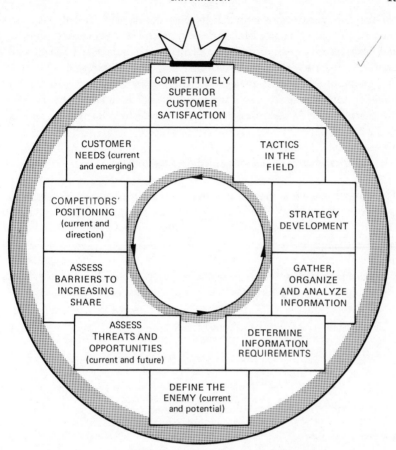

Figure 1.2 The competitive intelligence and strategy wheel

When considering customers' needs, many companies focus principally on the implications of changing needs for the physical product that they provide. Because products often become similar as markets mature, it is important to retain product differentiation by entrenching a process for innovation, thereby ensuring a constant stream of new ideas to keep the products different in a way that customers consider significant.

There are also opportunities to satisfy customers' needs in non-product areas, which has long been a neglected component of the marketing effort of most companies. For example, few suppliers fully appreciate their customers' strategies. They can assist their customers achieve their objectives in areas such as cost reduction, improved efficiency and differentiation of their offerings. To do this, companies should rethink their approaches to service, both before and after the sale. Examples where companies have identified with the strategic requirements of their customers and upgraded service provision include firms in the retail grocery industry and in automotive parts using electronic data interchange (EDI) to expedite customers' orders without paperwork; Procter and Gamble's Direct Product Profitability (DPP) which helps retailers improve their profits; and Scandinavian Airlines' (SAS) program to take off on time, thereby fulfilling the customer's expectation of arriving at the destination when promised.

1.8   Information for a Competitive Advantage

The competitive arena may be described by the three corners of a triangle, representing the firm itself, customers (including intermediaries) and competitors. Each element of the triangle requires thoughtful analysis and thus has its own series of information requirements, as described in figure 1.3: market research between the customers and the organization, competitive market research between the competitors and the customers and competitive intelligence between the firm and competitors.

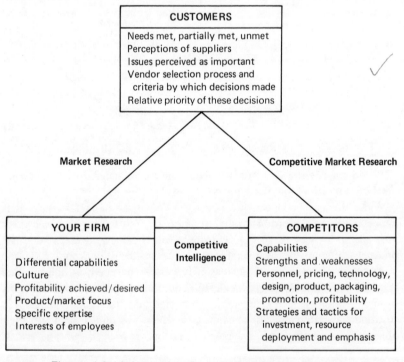

Figure 1.3   Information for a competitive advantage

Many organizations spend much time conducting market research and competitive market research – principally purchase, motivation, attitude and perception studies – to understand two sides of the triangle. Few conduct competitive intelligence and if they do, often they lack an understanding of what data they should gather, why they are obtaining them, and what they plan to do with them once they have them. With much competitor data available, it is a considerable challenge to separate the relevant from the irrelevant and to know where to probe for more depth. Much of this difficulty would be alleviated if analysts recognized that an important aspect of competitive intelligence is the formulation of questions, to which answers can then be sought. Typically, the intelligence gatherers obtain all the information about competitors they can and are then unsure about what is important, what will make a difference to their companies and what to do with what they have obtained.

Before you conduct competitive intelligence, understand the critical success factors in your industry. Your customers and intermediaries should help you define many of these, but the understanding of some is dependent upon an astute examination of industry concentration, scale, scope and economics – including proximity to raw materials or market – and issues such as the availability of a quality labor pool and the process of innovation and commercialization in the industry. Having identified these factors, examine how competitors are positioned in respect of each. This will help in formulating some of the questions to which you do not yet have answers. Others can be identified through the development of a 'shadow marketing plan', discussed next. It is likely that you will find you are able to complete only certain portions of the document, and you feel unsure about some important components of the plan. These gaps and areas requiring verification will help guide the formulation of questions to which your competitive intelligence must seek and find the answers. This is the information you really need.

1.9 Shadow Marketing

If you are to understand your competitors in detail and anticipate their actions, you should begin to think like their key executives. This requires that three tasks be undertaken:

- appointing individuals to profile and 'shadow' major competitors on an ongoing basis

- writing 'shadow marketing plans'

- conducting 'war games'.

Taken together, these tasks may be called 'shadow marketing'.

It is unlikely that most organizations have the necessary resources to examine and track all their competitors in depth, unless the industry is highly concentrated. For most, it is appropriate to list competitors and then make a clear distinction between those that will be monitored and those that will be analyzed – usually a small number, perhaps five or six. The competitors to which most attention should be paid are those that your customers see to be your major competition, which may not necessarily be those your company usually considers.

You should identify five or six employees who will work with you to defeat the competition. Assign one competitor to each. He or she should then become this competitor's 'shadow'. The task of each shadow is to monitor and analyze a key competitor, prevent major unpleasant surprises, prepare its business plans, and recommend changes in direction that capitalize upon that competitor's weaknesses. Over time, shadows should become individuals who begin to think as though they worked for the competitor. Competitors' shadows are discussed in more detail in chapter 2.6.

If you had your competitors' business or marketing plans, you could thwart their direction by putting your advance knowledge to work. Only a demented or unscrupulous operator would hand over their plans to you! But much of the information you need to duplicate competitors' plans is actually available to you from public, perfectly legitimate sources. The competitor's marketing plan that your company could prepare from these sources is called a 'shadow marketing plan'. The person shadowing each competitor should write the marketing plan using the same format you currently adopt for your own plans. The 'shadow marketing plan' is examined in chapter 4.4.

Once the plans are completed and the shadows are familiar with the competitors to which they have been assigned, consider having a 'war game', where the objective is to establish from the shadows what their likely scale and focus of response would be (and hence what those of competitors could be) to your strategic initiatives, and what they might do independently to improve their market position. The output of such a workshop should be modification to your marketing strategies and sub-strategies, such as product, service, price, promotion, distribution, people and technology/R & D, and the development of contingency plans to cover alternative courses of competitive action. See chapter 5.6 for more information regarding 'war gaming'.

1.10 Keeping Practices Ethical – Competitive Intelligence vs Industrial Espionage

If you are to develop superior strategies you will need quality competitive information. The temptation may be to acquire this information from whatever sources are available – including very 'marginal' ones. To draw the line between competitive intelligence and industrial espionage, refer again to the definition of competitive intelligence:

'Competitive intelligence is the process of obtaining and analyzing publicly available data'.

It is the *public* availability of data that distinguishes the two. If anyone could legally gather the data – if they only knew where to look, what to ask and how to ask it without misrepresenting themselves – then the activity can usually be considered legitimate.

I conducted a survey (with elements similar to those of the Wade System of Gradation of Information Sources*) of 175 US executives engaged in competitive intelligence, and found that most will not undertake distinctly unethical practices. As shown in table 1.1, reading published material was considered to be acceptable by virtually everybody, and most of those people in goods producing industries would have considered conducting patent searches. (However, be aware that some companies patent their mistakes as disinformation. Patents should thus be examined principally for their strategic value – showing how and where competitors are committing resources, not the technical specifics of the patent.) Many other areas were seen to be clearly above or below board (for example, no one was prepared to undertake blackmail or extortion to achieve their information objectives!).

However, there are gray areas where the designation 'public availability' is not completely clear and these can differ by country, according to the laws in specific jurisdictions. Discuss any areas of concern with your legal department.

Perhaps the most frequent area of uncertainty is whether or how to debrief former employees of competitors about their competitive knowledge. Approximately 20–30 per cent of respondents seemed unsure of the ethics of specific activities, such as visiting competitors' exhibits at trade fairs without disclosing their full identity, overflying a competitor's plant or hiring former employees of competitors for their special insight.

Although most companies routinely practice ethical behavior in the

*W. Wade, *Industrial Espionage and the Misuse of Trade Secrets*, Advance House, 1965.

Table 1.1   Responses to competitive intelligence questionnaire

Competitive intelligence element	% would do	% would not do
[*Would you ...*]		
Review articles in trade financial press	99	1
Analyze financial reports	98	2
Analyze competitors' advertising strategy, execution, targeting	95	5
Obtain stockbrokers' reports	88	12
Search on-line, third-party computer databases	88	12
Attend trade fairs and competitors' exhibits, stating who you are	88	12
Obtain stock-offering prospectuses	86	14
Review competitors' employee-hiring advertisements	85	15
Hire consultants from major firms, enquiring as to the methods they would use	85	15
Interview suppliers common to your firm and your competitors	81	19
Conduct reverse engineering of competitors' products	79	21
Debrief former employees of competitors	71	29
Visit suppliers working both for you and your competitors to see if unusual activities are taking place	69	31
Conduct patent searches	67	33
Attend trade fairs and visit competitors' exhibits, without disclosing full identity	59	41
Hire specific employees from competitors to gain special insight	44	56
Visit competitors' plants, without revealing the objective of so doing	40	60
Rent a plane to fly over a competitor's new plant to determine size, purpose, techniques to be employed	19	81
Hire consultants without enquiring as to their methods	6	94
Rummage through competitors' garbage	6	94
Remove competitors' plans, diagrams or samples without their permission	4	96
Place false advertisements for hiring employees – interview competitors' staff	3	97
Eavesdrop on competitors (electronically)	1	99

Table 1.1 *continued*

Competitive intelligence element	% would do	% would not do
'Plant' an employee on a competitor's payroll	1	99
Employ blackmail or extortion to achieve information objectives	0	100

conduct of their competitive intelligence, a minority do not feel bound by moral behavior. One executive in a major electronics firm in the US's Silicon Valley justified his attitude as follows: 'I am at war with my competitors. I will do anything at all to beat them. Anything.' He went on to say that he was sure his competitors were analyzing his firm with whatever data they could obtain from all possible sources and that he would have to do the same to remain at least at parity with the 'enemy'. Fortunately the numbers of the group to which this executive belongs seem small. Fewer than 10 per cent of respondents in my survey were prepared to undertake distasteful activities such as rummaging through competitors' garbage and stealing their plans, diagrams or samples. These are the ones to protect against in your own counter-intelligence program! As Kissinger said: 'even paranoids have enemies'!

■ In spite of the fact that virtually all corporations consider their executives to be honorable, there have been significant cases suggesting that not everyone is playing by the same rules. US reports document:

● an attempted exchange of the marketing plans of a toothpaste manufacturer for cash in the men's washroom at J.F. Kennedy airport

● the overflying and photographing of a new petrochemicals plant to determine the design, flow-rates and by-products (advanced photography of the type previously found in the aerospace and spy industries is now in the public domain)

● the alleged overflying and photographing of a new Procter and Gamble cookie manufacturing plant, perhaps to determine plant layout, capacity and technology

- the alleged observation of a competitor snooping through packaging material at a supplier for Procter and Gamble's Duncan Hines cookies

- increased competition for Air Cruisers, a manufacturer of inflatable life rafts, after a competitor obtained design and testing data from a federal authority under the Freedom of Information Act.*

■   Even the most ethical of firms may have unethical employees who can damage the firm's reputation. An attractive female employee of a major aerospace firm told me that she visited a restaurant near a large competitor seeking to gain competitor information. At the end of the day, the competitor's workers entered the restaurant and she engaged an eager man in conversation. After pleasantries, she steered the discussion to her areas of interest, believing she would soon obtain the required information, when the 'competitor' flashed his FBI badge in front of her and asked her to explain her interest in secret information. It took considerable effort to reassure the investigator that she was neither a foreign spy nor undertaking espionage. Fortunately for her and her company she succeeded in convincing her accuser, but the potential was there for the situation to be very damaging. Employees need to be sensitized to the impact of their information-gathering activities, and policies and procedures should reinforce this. My survey suggests that the existence of policy manuals can serve as a deterrent to unethical behavior. Several respondents indicated that they would not undertake obviously wrong activities, not because they were contrary to their moral code, but because company policy forbad them.

While there are some people who have difficulty determining how they might gather the information they need, there are usually people within the organization who will consider any competitive intelligence activity to be unethical or immoral. Usually this stems from a lack of knowledge about competitive intelligence and its dependence on public domain sources. Because it is important to have everyone in an organization 'on side' in the competitive intelligence program, you need to help uncommitted

---

*B. Schorr, 'How law is being used to pry secrets from Uncle Sam's files', *Wall Street Journal*, 9 May 1977, p. 1.

employees appreciate that competitive intelligence is no more unethical than market research, which obtains its information from publicly available sources external to the company; or financial planning, which depends on information from sources within the firm. Competitive intelligence uses both categories of information sources (internal and external) and does not need to depend upon unethical data. All that is needed to obtain a competitive advantage is readily available from a wide variety of legitimate sources. No one needs to crawl through the competitor's plant in the dead of night clutching a flashlight and spy camera! It could well be that most information is available in the public domain – and it is certainly easier to obtain. Even in the super-secret world of intelligence agencies and military and space secrets, there is considerable use of public information. According to Admiral Ellis Zacharias, Deputy Chief of US Naval Intelligence in the Second World War, the US Navy obtained 95 per cent of its intelligence from public sources and only 5 per cent from borderline and secret sources.*

■ Sometimes, public sources and secret sources are used together to obtain the required level of intelligence. A few years ago, an outbreak of a rare form of anthrax in the Soviet Union had the CIA wondering if it was an act of nature or a product of the Soviets' germ warfare experiments. It appears that they reviewed as many local newspapers as they could to see if they could identify widespread and unusual deaths of cattle. Where these were reported, the CIA mapped the locations and the result identified an area roughly approximating a circle, the centre of which was a reputed germ warfare facility. At this point field operators could be sent in to conduct a more detailed analysis, perhaps securing infected animal tissue for examination ... In this instance, the reading of published information was a cheap, low-risk way of defining issues, with greater depth being provided by more expensive and risky on-site investigation. Business can use information in much the same way, except that the local investigation obviously will need to depend upon publicly available information, such as gained through plant tours, interviews and reverse engineering of competitors products (where the design, technology, cost, quality, and assembly process is determined from a close examination of teardown of the product). In the photocopier industry, for example, many recognize the importance of reverse engineering.

* E. M. Zacharias, *Secret Missions: The Story of an Intelligence Officer,* G. P. Putnam's and Sons, 1946, pp. 117–18.

Insiders used to joke that Kodak could always depend on an assured market for at least two of its high-priced photocopiers – one would be bought by Xerox and another by IBM!*

   This chapter has introduced some of the concepts that will be developed in the course of the book. The central theme is that companies need to focus more on their competitors than they have in the past if they are to improve their market and profit positions. This new direction will require better competitive information than most firms have presently. The next chapter considers a procedure for conducting strategic competitive intelligence to provide the necessary information.

* G. Jacobson and J. Hillkirk, *Xerox, American Samurai,* Macmillan, 1986, p. 233.

2 The Process of Competitive Intelligence

- The objective of competitive intelligence

- Defining the competition

- Establishing a roadmap for the process

- Securing management and staff support

- Required budget and resources

- Staffing the competitive intelligence function

- Inputs, outputs and sequence of activities

- Understanding critical success factors for market share transfer

- Understanding your own firm – a necessary first step

Competitive intelligence requires a clear understanding of the strategic context within which the firm is competing. It is not good enough to define the objective of the intelligence operation as 'gathering information on competitors', although this is frequently the reason for undertaking it that many companies articulate. Their main concern seems to be the management of competitive risk: how to make sure that competitors do not do 'something' unforeseen. Such unclear objectives carry with them the seeds of considerable wasted effort, high expense and the possible frustration of those conducting the intelligence.

To succeed with competitive intelligence requires:

- the development of clear objectives for the intelligence operation

- understanding of what constitutes the competition

- that a roadmap for the process is established

- senior management support and a motivated organization

- sufficient budget and focused effort

- that talented employees conduct the intelligence.

2.1 The Objective of Competitive Intelligence

Competitive intelligence should have a single-minded objective – to develop the strategies and tactics necessary to transfer market share profitably and consistently from specific competitors to the company. Some corporations may have other intelligence objectives, such as identifying and analyzing acquisition targets, retaining high market share levels, finding approaches to increase overall industry profitability, gathering 'nice-to-know' information as a security blanket or developing tactical competitor and customer information; but most companies will find the above objective to be appropriate.

This objective requires that a formal process be established for understanding your own company and those of competitors, and then developing strategies and tactics to defeat them. It also means that the company must target specific firms from which it expects to gain market share – essentially deciding which companies will be the losers if it is to win. This makes a departure from conventional strategic thought which often does not consider the source of business if the plans are to be successful. Although what really constitutes the competition at first may seem obvious, defining the competition is often not straightforward.

2.2 Defining the Competition

What is the competition? Is it all the currently existing companies in the market, or a sub-set of them? Could it be that a substitute product or service represents competition, for example plastic siding which is replacing aluminum? Could the competition consist in an alternative use for disposable income? – an important consideration for vendors of large consumer durables or companies competing for business expenditures on capital goods or management services. Is the most severe competitive threat not from current competitors but new start-ups, companies diversifying or forward- or backward-integrating, or those entering the market from abroad? If a company was to analyze all current and potential competitors, virtually any budget available for the exercise would be strained. Competitive intelligence must focus analysis on those firms that represent the greatest threat and those that offer most opportunity for market share gain. Other firms can be monitored, but only a few companies should be *monitored, tracked and analyzed* for competitive advantage. In some cases, such as the insurance or financial services industries, the large number of competitors may make it appropriate to analyze logical groupings of firms.

Competitive warfare is being waged in the mind of the customer. That is the competitive battleground. That is where market share is won or lost. Thus, the definition of which companies are truly the competition should be established by finding out with which firms or groups of companies customers consider your firm to be competing. Specific competitors may well vary across market segments as customers define competition differently. For example, BMW's 3-series automobiles may be seen by potential baby-boom customers to be competing with Saab and Volvo, while their 5- or 7-series cars may be seen by middle-aged customers to be competing with Mercedes Benz or Jaguar.

In addition, competitors defined by end-users may be different from those identified as such by intermediaries. For example, a vendor of carbon brushes for electric motors may well be using the same middleman as suppliers of armatures, commutators and other apparatus for electric motors. These middlemen may be exclusive agents, and thus no competition in product form exists at the intermediary level, yet indirect competition for the time and attention of the agent may well exist.

Defining competitors depends upon:

- the mapping of product-market boundaries in the mind of the end-user – the key battleground

- the categorization of the product-market into product-market segments (analogous to competing for control of specific zones of the battlefield)

- the positioning of products within these segments.

Product-market boundaries should be based upon the perceptions of customers: with which products do they think your firm competes? This determination can be made by observation, experimentation, surveys and interviews. For example, researchers can observe consumers in action in a supermarket and determine which products they consider before making their final selection. Marketers might vary their marketing mixes in specific controlled test markets and determine the impact of specific changes on sales of competitive offerings. More typically, marketers can conduct surveys or interviews with end-users and intermediaries to determine:

- their top-of-mind listings of competitive products;

- their assessment of which products they would consider to be competitors for a predetermined list of offerings;

- the brands of products they would typically consider using in specific usage situations, such as which beverages they would consume while watching a sports game on television, while on a picnic, while at a party, and so on;

- the performance of products in respect of the buyers' main selection criteria.

The last-mentioned approach to defining competition can lead to several applications. First, it can be used to map the product positioning of vendors in 'product space'. It can also be used to define areas of competitive strength and weakness, and what needs to be addressed to correct deficiencies. You can map the positioning of your products, service and company relative to competitors by researching the key purchase criteria (why people buy products in this category) of your target market and then establishing how competitive offerings rate in respect of each of these criteria. Some managers do this by 'gut feel', but objective research is better if the depth of the attitudes and perceptions of customers which influence their decision-making is to be revealed.

Figure 2.1 is based on a two-dimensional product space, with the two main, hypothetical purchase criteria of end-users listed along the two axes. It illustrates the perceptions of young, affluent customers in the automobile market, and suggests that speed and appearance are their two main reasons for buying vehicles of this type. On this interpretation, Porsche 944, Corvette and Toyota Supra may be seen to be competitors, while Mazda 626, Nissan 300ZX and Toyota Celica compete within another category.

Another approach to charting the results or the perceived rankings of three specific automobiles in respect of targeted customers' purchase criteria

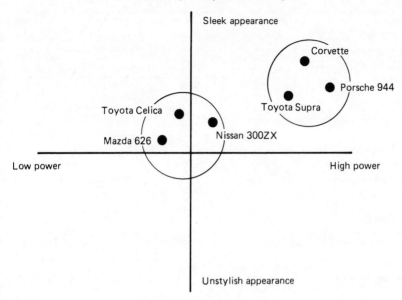

Figure 2.1 Product space

within a given segment is shown (in order of importance) in figure 2.2. This suggests that Vehicles H and O are likely to be seen as direct competitors with one another, but Vehicle X may well compete with other automobiles. It also implies that there may be an opportunity for Vehicle H to capture more sales from Vehicle O by modifying the reality and/or perception of the product's relative economy, durability and comfort.

Monitoring the direction of competitive thrusts in the minds of customers is as important as the one-time assessment. That is, the perceptions and attitudes of customers (and the trade/intermediaries) should be tracked, and competitive inroads on your own 'territory', or signs of competitors' positions weakening, should be noted. This will help you define the 'enemy' more explicitly. For example, in figure 2.3, Company A should defend against customer loss to Company R, while seeking opportunities to benefit from the 'high ground' it holds relative to Company Z.

2.3 Establishing a Roadmap for the Process

To develop a competitive edge:

- First you need to be able to see your company, your products and your services and those of your competitors as others do – especially your

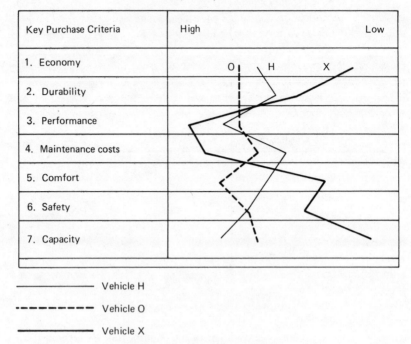

Key Purchase Criteria	High	Low
1. Economy		
2. Durability		
3. Performance		
4. Maintenance costs		
5. Comfort		
6. Safety		
7. Capacity		

———————— Vehicle H

---------- Vehicle O

———————— Vehicle X

Figure 2.2 Product positioning

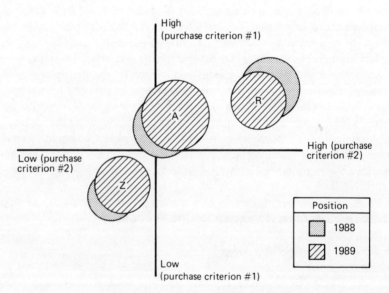

Figure 2.3 Defining competitors

customers . A thorough charting of the minds of your customers will tell you what types of competitive information you require and thus what questions you need to answer. For example, if your research indicates that customers view price as a very important attribute in a product, and they see your competitors as offering more attractive prices or pricing structures, then you will want to understand why this is so. Are you running a sufficiently lean operation so that your prices are as low as possible? Do competitors have lower input or processing costs, and if so, why? Do competitors have lower financing costs – a source of competitive advantage? Do they have a market penetration pricing objective, while you have a profit maximization approach to pricing? You will wish to build a competitive income statement, and see what you can do to improve your situation. Whatever your customers tell you, this is the starting point in competitive intelligence: *start in the mind of the customer* and work back to establish why it is that competitors enjoy the positioning they do, and what they are likely to do to change it in the future.

Figure 1.2 provided detail regarding this and other elements of the process. Market share transfer requires that an organization be able to achieve competitively superior customer satisfaction and make persuasive and true benefit claims to potential customers. This is illustrated in the diagram at the top of the circle by a crown – customer satisfaction is king. What the organization thinks it provides is irrelevant; what the customer sees to be important is vital. The improvement of customer satisfaction requires a solid understanding of the needs of current and potential customers, how those needs are changing over time, and the extent to which the industry in general, and specific competitors in particular, address those requirements. In some technology-driven industries this assessment is not very easy, because suppliers develop features that competitive offerings do not have, and seek to sell their products on this basis. For example, some private branch exchanges (PBXs) have a multitude of features which many customers, particularly those in small businesses, do not consider necessary; some just want 'plain old telephone service' – reliable voice communications – but vendors offer tremendous numbers of 'bells and whistles' in over-engineered products, and seek to command prices to justify these additional features. Once some customers see what the additional features are, they can be converted from their preference for more mundane systems, but the selling effort is often intense and the purchase decision is not always a rational economic one. Market research would need to be carefully designed to ensure that such technology-driven situations receive appropriate treatment.

- Next, the organization should examine its positioning in respect of customers' key purchase criteria, and relate this to competitors' positioning as discussed in chapter 2.2 above. An examination of the barriers that exist to increasing market share should follow. This question might be focused by answering the following: 'Why is your market share not twice the level it is? What is constraining it?' Hopefully, a thoughtful review of the market research and the application of experience and judgement will reveal competitive product, market, service, technology or other threats that need to be addressed and/or opportunities that exist for market share increase. Objectives should now be assigned for market share transfer (how much and by when) and the level of resources that will be made available to achieve this goal.

● At this point the 'enemy' should be defined. From which firms (or logical groupings of firms) is market share to be taken? Which companies represent potential threats for market share loss? These are the companies that will be the focus of competitive intelligence. Others can be monitored on occasion to establish that the decision taken to exclude them from the detailed analysis was correct. This is important. Any competitive intelligence program whereby a company attempts to gather considerable competitive information and analyze the competitive strategies of too large a number of companies runs the risk of failure through information overload.

■ Take the case of GTE. One of the first companies to recognize the importance of competitive intelligence, GTE implemented its 'BEST' program in a number of divisions. The objective was to gather the information necessary to improve its operations relative to its competitors. In 1981, GTE Sylvania implemented a computerized Management Information of Competitor Strategies (MICS) program to track 51 competitors on a continuous basis.* It seems to have been overwhelmed with information, to have experienced difficulty with updating the information and would probably have been better served by focusing its resources more narrowly.

I suggest that most companies should be able to limit the number of serious competitors (or competitor groupings) they monitor, track and analyze in detail to five or six. More than this and the process could become too unwieldy and resource-intensive. Any attempt to gather all information on all competitors in all regions from all sources, and then to analyze this intensively with the fairly limited resources of time, money and people

* *Business,* July–September, 1983, pp. 57–8.

most companies devote to this practice, is almost surely doomed from the outset. Rather, start small. If the system involving five or six firms proves easily workable, then it can always be expanded to cater for more companies.

- Information requirements should be determined next. What are the questions to which answers must be sought? What information will make a competitive difference? As recommended in chapter 1.9, write a shadow marketing plan of your key competitors using the format of the business plans you use for your own firm. This should help you establish what you know and what you do not know about your competitors. By going through such a process, you should be able to develop a series of questions for which answers must be obtained, and hypotheses which must be confirmed or refuted.

- Next, the relevant data must be sought and found, organized into a system and analyzed for what they reveal about the competitor and what implications they hold for an organization. From this, modifications to existing business strategies can be made, new strategies and sub-strategies developed (product, price, promotion, distribution, service, people, technology/R&D), and tactics implemented. There should be an ongoing review of what is working in the field and what is not, and this should feed into the market research and the assessment of barriers to market share increase.

This process is continual. The cycle should be repeated at least annually. (Data on key competitors should be gathered more often, though, but the analysis should occur as part of the business planning cycle.) It integrates information from market research with that of competitive intelligence and an organization's own internal plans to arrive at competitively superior strategies and tactics and, ultimately, customer satisfaction.

2.4 Securing Management and Staff Support

The commitment of management and staff to the competitive intelligence process is vital if the organization is to become truly competitive. There is a vast storehouse of competitive information within a company that is waiting to be accessed, but barriers must first be removed. The main roadblocks that must be overcome include:

- uncertainty about how the information is going to be used;

- skepticism about competitive intelligence and the results that can be obtained from the process;

- lack of time, budget, human resources and the assignment of a low priority to competitive intelligence in relation to other required activities.

Some employees providing information about competitors may feel that anything they provide could be used to judge their output relative to the performance of competition. Because they are reluctant to compare their performance with other companies, they may withhold information.

At the outset of any competitive intelligence program, there are likely to be skeptics who doubt the usefulness and the validity of the program. Perhaps these are people who doubt anything new; perhaps they have witnessed too many new approaches that promised salvation of the company only to be subsequently discontinued. Whatever their reasons, they need to be convinced of the merits of competitive intelligence and why it is vital for the continued growth of the firm.

Many of those most able to supply the needed information may consider that they have insufficient time to comply now and too few human and financial resources to provide ongoing support to a program. They may consider 'fire-fighting' and other pressing activities to be more relevant and thus accord them a higher priority than competitive intelligence.

All these barriers can be lowered or eliminated if the senior executive of the company communicates the need for competitive intelligence effectively to his/her employees. At the outset of the program, such executives too may not fully appreciate the benefit of investing time, attention and budget in competitive intelligence. They may have come to power as a result of their effective management of business during the market growth era that stimulated sales and profits in the 1960s and 1970s. They may not see that economic conditions have changed and that the old rules of business are simply no longer good enough to achieve the required growth in the 1980s and 1990s. They may therefore need to be convinced that an integrated program of competitive intelligence could yield the results they seek, and, moreover, that if competitors conduct this activity while their company does not, not only may opportunities be missed, but competitive threats will surely grow.

Senior management may still be unconvinced. Because competitive intelligence may be a new concept to the company, funds for this program are likely to come under close scrutiny. Executives may want to know what the payback will be on such an investment. The definition of market share transfer objectives and its associated timing could enable the development of a payback schedule. However, deeper commitment is likely to be obtained if executives 'buy into' the philosophy, in much the same way as they presumably think that financial planning and marketing planning are 'good things to do', even in the absence of financial analysis to prove it. I am not aware of a single firm that has examined the paybacks on the huge amounts of time committed to planning, but virtually every company (apart from Paul Newman's!) does it.

Management, once convinced of the merits of competitive intelligence, should issue a 'white paper' to the organization which provides employees with the following information:

- that the organization has a new focus: competitive intelligence

- what the reasons for this focus are

- what the objectives of the program are

- who will be responsible for co-ordinating the program within the company

- what is expected of all employees (limited investment of time and support in response to specific directed questions from the co-ordinator(s), and in the event that a significant competitive threat emerges in the marketplace that they would be expected to report it to the co-ordinator(s))

- that, when requiring competitive information, they can themselves use the system to gain the insight they seek

- the specific timing of the key milestones.

An approach similar to this was reportedly followed by GTE's President when implementing the 'BEST' competitive intelligence program within GTE divisions.

2.5 Required Budget and Resources

How much a company should invest in competitive intelligence depends on several factors, including:

- whether the company is in a service or goods producing industry

- the stage of the industry's life cycle and the level of competition in the industry

- the competitive position of the firm

- the amount the company stands to gain from the intelligence effort.

- In general, firms in goods producing industries will need to have a greater competitor focus than companies providing services, for three main reasons:

  ★ Service industries are often differentiated primarily on the basis of the service provider, rather than the service offered. Relationship management is central to customer retention, and the orientation of the service provider should therefore be towards providing and positioning services of outstanding quality to targeted market segments. The competitive focus should thus be directed on competing for the best people and training them to develop and manage their customers and their current and emerging needs as well as possible.

  ★ Goods producing industries are often capital intensive and require a minimum throughput to cover the investment in plant and equipment. If market growth will not provide the required sales levels, volume must come from competition – plant usually cannot be rapidly or profitably resized to provide for available sales. This usually requires an intensive competitor focus. (In contrast, service producing industries typically have high variable costs which can be adjusted to the available workload, often without dramatically affecting profitability.) In addition, because of the lengthy time horizons involved in planning, committing and implementing investment, competitor monitoring and analysis is required to ensure that competitors do not exploit opportunities to which funds will be applied. Many other aspects of goods producing industries are essentially service in nature, such as managing channel and customer needs and relationships – which requires that the company has a customer as well as a competitor orientation.

  ★ Goods producing industries more often have concentration of competition while service providers may have widespread competitors – in part the result of more limited barriers to entry. Goods producers can thus readily identify their key competitors. In some service industries, individual competitors may have very modest levels of market share, in which case service providers may need to aggregate similar types of competitors and focus on their ability to address customer needs of the type that the company is seeking to address.

- When the industry is growing rapidly and there is considerable change in product, technology, channels of distribution and customers' needs, companies should focus primarily on the customer to ensure that they obtain and retain as much as possible of the emerging opportunities. A competitor focus could yield insight into aspects of change and how their firms were seeking to address the market, but, depending upon the rate of change, the analysis may provide too little too late to assist in meaningful strategic direction.

When change is taking place slowly, a competitor orientation is vital to addressing market opportunities, because insight obtained from a close examination of competitors' strategies can be applied in a timely manner for competitive advantage.

• In addition to industry growth, relative market share affects the investment in competitive intelligence. In figure 2.4, industry growth is charted against relative market share and six regions are identified. Different competitive strategies are apparent in each one, as noted in table 2.1. In Regions 1 and 2, the company has a strong market position that must be defended against competitive inroads. A considerable customer focus will help identify the weak points which a competitor might exploit, and provide information necessary to retain market share. In Regions 5 and 6, companies will have very weak competitive positions, and will need to focus their resources to gain a breakthrough or develop a niche for a tenable advantage. This focus applies to both customer and competitor information development. In

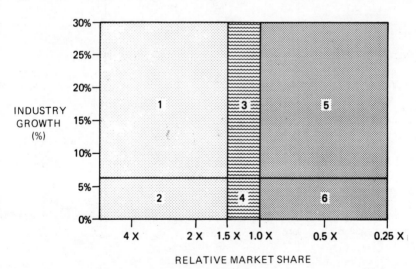

Figure 2.4   Customer vs competitor focus: when to have which orientation

Table 2.1 Strategies and focus stemming from market share:industry growth matrix

Region	Position	Market growth	Indicated strategy	Focus: Customer vs competitor	
1	Dominant	High	Defend, build	Considerable	Selective
2	Dominant	Low	Harvest, segment	Considerable	Selective
3	Unstable	High	Offensive	Moderate	Considerable
4	Unstable	Low	Selective offense	Focused	Considerable
5	Weak	High	Acquisition / merger, breakthrough or exit	Focused	Focused
6	Weak	Low	Niche or exit	Highly focused	Highly focused

Regions 3 and 4, the battle is being waged by firms with roughly equal market share. They will need to have a considerable competitor focus if they are to outwit, outmaneuver and outflank the competition without huge additional investment.

Figure 2.5 illustrates whether a company should have a customer or competitor focus, or both, according to the region of the growth:share chart in which it participates.

• Having determined the nature of its intelligence focus, a company should be in a position to determine the objectives of the intelligence program and assign resources to achieve the objectives. Table 2.2 suggests possible levels of investment in the annual operation of a competitive intelligence program, including relevant market and competitive research, manpower (and fringe benefit) costs and computer charges. The first year of operation of the system could prove considerably more costly, perhaps exceeding ongoing operating costs by 2–3 times that amount – including the investment in computer programming. Ranges are provided to reflect the differences in markets, need for competitive information and management priorities.

Firms in service industries should re-examine their market intelligence systems for areas of improvement before investing heavily in competitive intelligence, and the scale and scope of the intelligence program should be based upon the findings of their market research, which could lead many service providers to focusing on two main competitive issues – personnel recruitment and manpower training for strategic emphasis – and other issues for tactical deployment, such as pricing histories, win/loss reports, key individual profiles, and so on.

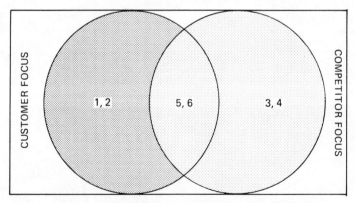

Figure 2.5   Customer vs competitor focus by region

Table 2.2 Possible operating budget for a competitive intelligence program

Type of company	Regions of matrix	Objective of intelligence	Annual investment (1988 $)	
			Corporate (each country)	Each division
Multinational multidivisional or national company	1,2	Defensive, share retention	200–250,000	100–200,000
	3,4	Offensive, share retention	250–400,000	200–400,000
	5,6	Focused growth	100–150,000	100–150,000[a]
Local goods producing company	1,2	Defensive, share retention	25–50,000	25–75,000
	3,4	Offensive, share retention	50–100,000	75–150,000
	5,6	Focused growth	25–50,000	75–150,000[a]

[a] As required.

The above figures are intended for illustration only, and should not be taken to define categorically the required level of investment by all firms in all markets. In addition, several small and medium sized companies may make a much more modest investment and could obtain significant returns by adopting many of the principles identified in this book, undertaking periodic as opposed to ongoing intelligence, focusing intelligence activities and using outside consultants to undertake specific tasks, often a cost-effective alternative to adding full-time personnel. Consultants can assist with setting up the computer systems, conducting competitive market research and supplemental intelligence, and developing competitor profiles. They can also assist with strategy development.

2.6 Staffing the Competitive Intelligence Function

The competitive intelligence function should be staffed both at the corporate level and at the level of the divisional business unit. Typically the corporate staff prepare competitor profiles that mirror their competitors' corporations, while the divisions add value to these documents and apply them in the context of their businesses. Where organizations do not have many divisions, the separation in function between corporate level and division level analysis may not be necessary.

At both levels, it is appropriate that the staff be competent analysts and that the key positions be used neither as a parking lot for people without the requisite skills, nor as a training ground for very junior staff. Several companies have adopted a competitive intelligence committee for both corporate and divisional analysis. This seems to function particularly well when staffed with individuals with a similar background. The committee should have five or six members, drawn from marketing, market research, corporate planning and general management positions. Not having staff from functional areas such as manufacturing, treasury, finance, purchasing, human resources and so on, could limit the amount of information provided to the committee, because of the barriers to competitive intelligence referred to in chapter 2.4.

Conducted by a few individuals with common marketing/strategy backgrounds, the analysis will reflect a heavy strategic emphasis. Moreover, each of five or six individuals in the competitive intelligence committee can be assigned a competitor to analyze and shadow. In the Second World War, both sides monitored the enemy and tracked the history of the battles fought by key commanders. Then, prior to developing the plan of attack, the strategist would counsel with the 'shadow', and try to determine the likely outcome of various moves. This can be done successfully in the business arena, too, and requires, therefore, that one individual be assigned the task of co-ordinating the gathering of data and information about a specific competitor, and then developing the relevant analysis and noting the strategic implications.

2.7 Inputs, Outputs and Sequence of Activities

The competitive intelligence program should have the inputs, outputs and sequence of activities identified in figure 2.6.

- At the outset, senior management should identify (or be led to the identification of) the need for competitive intelligence, communicating this effectively through the organization. An individual or, where dictated by a sufficient scope of operations, a committee should be appointed to co-ordinate and execute the competitive intelligence program. A system should be established to receive data input and facilitate data organization that enables information to be archived and accessed for tactical response and strategic analysis.

- Then, the committee should establish which companies information is required about, and what needs to be known about each firm. This assessment should be based on research that examines competitive positioning in respect of key purchase criteria and should not rely exclusively upon the subjective experience of the executives undertaking the task.

- Next, data should be obtained from sources within the company and external sources – in that order. Many companies already have much of the competitive information they are seeking, but a lack of co-ordination and focus fails to reveal the knowledge. Yet this could prove to include the most crucial information and is perhaps the least costly to obtain. In addition, it is often 'fresher' than some external information, such as that obtained from a review of trade or general publications. As 3M does, start first with internally available information, and then work from the inside of the company out, going next to secondary data sources (published material) and finally to primary sources for answers to specific questions. In this way, the cheapest source will have been accessed first, and the most expensive last.

    The data should be organized in the system, and responses to requests for information on subjects such as pricing histories for preparation of bids to major customers produced as required, listing allowances previously provided in launching new consumer food products to supermarkets,

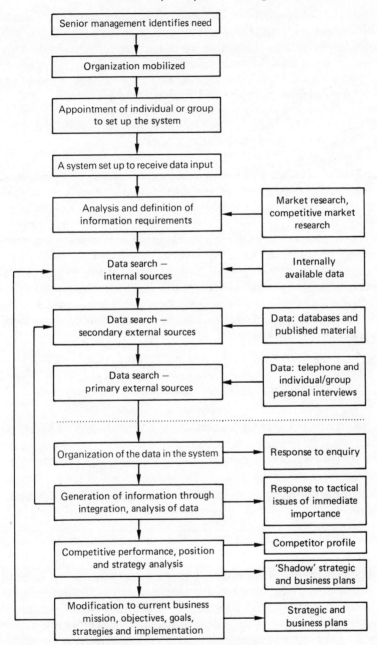

Figure 2.6 Competitive intelligence program: inputs, outputs and sequence of activities

patents previously issued, cost structure of financing and other issues that could yield a negotiating, strategic or tactical advantage. It is likely that, in the course of the information generation, specific short-term tactical issues will emerge which require immediate attention. Clearly, the intelligence committee should ensure that a mechanism be established to ensure that such information is communicated to those who should know and who are in a position to take appropriate counter-measures.

The cycle of data gathering and information generation should continue on an ongoing basis, or be repeated at least every quarter.

- Competitive assessments of relative company/business unit performance, positioning and changes thereof, and strategy analysis, should be undertaken next. This should lead to the development of competitor profiles and the development or completion of shadow marketing plans (that may have been used at the outset of the process to aid in identifying key information requirements). Implications of this analysis should lead to modification to, or confirmation of, the strategic business plans of the company, which gives the competitive intelligence program its strategic impact and without which the exercise will have been interesting, but ultimately useless. Additional detail regarding the method for accomplishing these tasks is provided throughout the following chapters.

- Implementation of the plans should follow, and this aspect of the process should be repeated periodically, usually annually before the strategic business planning cycle.

The dotted line in figure 2.6 separates the components in which research or data are fed as input to the system and those where output follows from data organization, information generation and plan development.

2.8 Understanding Critical Success Factors for Market Share Transfer

Gaining and maintaining a competitive edge meant dominating customers' minds in respect of key dimensions: their main purchase criteria. A clear understanding of what these criteria are can lead to the development of a listing of some of the most important factors which are critical to success in the industry. Key purchase criteria are a demand-side perspective. The ways in which companies can address these criteria constitute critical success factors in the industry. These may be developed directly from purchase criteria alone or from subsequent evaluation of the implications of the criteria based, for example, on industry economics and alternative approaches to achieve the benefit of differentiation, as articulated by customers. To illustrate: customers often describe price as an important criterion for purchase, which could lead to a consideration of the margins in the industry and what enables firms to compete on price, including an assessment of:

- the source and timing of financial resources (how long before the investor/parent expects a reasonable return?)

- access to faster, more productive design and production equipment or operations

- lower cost components or approaches to assembly

- appropriate labor-to-capital ratios

- proximity to raw materials or markets

- contractual or ownership linkages with key suppliers

- channel and promotional efficiency

- overhead cost structure

- pricing based upon full cost absorption vs incremental costing or other approaches, such as pricing to competition.

Other than price, the second most frequently noted factor which could cause an increase in market share for a participant is 'quality'. Everyone loves quality. But what does it mean? Quality means 'conformance to the customer's requirements'.* Essentially: quality is the difference between what customers *expect* from a product and what they *perceive they receive*. Both Coke and a BMW are probably seen by most consumers to be high-quality offerings, but 'quality' may mean very different things to purchasers. Quality in Coke is probably interpreted as its meeting requirements for consistent formulation of a desirable taste; while in a BMW it may mean absence of defects, rapid transportation, and close parts tolerances (good fit). Because the quality is seen from the perspective of the product/service purchaser, as opposed to the provider, the definition of quality should be determined by researching consumers. Then, based on their direction, the various components that comprise 'quality' can be

*P. Crosby, *Quality is Free*, Mentor, 1979.

further evaluated as success factors. For example, if reliability and durability are central elements in a definition of quality in a washing machine, an examination of the research, design and manufacturing issues that lead to superior reliability and durability can be determined.

Once a listing of the main factors which could drive market share transfer has been developed, ask: 'If we performed in an exceptional manner in all categories, would we transfer considerable market share from the enemy to us?' If the answer is 'No', or a half-hearted 'Yes', then the list of success factors is incomplete. Further barriers to market share increase need to be identified. Ask: 'Why do we not have twice the market share we do?' At this point issues such as the company's reputation, customer relationships, government support, fast commercialization of technology (short 'windows of opportunity'), rapid adoption of process improvements, and other factors may emerge. Consider, too, the role each of the key stakeholders plays in a firm's success in the industry (commitment of employees, availability of the latest technology from suppliers, etc.) and issues associated with the business environment of the firm (knowledge of latest technological developments, addressing emerging social concerns, legislative barriers/aids to growth, and so on).

Attainment of superior performance in respect of the critical success factors should be the main goal of all companies, and management should measure the firm's performance in respect of these factors. This should be the central focus of all monitoring and control within the organization; a major reorientation in the way most companies currently measure performance – guided principally by requirements for financial control and regulatory compliance (and, in some companies, for examination of individual performance). All these issues are obviously important, and need to be controlled, but the achievement of a dominant competitive position requires that the key factors affecting competitiveness be the ones that receive most scrutiny.

Measurement should occur both within the organization and in the marketplace, to determine whether positive changes in reality are being perceived by the end-user and intermediaries. This examination should include a consideration of competitive performance in respect of key purchase criteria – leading to an assessment and tracking of competitive positioning.

2.9   Understanding your own Firm – a Necessary First Step

At the outset of the process, there may be considerable enthusiasm to gather data on competitors while lacking a fundamental understanding of your own firm. The previous step (chapter 2.8) should have yielded a thorough examination of the industry environment within which the firm participates. An investigation of your own company should follow, to establish how well it performs in the light of critical success factors.

- Some companies set about their competitive analysis in reverse order. One client provided me with a detailed list of over 30 elements that he wanted to examine in each of 5 major competitors. I asked if this information was known for the client's own firm, and he told me it was neither available nor measurable internally. The client then understood the improbability of obtaining the information he sought, since he recognized that if he was unable to measure such specifics within his firm, it was unlikely that information of this sort on competitors would be available anywhere, least of all in the public domain!

A list of questions is presented in Appendix 1 that could prompt you to gain an understanding of the history, evolution and strengths and weaknesses of your company. This would guide you when you consider what needs to be changed in order both to address needed operating improvements and to ensure that competitive challenges are successfully pursued.

3 Gathering Competitive Intelligence

- How many competitors should be monitored and analyzed?

- Distinguishing relevant from irrelevant information

- Sources of competitive information

- Government filings and the Freedom of Information Act

- How to gather published information

- How to search on-line databases

- Conducting telephone interviews

- Conducting personal interviews

- Gathering information at trade shows

- Involving your own employees in the intelligence program

- Validating information and confirming its accuracy

- Keeping your secrets secret

3.1 How many Competitors should be Monitored and Analyzed?

In chapter 2.6, it was noted that a competitive intelligence team should comprise five or six members to help undertake the intelligence operations, analyze the data and serve as 'competitor shadows'. This implies that five or six companies, too, should be monitored in depth. If analysis of a larger number is attempted, the level of detail and insight could suffer − usually it does, particularly if the team members are doing the work as 'part of their jobs' rather than being dedicated specifically to the task.

This is not to suggest that no more than six companies (or logical groupings of firms if the industry is highly fragmented) can be tracked. The competitive environment should be monitored for signs of strategic change, but, to keep the project scope manageable, key strategic issues should be tracked, which should reveal the key competitors of the future. This horizontal cut of the information pie should help you establish if those companies that were selected as being the most critical to analyze (see chapter 2.2) are still those that represent the greatest threats and/or opportunities to your own firm. That is, you should be watching for signs that the competitive equilibrium is about to shift by scanning for information such as changing industry concentration, new ownership with long time-horizons and deep pockets, investment in production capacity or major research and development projects, and other issues related to the key success factors in the industry. This could reveal that new major competitors are looming in your served markets and that you should elevate your treatment of these firms by changing from a horizontal scanning of key issues, to a vertical search for specific information, perhaps replacing one or more of the companies that are currently on your 'hit list' with these emerging companies.

In summary, then, more than six firms can be monitored for strategic change by scanning for relevant information, but detailed analysis should only be attempted for five or six companies to avoid the problem of information overload.

3.2 Distinguishing Relevant from Irrelevant Information

Important information is that which enables a company to *predict* the next steps competitors may take to satisfy customers, either in a strategic, long-term context, or those of a tactical, short-term nature. Irrelevant information is that which provides neither insight.

Relevant information is thus distinguished from irrelevant according to the focus of the user and the intended purpose of the information. As discussed in chapter 1.9, the most relevant strategic information is that which leads to completion of the shadow strategic or marketing plans, because this information can lead to consistent market share transfer. Usually, executives will want a strategic focus. On the other hand, functional department heads or line managers generally prefer more detailed tactical information, the requirements of which vary depending upon the nature of their work. For example, pricers will want to know all they can about competitors' pricing changes. Purchasing managers will want to understand competitors' procurement policies. Sales Directors will want to know what competitors are doing in their key accounts, and so on.

Therefore, it is important that the intelligence group define at the outset of the project who their key users are going to be, because the users will affect the type of information collected and the purpose to which it is put. If line managers are to be the principal users, for example, their system will require the development and timely updating of a more detailed information base than would be required by strategic users.

In setting up and running the competitive intelligence system, it is likely that a vast amount of data will become available. To distinguish the important from the inconsequential, the analyst must ask questions of the information users at the start of the project and then seek out the data or

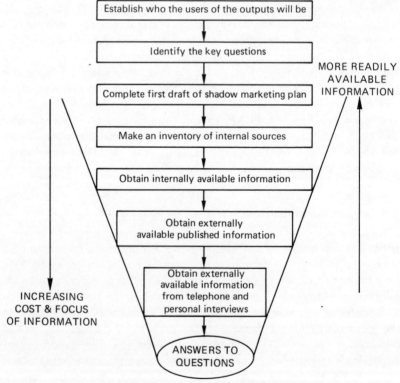

Figure 3.1 Finding the right information

information to provide the answers. This process is described in figure 3.1. To do the reverse – to find all the answers to questions which have yet to be formulated – could result in the process depicted in figure 3.2. It will lead to the intelligence group gathering endless amounts of information, never knowing when their task is complete. Respond to executives who say: 'Find out all you can on Company X' by asking: 'Why are we doing this?

The President: Make us more competitive!

Vice President: Get the information we need to become more competitive!

Director: Gather information on the competition!

Manager: Find out everything about all our competitors!

Analyst: TILT!

Figure 3.2   The workload builds ...

What specifically do we need to find out about Company X? What will we do with the information if we know the answer? How much time and money are we prepared to spend to find this out?'

3.3   Sources of Competitive Information

All sources of competitive information may be categorized into three groups:

- what individuals within your own company have observed;

- what third parties say;

- what competitors communicate about themselves.

Internal Sources of Information

A vast amount of information already exists within your firm – perhaps as much as 80 per cent of what you need, depending upon the size of your company and the level of awareness and sensitivity of the staff regarding the subject matter. Most of your employees will have monitored competitors informally over the duration of their careers. What is different now, is that you are seeking to formalize the process, share competitive insight and find new ways systematically to transfer market share from the enemy to your company. You are making competition the central core of strategy development, not the peripheral element implied by an informal monitoring. You need now to tap into the informal internal network of information – the most cost-effective information source. Begin by seeking information from the inside of your company and then work out to progressively more expensive sources: first to published, secondary information, then, still in search of an answer to an elusive question, to primary research (conducting telephone and personal interviews, principally).

Start your search for internal information by finding out who knows what about your competitors. Take an inventory of the internally available information using a form such as the one described in figure 3.3, sent with an appropriate covering letter outlining the objective of the contact and referencing the competitive intelligence program that will hopefully have been communicated to the organization by a senior executive by this time. Once you understand the availability of specific types of competitive information within your company, and have formulated key questions about your competitive environment, identify the people internally who are likely

NAME: _____   TELEPHONE LOCAL: _____

TITLE: _____   E-MAIL ADDRESS: _____

DEPARTMENT/DIVISION: _____   DATE: _____

COMPETITOR'S NAME: _____

DIVISION OR PRODUCT LINE WITH WHICH WE COMPETE: _____

COMPETITOR'S SHARE OF THE MARKETS WE SERVE: _____

Do you maintain information files on this company? (Y/N)	How often are files updated? (M/Q/Y/ other)	What are the major file headings or categories of information captured?	Identify the major published and personal sources of information used	Are competitor information reports prepared? (Y/N)	How frequently are reports updated? (M/Q/Y/ other)	Reports tactical or strategic? (T/S)	What unpublished or undocumented competitive information do you know about? Please list general categories or areas of knowledge

Figure 3.3   Inventory of internally available competitive information

to provide the answers you need and set up appointments to review the published and unpublished information in their possession. Conduct interviews with them. Table 3.1 lists typical areas of competitive knowledge, some of which you may wish to cover in your discussions, depending upon the issues that are of most relevance to you.

After obtaining an initial understanding of the competitive knowledge of your company's employees, you should consider how best to involve them in the competitive intelligence program on an ongoing basis (see chapter 2.4).

Third Parties

Third parties are the next major source of competitive information. Many are likely to be friendly contacts because you already deal with them, perhaps making them amenable to helping you with your information development. Typical third parties and their areas of competitive knowledge are listed in table 3.2. Currently, many of these organizations are asking your company for information. Consider how you can make this more of

Table 3.1 Internally available competitive information

Internal departments/personnel	Typical areas of competitive competence/knowledge
Engineering	Reverse engineering of competitors' products; cost of production; technical excellence relative to your offerings; direction of technology
Finance and treasury	Cost of funds; relationships with financial community; financial analysis
Human resources	Key performance criteria for success in the industry; key executives in competitors' companies; organizational structures; employees within your company who have worked for competitors
Information centers	Published data; informal librarian network
Manufacturing	Assembly methods; labor-to-capital ratios; unionization; labor rates; state of employee relations; key manufacturing weaknesses/strengths
Marketing	Level of media expenditures; media strategy; target markets; marketing mix; market share performance; competitive product and division level strengths and weaknesses; barriers to increasing market share held by competitors; strategic direction
Procurement	Relationships with strategic suppliers; estimated costs of obtaining key components; specific sources
Public relations	Level of 'unpaid' media exposure; media relationships; strategies articulated
Research and development	Core technical competence; emerging technologies under development
Sales	Relationships with key accounts; types and timing of programs usually planned; usual reflex actions to your/other competitor innovation in product and price; key sales staff profiles; competitive sales culture

a 'two-way street'. For example, when financial analysts contact the senior financial officers in the firm, they should be asked pointed questions in much the same way as they seek to gain answers to their own. If they do not know specific answers, they could be encouraged to find them out.

The advertising agency should be expected to develop competitive

Table 3.2   Third-party sources of competitive information

Third party	*Typical areas of competitive competence / knowledge*
Advertising agencies (your own)	Competitors' media expenditures, positioning, product / market strategies
Bankers	Competitors' financial dealings
Consultants	Competitive intelligence programs; competitor profiles; specific information
Customers	The Ultimate Information Source: for competitive positioning, new competitive products and programs, purchase intent, awareness...
Distributors	Trade programs; distributor margins; support received by competitors
Editors and journalists of trade or general press	Loquacious sources of general competitor insight
Equipment manufacturers	Installed base; technology employed; productivity rates
Financial analysts and stockbrokers	Financial and product / market strategy; understanding of stock valuation and reasons for discount or premium vs your company
Government	Usually helpful about overall industry rather than individual competitors
Labor unions	Contracts, labor conditions
Lawyers	Interpretation of court rulings involving competitors; competitors' court-case orientation — aggressive pursuers of court action, avoiders of legal battles, or neutral
Patent attorneys	Patents issued to competitors and the strengths and weaknesses of the patent filings
Previous employees of competitors	Focused competitive insight
Suppliers — ingredients, services, packaging, other	Costs, quality and amount of inputs; competitor procurement priorities; recent requests for offerings not usually supplied
Trade associations	Shipments; focused competitor information

positioning discussion papers and to assist in identifying key questions to be resolved about competition; as should the public relations agency, lobbyists, lawyers and perhaps other professionals employed by your organization.

- Former employees, particularly those who work for your own organization, should be sought out and interviewed. (This may involve the human resources/personnel department in identifying who to contact. If they cannot help, which is often the case, their systems need modification.)

- ■ I recently conducted an analysis of major corporations to assist a client buy into an industry. One of the most helpful sources of information proved to be a former senior executive who had been forcibly retired from the acquisition candidate and was willing to shed light on his former company.

Competitors Communicate

Competitors say a great deal about themselves for one of three main reasons: because it is required public disclosure, from personal ego or corporate prestige considerations, or because they *must* communicate to do business (customers, trade, etc.). This information is frequently published and may be obtained via search procedures in the library, from a clippings service, or from a computer database. One particularly helpful US source is The Wall Street Transcripts (120 Wall Street, New York, NY 10005. Telephone: 212-747-9500), which captures verbatim responses of senior executives to the questions posed by financial analysts. Such information not only helps in understanding the strategic direction of competitors, but could help profile the senior executives. You may wish to give items such as speeches made by competitors' senior executives, past copies of Wall Street Transcripts, recordings of their TV and radio interviews, their curricula vitae and other relevant personal information to a psychiatrist for as detailed an evaluation as is possible with published material. Incomplete elements of the profile could be developed by identifying questions that need resolution. Profiles of one or more senior executives could help you identify patterns of behavior and decision-making processes – information that could be employed to strategic or tactical advantage in the market. What do they do under stress, as they would be, for instance, in a takeover attempt? Do they challenge the status quo or accept it? – important issues when introducing a new product or price. Do they have intellectual or psychological 'blindsides'? Are there areas or activities which cause them to be uncomfortable and comfort 'zones' to which they gravitate when under pressure (usually the areas from which they have been promoted)?

Competitors' communications may be captured in sources such as:

- ● Advertisements

- Annual reports

- Company newsletters

- Court cases

- Filings with environmental protection agencies, health and safety protection agencies, municipal or city planning boards, equal employment opportunity co-ordinators, labor relations boards

- Financial filings with regulatory authorities or the government

- Financial press

- Local or regional press

- Magazine articles

- Patent filings

- Popular press

- Product literature and brochures

- Recruitment advertisements

- Regulatory hearings

- Technical papers.

All these sources should be reviewed for the information they convey about competitors' activities and plans. Advertising is a particularly informative source, because it presents the results of the competitor's market research, strategic thinking, target market, selling propositions and positioning all in one brief piece of celluloid, paper, magnetic tape or whatever. However, by the time you see the advertising, it may be a little late to do much except take short-term, reactionary measures to defer the impact of a competitor's thrust, until you have had time to address the issues raised there.

Companies say a great deal about themselves in annual reports and financial filings with regulatory authorities, such as the Securities and Exchange Commission in the US and Companies House in London, England.

Much of this is helpful in the development of a competitor profile, but the usual market and financial emphasis is on what has already occurred, not on the future. To arrive at an understanding of what the competitor will be doing next, you need to examine sources that allow a longer time for the development of an appropriate response, typically those that shed light on activities that occur very early in the value chain. Much of this information will come from technical papers presented at conferences, patent filings and local or regional newspapers. Engineers and scientists often seek peer group approval at conferences where they discuss the nature of their work – often a good indicator of future investment emphasis in their companies. Your own technical staff should be directed to obtain relevant information at these events.

Patent filings are another good source of future market activity. Not all patents should be treated literally. For example, companies in the pharmaceutical industry are known to patent errors, perhaps in the hope of misinforming competitors or refining the mistakes into workable products later on. Patent searches will nevertheless indicate the areas of emphasis of a competitor's research and development program, even if the specifics are not always accurate. Because of the rapid pace of technological change and the ease of duplication of the benefits of the patented products, if not the patents themselves, some companies are no longer patenting their innovations, preferring to surprise the market and develop a strong positioning in the minds of customers before competitors have had a chance to emulate them.

Local and regional newspapers monitor issues that affect their local constituency. Companies often choose to locate in a town, believing labor there to be more loyal or hard-working than that in larger cities. The local newspapers, or indeed the community papers in the cities, monitor the companies that most affect their region's tax base, level of employment and quality of working life.

> ■   I recently concluded an assignment for a client wishing to produce a specific category of custom-made electronics. I was informed that the project was 'super-secret' and that the client wished to keep his company's name confidential in the execution of the project. Imagine my surprise when I opened the community newspaper delivered to my front door and saw my client with his arm draped around one of the 'super-secret' machines that had been installed. The commentary described the objective of the project, the number of machines that had been bought, the productivity of each unit, how much employment would be added to the facility and more –

information from which several competitors would have benefitted!

■ On another project, by reading the local press I was surprised to find considerable Congressional interest in a competitor's plant, one with significant local employment and proprietary technology. The local Congressman was on record that he was against the Department of Defense's interest in having two sources for major contracts, presumably because this plant had a major contract and employment would be undermined by second-sourcing. Following up on the contacts revealed in the article led to an understanding of the extensive political support available to the competitor – an area our client had all but ignored. That client is now much more diligent about 'working the Hill', lobbying for their position in Congress and with the Senate.

Competitors say much to damage their future prospects. Few are alert to the wartime saying: 'loose lips sink ships'.

■ A few months before Colgate were about to introduce their toothpaste-in-a-pump in Canada, an article appeared in a mass-circulation Toronto daily's consumer affairs column which discussed the pump project, the target market, the media expenditures and frequency of airing, the pricing of the pump and the coupons that would be issued (I received a 75 cent coupon as promised a few months later). As a Brand Manager for Crest, Colgate's major rival, this would have presented me with the information I needed to:

  ● establish if the consumer and trade perceived merit in having toothpaste dispensed in a pump format, and the specifics of their needs, if positive indications were received;

  ● develop tactical approaches to blunt Colgate's thrust, perhaps by 'pantry loading', providing consumers with significant incentives to purchase high volumes of Crest for future usage, which would be likely to lessen their interest in trying the Colgate pump when that was introduced;

  ● develop strategies to enter the market, now that time had

been bought by the tactics described above, which could include the purchase of machinery and packaging, or having the product produced under contract packing agreements.

What would you have done?

Had the Crest marketing department been alert, they could have discovered the pump threat from Colgate even before reading the article in the press. By keeping in contact with key strategic suppliers, reading trade publications and attending trade shows, they should have been able to establish the likelihood of this packaging machinery being introduced, and find out Colgate's position on the product. At the time of its launch, there was just one major manufacturer of the pump machinery, a European firm. The purchasing department should have known about them and interviewed them. Knowing the aggressive management team at Colgate and the organization of their marketing department could have helped Crest to conclude that Colgate would not only introduce the pump, but perhaps attempt to secure global exclusivity on it.

Recruitment advertisements are an excellent source of information on the skills the competitor seeks in order to be more competitive in the future. Sometimes it can reveal an entire new strategic direction.

■ Through the monitoring of employment advertisements, a client became aware of the decision of a supplier to the automotive aftermarket to exit the production end of the business, moving instead to company-owned service outlets. By scanning the coverage of the advertisements, the client was able to establish the coverage of this service-oriented program – principally in the US South at the time. This led our client to consider emulating the service aspects of what it had learned. Unfortunately, it failed to understand the importance of information uncovered regarding the competitors' exit from production. Had it done so, it would probably have bought the competitor's aging plant and retired it, thus preserving profitable market dominance. Although still in a strong position, the client has been weakened by a Japanese firm which bought the competitor's plant at a modest price and has recently become very price competitive.

3.4 Government Filings and the Freedom of Information Act

Filings companies must make with specific government departments can often be accessed under 'sunshine' provisions by which governments open their files to public scrutiny. Currently, the US Federal Government has the most open access, but more information is becoming available after legislation in other countries – Canada's Access to Information Act and the UK's Data Protection Act, for example. In the UK, a Freedom of Information Act is also being considered.

The information that can be gleaned under these laws can be more than useful – it can make a fundamental difference to the competitiveness of a company.

■   For example, in a celebrated US case, the Freedom of Information (FOI) Act was used by a competitor to gain knowledge and design details without incurring high research and development costs. Air Cruisers had filed a design for a 42-person inflatable life raft with the Federal Aviation Administration. Approval, they thought, would give them a competitive advantage. Although approval was granted, a competitor, Switlik Parachute Company, apparently obtained portions of the Air Cruisers submission – under protest by Air Cruisers, who had learned of Switlik's interest in procuring a large amount of what they considered confidential technical documents. This information may have helped Switlik design their own raft and win a major European contract award in competition with Air Cruisers.*

■   A company considering capacity and plant design of a competitor in the petrochemicals industry made an application under the FOI Act to the Department of the Environment and secured information on effluent discharges that helped provide the understanding they needed about their competitor's operations.

The Freedom of Information Act is not supposed to reveal 'trade secrets and commercial or financial information obtained from a person and privileged or confidential' (Exemption 4). In practice, as described above, it sometimes does. Make applications for FOI filings through third parties,

---

* B. Schorr, 'How law is being used to pry secrets from Uncle Sam's files', *Wall Street Journal*, 9 May 1977, p. 1.

because a direct filing of your own is subject to a reverse FOI search, revealing you as the party seeking the information.

The US government must advise in ten days whether your request is approved or denied. If denied, the decision can be appealed, often successfully.

- In the US, organizations such as FOI Services Inc, 12315 Wilkins Ave, Rockville, Maryland (301-881-0410) do work of this type. More information about the FOI Act and applying can be obtained from the FOI Clearinghouse, P.O. Box 19367, Washington, DC 20036 (202-785-3704). Ask for the free brochure 'The Freedom of Information Act — What it is and how to use it'. Other relevant publications are available from the Superintendent of Documents, US Government Printing Office, Washington, DC 20402 (202-783-3238). Ask for the 'Freedom of Information Requests for Business Data and Reverse-FOIA lawsuits' and 'A citizen's guide on how to use the FOI Act and the Privacy Act in requesting government documents'.

- In Canada, obtain the Access to Information Register from the Canadian Government Publishing Centre, Supply and Services Canada, Ottawa, Ontario K1A 0S9. This provides guidance on how to contact specific individuals about the information you need.

- In the UK, obtain information about the Data Protection Act by contacting the Data Protection Registrar, Springfield House, Water Lane, Wilmslow, Cheshire SK9 5AX.

When applying for government documents, you will usually need the support of the government employee if you are to get exactly the information you seek. Any reference to the FOI Act or its equivalent in other countries could sink your chances of co-operation, so try to gain what you need without resorting to the time-consuming provisions of the legislation. Know what you want before you call. Can you describe the record or information you seek? Do you know the contract numbers or the numbers of the forms? (Much information of this type can be identified within your own organization, by establishing what forms your company files with which government departments.) This will prevent the phenomenon of endless referral loops which often follows undirected requests for information to the government – any government.

3.5 How to Gather Published Information

Published information, although an important competitive information source, is relied on for too much competitive insight by most companies. This is not surprising since published information is available with little effort, is easy to organize, and does not require interpersonal contact, which some researchers or analysts prefer to avoid, especially when obtaining sensitive information. Published material, however, often suffers from significant deficiencies, particularly from the fact that the data have been gathered for purposes other than your own, often to inform and entertain a mass audience. As such, it often lacks the clarity and insight you need to assemble your own strategic conclusions. Resist the temptation to gather mountains of published material, thereby deferring other research, and the development of conclusions and implications for your company. Get out from behind your desk and ask the specific questions to which you need answers.

Nevertheless, published information must be obtained in any integrated intelligence operation. Start at the most general sources and work to the progressively more specific. This is an appropriate order in which to review sources:

- published information about competitors already available within your company

- directories and indexes for background company information

- indexes for articles published about the competition

- directories published by financial brokerages to identify the companies they cover

- third-party, 'off-the-shelf' studies

- financial filings, annual reports

- company-produced literature, such as product brochures, employee/ mass publications

- **on-line** databases to search specific key words – for information such as that described above, and more specific product, market, personnel, advertising and technical information in response to the issues that you need resolved

- key publications, which should be subscribed to and monitored on an ongoing basis.

You will learn of additional publications to obtain from the published information you gather and during the course of your interviews. That is, the process of obtaining published information cannot, and should not, be divorced from subsequent stages of the intelligence operation.

Background competitor information can be obtained from sources such as those referenced in the appendices for the US, Canada, the UK and Japan. Some of the more prominent background sources in the US are:

- *Moody's Industrial Manual*, Moody's Investor Services
  General information regarding history, products, plants, financial statements, corporate officers

- *The Million Dollar Directory*, Dun's Marketing Services
  General information for annual sales, number of employees, products made, officers and directors

- *The Directory of Corporate Affiliations*, National Register Publishing Company
  Affiliations between corporations, divisions and subsidiaries – essentially, a review of who owns whom

- *Standard and Poor's Register of Corporations, Directors and Executives*, Standard and Poor's Corp.
  Company history, subsidiaries, products, plants, financial statements, officers

- *Standard Directory of Advertisers*, National Register Publishing Company
  Lists of advertisers, advertising budgets and sales

- *Business Periodicals Index*, H.W. Wilson Co.
  A wide variety of trade publications and periodicals are indexed

- *F&S Index of Corporations and Industries*, Predicasts, Inc.
  Information indexed from periodicals and newspapers in the US and internationally

- *Ulrich's International Periodicals Directory*, R.R. Bowker
  Directory of periodicals to identify which ones merit subscription

- *Ayer Directory of Publications*, Ayer Press
  Directory of periodicals to identify which ones merit subscription

On-line database services (discussed in chapter 3.6, next) can provide additional background information.

3.6 How to Search On-line Databases

The gathering of published information has changed significantly from the days when you could only carry out such work in the library because you needed access to its books and other reference material. The inconvenience of obtaining published information led many managers to search only the most readily available or accessible information sources. The advent and proliferation of on-line databases has changed both the amount of information and the hours of access – information availability is now almost continuous. Certainly the library still plays an important part in the information search, but much of the 'front end' research has been replaced by over 3,000 databases available from over 450 on-line services around the world, which offer the intelligence professional an opportunity to sort through mountains of data to locate those that are vital instantly.

The typical research process involves the on-line identification of the articles that are desired reading material and then off-line gathering of the articles from search procedures in the library or through inter-library loans. Many of the key databases are not full-text – they provide only the abstracts and citations of articles to indicate their relevance to your information search. Until more databases are full-text, you will continue to need your Information Centre and the library network.

To get started you will need a terminal or a personal computer with a modem and communications software. If you already have a personal computer, it can be adapted for data communications by purchasing and installing an internal or external modem and communications software. Either approach is relatively inexpensive. Hayes modems and software are regarded by many as an industry standard. It is worthwhile buying a 1200/2400-baud modem in order to speed up information reception. Although some database vendors charge you more for transmitting data faster, it is still cheaper for you to stream the data into memory and then review the material off-line. Not all vendors, however, offer 2400-baud transmission, so your modem should allow for lower rates of reception, too.

Once the hardware is in place, the next step is to obtain a database subscription through a single or multiple database vendor.

See the appendices for a listing of a selection of vendors, or purchase a directory of databases such as the comprehensive 'Directory of Online Databases', Cuadra/Elsevier, 52 Vanderbilt Ave, New York, NY 10017 (212-370-5520). Selecting from the many databases is made a little easier because several databases are sold through a few major database vendors such as Dialog (Palo Alto, California), BRS (Latham, New York), Mead Data Central (Miamisburg, Ohio), Pergamon Infoline (London, England) and others identified in the appendices. Gateways exist to enable access to multiple vendors, often in a menu-driven interactive manner, from services such as EasyNet offered by Telebase Systems (Narberth, Pennsylvania) and Business Computer Network (Cardiff-by-the-Sea, California). Gateways automatically select the 'most appropriate' database and then search and display information.

You may need instruction on how to use databases effectively. Although the handbooks provided by vendors are self-explanatory, you may wish to benefit from the free or low-cost courses of instruction offered by many suppliers — enquire from your local representatives of the major vendors, such as those listed in the appendices. Becoming familiar with the search procedures for one supplier should enable you to search the databases of others — the basic procedures are similar and easy to master.

The search routines require that you sign onto the system, select a specific database, choose the key words you wish to examine and then print your output. For example, if you were seeking to establish if Acme Industries would enter into the fiber optics industry, you might search for the following key words: 'Acme', 'fiber', 'optics', 'strateg?' (which is the way to reveal all articles with the word strategy, strategic, strategies, etc. on Dialog's databases). To find the articles that interest you, you would then link the output from all these search terms. This should reveal a few choice articles and perhaps a few bizarre ones. In one recent investigation, I was researching competition in the market for membrane switches and was surprised to find an article on expediting the hatching of chickens – something to do with them penetrating the membranes of their eggs. Other key words I was looking for were in this one, too!

Your 'search strategy' is critical, because it defines what information you will obtain and what you will exclude from the database. Think about the approach before going on-line. For example, should you search surface mounted devices as 'surface (with) mounted (with devices' or as 'SMD' or as both? Are there other terms that could be substituted in some articles? In this case, 'surface mounted technology', 'SMT', 'surface mount' or 'leadless components' are words which could replace 'SMD'. Table 3.3 illustrates the specifics of a search. I used Dialog–PTS Prompt to provide published material on the strategies being adopted by Tektronix. This search and output cost $11.02 in 1984. Although it would be more expensive now, database access can still be quite economical – approximately $1–2.00 per minute of on-line time inclusive of all charges. A typical search will take perhaps 15–30 minutes.

A helpful tip about using databases for timely competitive information: you can make arrangements with a database vendor to 'electronically clip' relevant articles and send these to you on a periodic basis. Just identify the search terms and they will routinely run the search and send you the output as often as you specify. Also, you can save those searches you run often or on more than one database, and execute the search routine instead of entering all the material again. This can save you on-line time and effort.

3.7 Conducting Telephone Interviews

By the time you are ready to conduct interviews, you will have gathered and digested a large amount of published material. You will now be familiar with many of the key issues your competitor faces and will have obtained considerable background information, but you may be a little hesitant about conducting telephone interviews. You may need to overcome a few personal barriers:

● Nobody is going to hang up on you. Most people are pleasant and co-operative, and some will consider that they will gain from speaking

Table 3.3   An example of a database search

I typed the following:	*The computer responded:*
select Tektronix	**1** 471 Tektronix
	(meaning selection 1 identified 471 articles about Tektronix on the database)
s strateg? or prospect? or outlook or projection? *(s is the same as select on this database)*	13635 Strateg? 5569 Prospect? 3362 Outlook 3244 Projection? **2** 24987 strateg? or prospect? or outlook or projection? *(meaning selection 2 identified 24987 articles with the desired terms. Note that some articles have more than one key word, so the total is lower than the sum of the elements above)*
combine 1 and 2	**3** 19 1 and 2 *(19 articles identified that include Tektronix and key search words)*
type 3/6/1-5 *(3 = selection 3 above;* *6 = classification for length of output;* *1-5 = number of articles desired for review on-line)*	3/6/1 1079544 Business Trends: Color Graphics Terminals: Tek is on a raster roll. 3/6/2 1058791 Funds split on overseas moves 3/6/3 1042567 Companies: The Cable Service Supermarket 3/6/4 977951 The non-captive CAD/CAM displays market could reach $2.1 billion by 1987 or 30–35% per year 3/6/5 973705 Nonimpact color copier-printers are filling the needs of computer graphics market, which is expected to reach $17 bil in 1987, according to Creative Strategies International

Table 3.3   *continued*

I typed the following:	The computer responded:
print 3/5/1-19 *(print off-line and send by mail* *all 19 references in the longest* *format available – format 5)*	I received detailed output from Dialog that helped me identify which articles I needed to obtain from the library to review in greater depth.

with you, perhaps because they wish to learn more about their industry or simply because they want – and are rarely able – to talk about details of their work. You provide an interesting distraction from some of their pressures.

- Resist making assumptions about what people will tell you. Ask, and you may uncover a considerable amount of information. At first read this may seem obvious, but many researchers assume that a respondent either does not know or will not tell, even before posing the question.

Interviewing in competitive intelligence is an important part of the work. It is time-consuming and, at times, frustrating. But perseverance and dedication are likely to yield the results you see. Interviews and the information stemming from them are likely to influence your findings significantly more than the review of published material alone.

Good interviewing practice may, or may not, come naturally. Each person develops his/her own style in the interview situation in accordance with his/her personality, but many of its important skills can be learnt – how to listen, for example, and how to draw out what you need to know.

There are good and bad interview situations. Some bad interviews will be the fault of the respondent, some the fault of the interviewer. For example, anyone can talk with people, and if enough discussions take place a vast amount of data will have been collected. However, this is not the purpose of the intelligence operation. Good interviews must be highly directed and yield correct, accurate information (to the extent that the respondent knows the answers, or has 'correct' perceptions), relevant to the research objectives and obtained with the minimum number of interviews consistent with obtaining this information.

There are two basic types of interviews: structured and semi-structured. In structured interviews, respondents are asked fixed questions one after the other. These are prepared in advance and asked in a pre-arranged sequence. This type of interview yields comparable information from one interview to the next. It is similar in approach to a mail questionnaire and may be carried out using the telephone. Disadvantages include rapid tiring of respondents, inadequate depth of information, and no opportunity for the learning achieved by the research to date to be built into the questions. In general, structured personal interviews are not recommended, and should only rarely be used for telephone interviews. A preferable approach is to use semi-structured interviews, whereby the interviewer is directed by a guide, but the timing, format or nature of the questions is left up to the skill of the interviewer. A truly successful interview should leave the respondent feeling that he/she has just engaged in an interesting discussion, rather than an interview. The key is to let the respondents talk about what is important to them, while aiding their recall to ensure that they cover the topics for which you have planned a response.

Your first step will be to develop a contact list of individuals who may be able to provide the insight you need. In chapter 3.3, sources of information of this type were identified. You will need to supplement such a list of contacts through techniques such as the following:

- Reference trade directories.

- Milk articles for all the names you can. Articles will frequently quote sources who would be helpful contributors to your project.

- Contact authors of relevant articles to find out what information they had 'left on the cutting room floor' when they wrote their articles, and what the sources were.

- Segregate sources into 'friendly' and 'unfriendly' categories. Friendly sources would include your suppliers, government agencies, trade associations and your distributors and agents. Sources likely to be unsympathetic to your information needs include specific competitors and those companies or individuals that depend heavily on competitors for their livelihood, such as sole-source suppliers of products or services. Contact 'friendly' sources first, both to find out what they know and to obtain referrals to others.

- Make cold calls to the switchboard to identify contacts.

- Before you call anybody, prepare:
    - ★ an interview guide;
    - ★ a respondent profile.

An interview guide is required to make sure that you identify the main issues you would like addressed in the course of the discussion. The guide (or guides, if you are calling several different categories of respondents) does not have to detail the precise phrasing of the questions, nor their specific order. By having a listing of the issues, you will know when you have succeeded in the interview and when your discussion is complete. Do not attempt to follow the guide rigidly – a successful interview should allow some leeway in the issues that are covered if it is to reflect the areas that are perceived as important by the respondents. After you have conducted a few interviews, you should update your guides to reflect the knowledge you now have and the outstanding issues to be resolved. Only if you are seeking confirmation or validation of responses should you consider putting questions to one respondent that you have previously directed to another. Either ensure that your questions reflect greater depth or stop interviewing.

To ensure that your contacts yield considerable information over an extended period of time, you will need periodically to call some of the respondent back to obtain updates, verification, to review hypotheses or to ask directed questions about key issues that may arise in the future. You should systematize your contact network by preparing respondent profiles such as the one described in figure 3.4. This will enable you to remain familiar with the key items of interest to respondents and to do small favors to help them and cement your relationship, such as sending articles or information which you know will interest them. At the conclusion of each interview prepare a form to assess the conclusions from the interview and what actions should be undertaken. (A sample form is presented as figure 3.5.) Also, update the respondent profile where appropriate.

The articles you have read are targeting a mass audience and have obviously not been written to help you resolve your competitive issues. Although you will have obtained insight from these publications, customized information can only come from personal or telephone interviews. Good interview techniques are vital if the answers you are to obtain are to be usable and actionable. The following guidelines will help ensure that the discussion yields the information you seek:

- The quality of your style will improve with time, so start by doing the less important interviews first, so that you can 'warm up', adjust your approach and gain confidence.

- Introduce yourself and your reason for calling. Be honest and do not misrepresent yourself.

FROM THE FILES OF: .... PAGE # ....
CONTACT # ....

RESPONDENT _____

TITLE _____

COMPANY _____

ADDRESS _____

_____

TELEPHONE # _____

INITIAL APPROACH:
TELEPHONE COLD CALL ☐ TRADE SHOW ☐
REFERRAL: FROM ARTICLE ☐ PRESS ☐ INDUSTRY CONTACT ☐
DETAILS: _____

AREAS OF KNOWLEDGE   DETAILS/AREAS OF INTEREST
1. TECHNOLOGY _____
_____
_____

2. INDUSTRY/MARKET/ _____
DEMAND _____
_____

3. COMPANIES/SUPPLY _____
_____
_____

4. PEOPLE _____
_____
_____

HISTORY OF CONTACT:
DATES   AREAS OF DISCUSSION/REMARKS/AREAS OF SENSITIVITY
_____ _____
_____ _____
_____ _____
_____ _____
_____ _____

Figure 3.4   Respondent profile

- State early on that you are not seeking to sell anything, but would like to share views about aspects of the industry.

- If someone has referred you to this individual, mention who it was,

RESPONDENT _____

INTERVIEW DATE _____

CONTACT: TELEPHONE ☐   IN PERSON ☐

INTERVIEWER _____

PAGE #

CONTACT #

Interview guide
is attached

KEY FINDINGS

AREAS TO BE SUBSTANTIATED

ACTIONS TO BE TAKEN

SOURCES TO BE CONTACTED

NEW SOURCES IDENTIFIED & AREAS OF EXPERTISE

Figure 3.5   Conclusions from interview

even if the contact was only a few minutes previously elsewhere within the company. Such a bridge improves your credibility and acceptance.

- Prequalify the respondent to ensure that this is indeed the right person to be answering your questions.

- Establish if the person is busy. Such a basic courtesy is often overlooked and could lead you to make an incorrect assumption about the brevity of the interview or the quality of the discussion.

- If the person is busy or 'in a meeting', leave a message and mention a time when you will call again. You are imposing an obligation if you expect the respondent to call back.

- Provide an incentive to the person to participate in the discussion. Offer to share information where you can, and do so early on in the interview so that the individual understands that he/she has much to learn from you.

- Relate to the respondent as a peer, because this is the best way to ensure high volumes of quality information transfer. Resist the temptation to appear overbearingly powerful (even if you are!) or meekly submissive (which is usually transparent, because you are not, or you would not be engaging in this assertive program in the first place).

- Simple, open-ended questions are at the heart of good interviewing technique. Yes/no answers in interviews are seldom very useful. The good interviewer should begin all questions with one of the following six words: 'who', 'what', 'where', 'when', 'why', 'how'.

- Do not ask questions with great intensity in a rapid-fire manner, because this will kill the interview within a few minutes. Goodwill may enable the respondent to get past an initial onslaught, but in a few minutes, patience for one-way information transfer is usually exhausted.

- Obtain quantifications and explanations for the conclusions or information provided by the respondent. Qualitative statements yield insight but do not enable your company to respond. A comment such as 'Widget's sales are declining, and now they're introducing a larger, faster product' could be met with the rejoinder: 'When you say their sales are declining, by how much do you expect sales this year to be down compared to last year?' (Response.) 'Why do you say that?' (Response.) 'Mmmm. That's interesting. And when you say they will be introducing a larger product, by how much is it likely to be bigger?' (Response.) 'And how much faster than their current offering?'

- Where people do not know the exact answer to a quantitative question, narrow their range of uncertainty – the result is usually good enough for your purposes. Ask if the figure is likely to be greater than ... or less than ... to provide bounds to the uncertainty which you can confirm and narrow down even more in subsequent interviews.

- Cross-reference statements made in the interview, with others presented by the respondent earlier in the discussion, and with information available from other published sources or interviews you have previously conducted.

- If you are having difficulty obtaining a response to a key question, you might use knowledge you already have and seek confirmation of an hypothesis by taking a stab at the answer. For example, if you wished to know what micro-processor would be used in a new computer, you might say something such as 'I understand that Acme's new computer may employ an 80286 chip. Is this your information, too?' Many people feel uncomfortable when an inaccurate perception exists in the minds of others, and will immediately leap to correct your error, and perhaps confirm your sound intuition.

- Time the placement of key questions. In most industries and many Western countries, telephone discussions of 10−20 minutes are common with middle- to senior-level line managers. More than that and you have a bonanza − less and you have either a poor respondent, insufficient benefits to offer or a poor interviewing style. Around the 5−7-minute mark the respondent should be warmed up and ready for your main question(s). If you present it earlier you may get a truncated response. If you wait till later, you may never have the chance. Slip in the question without fanfare or tremulous voice and move on once you have the response you seek without dwelling on the subject.

- Restate key responses to make sure that you have understood and that there is no more detail the respondent wishes to add. For example, if the respondent says 'I buy about half my widgets from Company A,' you could respond 'You said earlier that you buy a total of 2,000 widgets per year. Is it correct to say that you buy about 1,000 each year from Company A?'

- To induce a respondent to go deeper into a subject when he/she thinks that the end has been reached, bridge to an in-depth question by suggesting that you may have missed something or wish to clarify specific points.

- Conclude the interview by asking: 'Is there anything I can tell you that you would like to know?' This usually brings respondents back to the issues in which they are most interested and leaves them with a last impression that you are helpful and co-operative.

- Ask if you can call the respondent back at a later time to go over some of your main findings. The person will probably be flattered and more than willing to participate. This could open the door to an ongoing relationship.

- Lastly, obtain referrals to others who may know about your particular areas of interest.

Even with these techniques, you are likely to experience pitfalls such as the following that must be overcome:

- An efficient secretary screens you. It may be difficult to articulate your mission and persuade him/her of the value of your cause. Try stating your name, company name and the fact that this is an important matter related to your industry that you would like to discuss with the boss. Brace yourself for not getting past all secretaries. If told that he/she is 'out of the office today', you could ask that your name and company name be recorded and placed on the employer's desk, and ask when would be a good time to call again.

- Occasionally the respondent may indicate that he/she is not interested in discussing the subject matter. Ask what his/her concerns are, and try to address them. If still unable to resolve the issues to his/her satisfaction, thank the respondent and conclude the discussion. Recognize that a disproportionately small number of people yield the vast majority of the insight you need – perhaps 90 per cent of what you need to know is supplied by 10 per cent of the people you interview, so do not be discouraged if you lose a few respondents along the way.

- The respondent may mention that someone has just entered his/her office and ask, 'Would you hold for a moment?' This may well happen a second, third and fourth time. Hang onto your patience and ask, if this is not a convenient time to talk, could you call back at a later, more suitable opportunity.

- Your respondent may be argumentative. Do not respond in kind.

- Although you may be very knowledgeable about the subject matter, try not to seem like a 'know-it-all'. Respondents have little desire to share information with someone who appears to already be in possession of all the facts.

- Occasionally the interview may go silent as the respondent decides how or whether to answer a key question. In moments such as these, keep quiet – let the silence continue. Your respondent will inevitably rush to fill the void, often with particularly revealing material.

- If the respondent starts talking in tangent to the core subject matter, gently guide him/her back to your areas of interest. Many interviewees are likely to present an emotive argument about the economy, the weather or the politics of the day. Confirm that you have heard the respondent's argument and then refer to a point he/she made earlier about which you would like to know more. Say something like: 'That's interesting, Mr. Bloggs. Returning to a matter you raised earlier, I was surprised that you consider Fotheringham Industries a candidate for a takeover. Why did you say that?'

Above all – listen. Speak for no more than 20 per cent of the time. Take notes. Do not tape-record the conversation without alerting the other party and, because it usually establishes a barrier to communication, it is not recommended.

3.8 Conducting Personal Interviews

Many of the above suggestions for conducting effective telephone interviews hold equally for personal interviews. There are three key differences:

- setting up the interviews

- the physical environment in which the interviews are conducted

- the detail of the information gathered.

Whereas you should be able to conduct and write up 15 good telephone interviews per day, you may only be able to do this number of interviews per week in person. Identify who you plan to meet in person and who will be contacted by telephone. Group the personal contacts together by region and have at least four names to contact for every day in which interviews are to be held. Phone companies in a single area and make interview appointments for a day 3–4 weeks in the future by saying 'I will be in your area on [month, day] and would like to meet with you to [review benefit].' Try to set a time. If the individual is unavailable, establish if you can meet for breakfast, lunch or dinner or, failing that, if someone else from the respondent's company can stand in for him/her.

Avoid falling into the trap of immediately interviewing a respondent who says 'OK, come now' when you phone, and then, after writing up the interview when you return, arranging another the same way. You can do one interview a day like this for weeks and feel that you are working hard.

When you contact the individual to set up the appointment, you may be told that you have no more than 30 minutes for the discussion. Do not be alarmed. When you conduct the interview, it is highly unlikely that the respondent will call for closure after half an hour. He or she may well be intrigued and your interview could last over 90 minutes. However, you should make sure that the key issues are covered by the 30-minute mark, just in case your interview is terminated.

When you enter the respondent's office, take cues from the environment to establish rapport and gain insight. Locate yourself so that the window is to your left or right, to avoid the possibility that either of you will squint into the light, limiting your impressions of facial expressions and body language. Try to ensure that the respondent has his/her back to the office door, so that anyone entering the office will be discouraged from interrupting the meeting. To reduce this likelihood further, close the office door when you enter. If the respondent takes a telephone call early in the meeting, you might ask for calls to be forwarded to the secretary.

By watching the respondent closely, you can establish which areas the person is particularly sensitive about. By registering such signs as crossed arms or legs, a hand put up to cover or partially obscure the mouth or a change of facial expression, later in the interview you can explore the reasons for sensitivity further.

You should take notes in your interview. Ask for permission first, though, as a matter of courtesy. (I have never known anyone object.) Keep notes during the interview as verbatim comments to avoid introducing biases or conclusions too early. Do not use big clipboards or leather-bound portfolios – make note-taking informal. Write quickly, or the respondent may lose his/her train of thought waiting for you to complete a sentence. Fill out and expand these notes immediately after the interview is complete to ensure that the maximum amount of information is recorded.

Personal interviews have important advantages over those done by telephone because they typically offer a longer opportunity for information interchange, they are more interpretative, and, importantly, allow the interviewer to present graphics, organizational charts, sketches or published materials for review and debate. Go to personal interviews with such material in your briefcase. If you have none, make sure that the interview is sufficiently important to warrant a personal visit – this is an expensive way to gather information.

3.9 Gathering Information at Trade Shows

When competitors gather at trade shows and present their products to the world, they offer a unique opportunity for gathering competitive intelligence directly. A few tips on conducting your intelligence operation at a trade show:

- Before going to a trade show, do your homework. Who is likely to be there from the competition? What are their backgrounds and areas of expertise? What products are they likely to be exhibiting? Prepare and memorize an interview guide.

- Before approaching the competitor's booth, do some reconnaissance, surveying the layout, organization and staff complement at the competitor's exhibit. Identify who it is you wish to interview.

- Visit the respondent's booth at a time that would be convenient for him/her to answer your questions in detail. Often this means visiting in off-peak hours.

- Select a respondent who appears to have had limited training or experience in dealing with the public. Such people are often to be found putting final touches to a piece of equipment that had the final touches attended to long ago – they seem to be studiously avoiding contact with the public and are present primarily to answer technical questions. Often they are the technical 'gurus' or 'boffins'. Usually, after initial resistance, they become very helpful indeed, not just on technical matters, but regarding many other aspects of the company.

- Do not misrepresent yourself.

- Keep your own secrets secret, but be prepared to provide information of mutual interest.

- Start with a review of products on display and then branch to a discussion of issues that are more relevant to you. Pick up product literature and other published material along the way.

- Go through the interview guide you have memorized. Do not take notes, but commit important details to memory.

- After conclusion of the interview, go to a remote area of the hall and immediately record your findings on 3 × 5-inch cards or a hand-held tape recorder. If you delay, many of the salient details will be forgotten, even though you may believe at the time that you will not forget anything. As for telephone interviewing, do not use a tape recorder without alerting the respondent – which probably rules out this method of achieving total recall.

- Make an overall assessment about the quality and positioning (both in the hall and from a marketing perspective) of the competitor's trade exhibit, presentation and personnel. Compare them to your own and decide how you can be clearly superior next year, if your conclusion is that you are at parity or close. Relative quality can be further assessed by anonymously interviewing trade show visitors, asking third parties to interview the key buyers (assuming they already know you) and doing traffic counts at all competitive booths (how many people are in the booths, how many are passing by?). Consider putting a third-party tail on key buyers to find out where they spend their time, how much time they spend there (use stop watches) and with whom they talk.

The likelihood of doing an effective interview at trade shows may be limited if you are, or think you are, known to the competitors, or if you feel uncomfortable about doing the interviews directly. If so, you may consider hiring one or more third parties to do interviews for you. Make sure you understand the tactics they will engage in and that they will represent themselves legitimately and in a manner with which you are comfortable.

3.10   Involving your own Employees in the Intelligence Program

As noted in chapter 2.4, a critical part of any intelligence program is ensuring that your own employees support your intelligence efforts. This can be aided by securing management support and ensuring there is adequate communication of the objectives and goals of the program to all employees. But it also requires you to:

- develop a reward system

- develop a negative incentive program for non-compliance

- provide clear, succinct direction, explaining what information is required, from whom, by when, and developing an effective approach for timely reporting

- establish a method of publicizing the program and communicating with employees.

Management must develop a formal positive and negative reward system. Perhaps the most effective way of doing this is to incorporate competitive intelligence objectives within job performance objectives and the annual review process. People should be rewarded for the competitive information they generate in their areas of expertise, especially if it helps them do their job better and if it contributes to the objectives of the overall program. For example, sales staff should be required to submit competitive data sheets that you have designed to reflect your information requirements. Those who do not, should receive negative stimulus through the performance appraisal process. Those who perform well might receive commendation in the annual review, in an information bulletin, or by means of a direct incentive, such as a prize for the most valuable and consistent supplier of competitive intelligence. You may even want to have an annual competitive intelligence award for individuals who have consistently provided information to help the company become more competitive. One firm of which I am aware gives an Apple Macintosh computer each month to the employee who submits the most valuable competitive information.

For the intelligence program to be successful, you need a well-developed system for asking focused questions of specific employees. Establish who the key contacts are for specific categories of information. Functional areas of expertise are quite easy to establish, because most companies are organized functionally, but frequently the information you need cuts across functional lines. Hopefully your human resources/personnel group will be able to tell you which employees have the insight you need and which have worked for competitors. If they cannot, do what you can to ensure that they modify their data capturing, so that they can provide information of this type in the future.

Consider setting up a newsletter to remove the mystery of the program and provide positive feedback. (However, be alert to the impact such a newsletter could have if a competitor somehow obtained a copy.) The newsletter could include coverage of continuing insight into competitive activity, your information requirements, what your company is doing to beat the enemy and cases where employee information has helped the company. If you have questions that require response from large numbers of employees, or an obscure requirement which you believe 'someone out there' might know, broadcast your need in the newsletter and indicate who employees should contact, and by when. (A major bank does this and it works well.) To establish urgent answers to vital questions, you may wish to use the company's electronic mail system, if you have one, and issue a general inquiry to all those who are on the system. (A very large communications company now uses this approach, and it, too, is achieving its objective.)

3.11 Validating Information and Confirming its Accuracy

Any successful intelligence program will be generating considerable amounts of data and, sooner or later, will find information from two sources that is apparently in conflict and, occasionally, information of a breakthrough nature – but, is it believable? Which source is right? Is the critical information correct? This can be established by validating two main factors: the source and the data themselves. The validity of the source can be determined by:

- the quality of the information that has been previously provided

- the reasons the source might have for providing you with the information (jilted employees, suppliers, and acquisition targets make unreliable sources, for example)

- whether or not the source possesses the information claimed

- the credibility of the source, which can be determined by asking questions for which you already have the right answer and then finding out why their answer differs, if it does (character references from others can also help ensure an accurate assessment of credibility).

The validity of the data can be determined by referencing other sources. If the data were from a print source, confirm them by asking focused questions in interviews. If the data were provided by people, cross-check with others. Scrutinize the data by cross-referencing the source's comments with data provided elsewhere during the interview.

If you suspect that the source is not in a position to know the information he/she is supplying, make sure that you are not being set up with misinformation. If you check with multiple sources at the same time and they all respond with the same story, without variation, and with no more or less color, it is likely that you are indeed being drawn into a competitive trap of some sort. For example, if everyone notes that Competitor A is about to roll out their successful Product X in Region R, suspect a feint, and that they may in fact be about to introduce it elsewhere first or not have the specified product at all. Alert your sales force to report the first sign of competitive activity directed towards your customers or potential customers. If ever you find yourself being led into a trap of misinformation, you may have an excellent opportunity to turn the tables and win a tactical battle. Keep a watchful eye, and do not think your competitors are not sophisticated enough to try such a stunt. They are and they do.

3.12   Keeping your Secrets Secret

Competitive intelligence is being practiced today to some extent by most major companies and increasing numbers of small to medium sized ones. Over half the Fortune 500 companies have attended executive briefings I have conducted in North America, and my European seminars are also filled. An association of competitor intelligence professionals now exists (The Society of Competitor Intelligence Professionals, 8375 Leesburg Pike, Suite 428, Vienna, Virginia 22180). Increasing familiarity with, and the spread of, the techniques and concepts of competitive intelligence bring a threat to your own company. You should be concerned that you minimize the amount of intelligence a competitor can conduct on your own organization. Perhaps you are now thinking of implementing or enhancing your company's traditional security systems to limit information theft and compromise – and you should. What happens to typewriter ribbons when they are used up? How is your trash disposed? Do any executives engage in practices that make them a security risk? When were your offices last swept for electronic bugs? Is the most sensitive information typed on a 'Tempested' (secure) personal computer or can competitors pick up the minute radiated emissions? (It is now possible to park a van in your parking lot and monitor what is being typed inside the building on conventional p.c. keyboards. To prevent this and other physical security leaks from happening, discuss your security with a consultant, and equipment vendors. (IBM, Zenith and Wang, among others, make Tempested systems.)

I suspect, however, that much more information is lost over the telephone, in conferences and in personal discussions than is ever stolen by intruders foiling guards, getting through authorized access zones and defeating identification systems. Many firms spend considerable time and attention seeking to perfect a security system against illegal activity. Few formulate programs to minimize the loss of information obtained quite legitimately from the company.

A program to counter competitive intelligence requires that you define what 'secrecy' means in your company. Many organizations are quite prepared to share much vital information with employees because they want the commitment that comes with a more complete understanding of the objectives and performance of the firm. Others prefer to operate on a 'need-to-know' basis, screening information from those without a legitimate requirement to be in possession of specific information. This can be counter-productive if it is enforced too rigidly.

It is appropriate to designate information according to its competitive sensitivity. Three or four levels of coding would enable different secrecy requirements to be reflected in a security plan.

Your security plan should recognize that the key resource most organizations mine, process and inventory is information, and it should thus seek to protect this 'soft' asset. The plan should:

- Identify what the key information is that you wish to protect. Typically this information should be that which has the most impact on your organization's future, such as technology under development, investment plans, capacity addition, equipment procurement, new business start-ups, acquisitions, divestitures and strategic, financial and operating plans. This should receive the highest level security access coding.

- Identify from whom each category of secure information must be protected. This requires that you understand from whom information could be lost, including current and past employees, suppliers and unrelated individuals. You should also examine the methods whereby loss could occur, such as inadvertent transmittal of information (usually the product of not being sufficiently sensitized to the importance of the information), the techniques employed by interviewers, and communication with one section of the public that could be accessed by another – your competitors – for advantage.

- Target each of the possible sources of information loss to ensure that proper sensitivity exists (particularly in the case of technical personnel, who derive esteem from peer group acceptance at symposia and industry conferences and have been known to communicate information that is unhelpful to the company's longer term interests), that non-disclosure agreements are signed to help deter past employees from information hemorrhage, that employees are briefed on the handling of interviewers, and that senior executives who communicate with the press have had professional media training to prevent them discussing issues they should not. It is likely that the media experts will tell them to identify four or five key points to make in an interview, and then, no matter what the interviewer's question, to find an appropriate way to 'bridge to an ace', finding one of the four or five prepared answers that most closely fits with the question.

- Establish the communications reception and delivery responsibilities of different levels of employees and ensure that the members of each cateogry know what information they should communicate to whom and that they receive only that which is appropriate to their level or the security code of the information.

- Appoint overall information 'gatekeepers', whose responsibility is to field calls from the press, consultants and others where the direct business purpose is unclear and, if appropriate, either to deal with the information request directly or to channel the individual to other employees. The switchboard operators need to have a brief checklist to help them decide when to send incoming calls to the gatekeeper. Procter and Gamble in Cincinnati, Ohio, appears to have such a mechanism. One company for which I worked did not. A plant manager was contacted by the press and, flattered by their interest in his business, he proceeded to discuss contentious issues which were subsequently printed in a mass circulation newspaper. The plant manager was exported and the rules of dealing with the press changed!

- Train gatekeepers in dealing with incoming calls, obtaining a list of questions in advance, and developing and communicating their agenda, not that of the caller.

After developing and implementing your security plan, you should test how well aspects of it work. Call up your own switchboard, and try to establish who is responsible for new product development at your company. See how they handle the call. Conduct interviews with the people to whom you are channelled, and keep notes so that you can upgrade your security plan. Conduct an on-line database search on your own firm – you may be surprised at what you learn, and you may pick up tips about which weaknesses need to be addressed. I often start off an assignment with such a search and my clients usually learn something new about their own companies from this process. In most cases there is no security plan, other than for traditional physical security and protection, but many firms are now taking action to address this shortfall.

4 Organizing Competitive Intelligence

- The competitive intelligence system

- The industry review

- The competitor profile

- The shadow marketing plan

- Benchmarking performance relative to competitors

- Benchmarking performance relative to excellent non-competitors

- Benchmarking in the minds of customers

The previous chapters have shown how to gather competitive information. Now organize your program by setting up the bare bones of the competitive intelligence system before you begin to gather the information, and then inserting what you find as it becomes available.

4.1 The Competitive Intelligence System

The information you gather should be organized according to a system that facilitates archiving, response to enquiry, system interrogation, tactical response and the preparation of key documents, such as competitor profiles and shadow marketing plans (see below).

As noted in chapter 3.2, at the outset you should decide if the system is to be primarily strategic or tactical in nature. A strategic system would require information to support the long-term objectives and goals of the organization, including allocating and directing resources; while a tactical system would seek to address the immediate imperatives of competition in the marketplace, such as responding to a competitor's new product introduction or price change. This suggests that an organization could choose to have more than one type of competitive intelligence system, or a hierarchy of systems, if objectives are both strategic and tactical.

The decision about which type of system to adopt will be determined by establishing who are to be the primary users. If you are serving others within the company, and the drivers and support for the competitive intelligence program are coming from line management, the use of the information will probably be tactical, requiring information such as competitors' prior win/loss records and pricing history on specific types of products/customers/situations. Having identified your targeted system users, conduct a survey of their needs to focus the system structure, data requirements, update frequency and other issues. Recognize that tactical systems may require 3–4 times more human and financial resources than a strategic system, because of the requirements for both more data and more current data.

In order to keep the costs of operating the system, principally personnel costs, within reason, try to focus your data gathering and analysis as much as possible (the user survey mentioned above will help). Although some companies do have a legitimate need for extensive on-line and full-text competitor databases, many would be better served by operating a system that combines manual and computer based approaches. One method of developing a system to serve your requirements is flowcharted in figure 4.1. This suggests that you establish the mechanism for data input and develop file structures in both manual and computer based systems before attempting to conduct extensive competitive intelligence. Once developed, sample data should be inputted and the system debugged before a wide-scale and, perhaps, multi-user approach is adopted.

You should develop your software based on a Lotus 1-2-3 or database management software package. Few companies will find it appropriate to build their competitive intelligence systems around the in-house mainframe systems, because these have been developed for accounting, financial planning and the order-shipping-billing cycle, not decision support. If you need to get your system operating as soon as possible, you may find it preferable to build the system yourself, rather than wait for your systems department to tackle it. This can be a valuable learning experience, and will enable you to modify the reports or any aspect of the system that requires evolution as you go.

When building the system, break it down into modules that cover the industry and specific competitors. Industry data should be organized

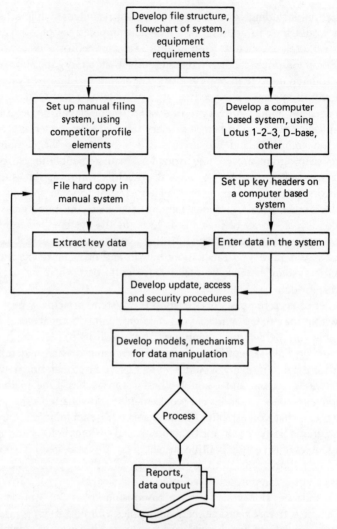

Figure 4.1   Setting up a competitive intelligence system

according to the key forces that affect industry profitability, which are presented below and discussed in the following section. Competitor data should be organized according to 'value-chain' elements and their outputs, essentially the key building-blocks of value in an organization (see chapter 5.6 for further discussion of the value chain).

Certain restrictions may apply to the information you maintain on individuals, depending on legislation in your country. In the UK for example, the Data Protection Act of 1984 may require you to register as a data user of personal data and to inform individuals that you have their personal data on file. Check with your legal department before establishing a database of personal data.

The following list is provided to guide the development of the system file structure, although it may need to be modified in line with your industry, business or priorities:

Industry

- Industry sales, operating profits, after-tax profits, return on assets and financial ratio analysis

- Industry concentration and relative market shares in all product–market intersections

- Rivalry among existing competitors

  - Number of market participants

  - History of strategic change and market share shifts

  - Proximity to market, labor and raw material

  - Unionized vs non-unionized segment growth

  - Production mobility

  - Capacity – availability and utilization

  - Capital vs labor-trends, trade-offs and costs per unit of production

  - Changing economies of scale and scope

  - Technology

  - Promotion

  - Pricing

- Bargaining power of suppliers

- ■ Supplier concentration and trends

- ■ Proliferation of innovation in the industry, and the changing role of suppliers in guiding the diffusion and price of innovation to their customers and end-users

- Threat of substitutes being introduced

  - ■ Emerging technical developments

- Threat of new entrants

  - ■ Trends in off-shore company participation in domestic markets

  - ■ Relative ranking of profitability, return on investment in this industry relative to others

  - ■ Company announcements of diversification intentions

- Bargaining power of buyers

  - ■ Purchaser concentration and trends

  - ■ Trends in agreements, supplier–purchaser alignments, discounts

- Threat of takeover / ownership changes (which could cause some firms to take actions which run counter to their long-term interests)

  - ■ Factors which would cause corporate 'raiders' to be interested in this industry

- Bargaining power of labor unions

  - ■ Trends in labor settlements, broad details of union contracts

  - ■ Number of grievances filed, and areas of coverage

  - ■ Safety and other areas of union concern

  - ■ Dues paid to unions

  - ■ Union membership and trends

- ■ Financial health of unions

- ■ Issues associated with barriers to acceptance of management direction

- Bargaining power and availability of skilled technical and management employees

  - ■ Remuneration packages, employment contracts, signing bonuses

  - ■ Number of graduates in key fields

- Threat of this industry receiving negative attention by special interest, political and lobby groups and social critics

  - ■ Number of positive, negative and neutral mentions of the industry in the press and the sources and timing of the references

- Threat of legislative or political action weakening the industry

  - ■ Number of positive, negative and neutral mentions of the industry in Congress and the Senate, the Upper and Lower Houses of Parliament, or the seat of government wherever your company does business

- Bargaining power of middlemen (including dealers, distributors, trade representatives, agents and wholesalers) and retailers

  - ■ Number and profitability of middlemen

  - ■ Trends, changing concentration

- Globalization of production, marketing, management

  - ■ Review of international media

  - ■ Emergence of global production

- Other generic issues relevant to your business

Company

- Design, research and development

- Procurement

- Manufacturing and operations

- Warehousing, transportation and physical distribution

- Sales and marketing

- Human resources and labor relations

- Finance and treasury

- Management

- Products

- Markets

- Key accounts and customers

- Channels of distribution

- Pricing

Each element should then be 'exploded' to categorize relevant details for each. Thus, for 'products', you would list all the competitors' different classes of offerings and their distinguishing characteristics, performance differences, customer perceptions and so on. The system should also have multiple elements for each entry to allow data to be tracked over time, revealing developing trends.

All data inputted to the system should be sourced, and cross-referenced to any manual files that may exist. This will enable data verification when someone says (as someone surely will), 'I don't believe these data. Where did they come from?'

The system should allow for the monitoring of changes in industry structure and attractiveness, and the development of competitor profiles, and should therefore make provision for the capture and tracking of relevant data elements – discussed next.

4.2   The Industry Review

A comprehensive competitive intelligence system should allow not only for the tracking and monitoring of the specific activities of individual competitors, but also for shifts in the key elements that drive the profitability of an industry, which should lead to the development of an industry review – the first element in any consideration of competition. Competitor profiles and an overview of your own firm and business position form subsequent chapters of an integrated document, as described in figure 4.2.

For the industry review, the system should provide the data necessary to develop a document describing the industry structure, its evolution to its present form, its outlook and the forces which will determine its profitability, such as those Porter has suggested*:

- the intensity of rivalry among existing competitors

- the threat of new entrants

- the bargaining power of buyers

- the bargaining power of suppliers

- the threat of substitutes being introduced.

Porter's Model has as its foundation the implicit assumption that monopoly power maximizes firm (and, obviously, industry – in a monopoly situation) profitability. The achievement of a monopoly position is constrained both within the organization and externally by real power imbalances and the company's perception of threats of possible monopoly reduction or elimination. To maximize profitability, organizations should therefore be seeking to achieve a monopoly position. No wonder, then, that so many companies keep a scorecard on market share – this is one measurement of industry dominance. While Porter has considered a selection of powers and threats that constrain monopolization, there are others which are also drivers or constrainers of profitability. These relate to the firm's power relative to *all its stakeholders* (forces with an interest in seeing the company succeed) and *all its competitive forces* (those that have an interest in the company not succeeding to its desired extent). These issues include:

- the threat of takeover/ownership changes (which could cause some firms to take actions which run counter to their long-term interests)

- the bargaining power of labor unions

*M. E. Porter, *Competitive Strategy*, The Free Press, 1980.

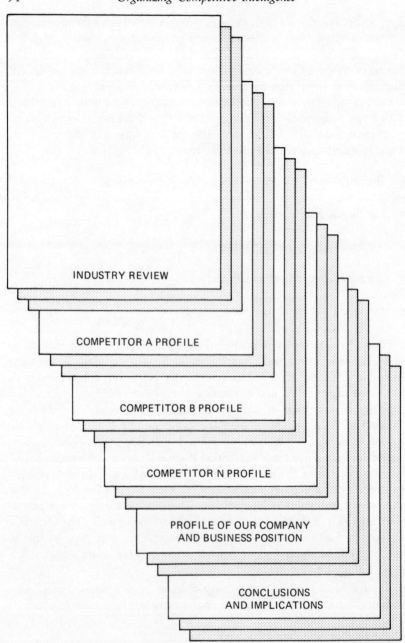

INDUSTRY REVIEW

COMPETITOR A PROFILE

COMPETITOR B PROFILE

COMPETITOR N PROFILE

PROFILE OF OUR COMPANY
AND BUSINESS POSITION

CONCLUSIONS
AND IMPLICATIONS

Figure 4.2   Reporting the system outputs

- the bargaining power and availability of skilled technical and management employees

- the threat of this industry receiving negative attention by special interest, political and lobby groups and social critics

- the threat of legislative or political action weakening the industry

- the bargaining power of middlemen.

All of the above elements should be used as headings of the 'Relative power' and 'Emerging threats' sections of the Industry Review, which could have a structure along the following lines:

- **The Business environment**

  - Regulatory, legislative, social, labor, technological, economic, tax and other issues as they impact on current and potential competitors in the industry

- **The Industry and its structure**

  - Development and evolution of the industry: industry concentration, technology, product, packaging, unit pricing/price structure, level of shipments to and from domestic and international markets (value and volume), industry profitability and return on investment, tax structure, core skills, level of integration, system selling, political position and 'support in high places'

  - Types of products available, features and benefits, sales by category, trends, major product offerings, level of differentiation, breadth of product lines, new product introductions (number and success rate, by vendor), standardization vs custom production, performance durability, differences in manufacture or assembly, patent protection, emerging technologies

  - Factors critical to success in the industry

  - Market participants and their market positions, market shares

  - Distinctive capabilities of participants and the reasons for their performance history (why do they have the market shares they do, why not twice or half as much?)

■ Firms responsible for the most important milestones in the industry's evolution (leaders vs followers vs opposers: which are the 'ones to watch'?)

■ How will the industry's structure be different in five years and which firms will benefit from this change?

● **Relative power of market participants**

■ Current and shifting power among existing competitors

■ Bargaining power of buyers

■ Bargaining power of suppliers

■ Bargaining power of labor unions

■ Bargaining power of non-union technical, management and other employees

■ Bargaining power of middlemen (including dealers, distributors, trade representatives, agents and wholesalers) and retailers

● **Emerging threats to industry profitability**

■ The threat of new entrants

■ The threat of this industry receiving negative attention by special interest, political and lobby groups and social critics

■ The threat of legislative or political action weakening the industry

■ The threat of substitutes being introduced

■ The threat of takeover/ownership changes

- **The market(s) for which companies compete**

  - Size (apparent domestic consumption), growth rates, segments (geographic, lifestyle/attitudes, age, income, family size, stage in the life cycle, marital status, ethnic background, purchase process, size of company, industry, and other industrial and personal demographic segmentation approaches), key accounts, sizes of city, cyclicality, seasonality

  - Outlook for demand in the market

  - Purchase decision-making criteria, unit and process

  - Market shares and direction of trends

  - Distribution channels employed, channel concentration, relative importance of different channels, regional differences, trends in channels of distribution, distributor margins, support accorded to different suppliers by channel participants (with reasons)

  - Promotion: media used, message conveyed and consistency – by segment, competitors' shares of media expenditures, allocation of media budgets, trade or direct sales push vs consumer pull strategies

  - Pricing: structures, rebates, discounts, terms, determination of pricing, degree of price competition, perception of value by customers

  - Technology: categories, systems emphasis, trends in development, trends in market acceptance, expenditures, competitors' shares of technology spending

4.3 The Competitor Profile

The next major requirement of the competitive intelligence program is the production of competitor profiles – documents which present a snapshot of the competitor at a specific time. Competitor profiles can be either corporate overviews, or divisional or product line profiles – or both.

In cases where companies seek to understand the competitor's corporation and lines of business, profiles are typically prepared by the corporate group and forwarded to divisions, who will add value and insight. In this way, the competitor is mirrored within a company by the individuals who are best able to interpret their competitive counterparts and who will be best able to analyze the information they need to make their specific business decisions.

The specification of key headers for the competitor profile should proceed from the most general to more specific areas of coverage. The following structure for a profile could be modified according to individual requirements:

- **The competitor's corporation**

  - History and evolution of the company, including acquisitions and divestitures

  - Mission and objectives (articulated and manifest)

  - Description of organization, locations, staffing, key officers, Board of Directors, product lines and share of sales and profits derived from specific product / service offerings, regions, countries, channels, key accounts, people, categories of customers

  - Positioning with channels, with end-users, with key suppliers

  - Distinctive capabilities

  - Strategic direction with regard to target markets, technology, products, promotion, positioning, pricing, portfolio of businesses and relative emphasis

  - Where relevant, issues associated with: culture (an organizational strength or weakness), strategic alliances, manufacturing, strategic suppliers, labor relationships, personnel reward systems, transportation and warehousing, sales force, marketing, finance, personnel, performance measurements (ratio analysis comparisons)

  If at the corporate level (if at the division level, record in an appropriate place):

  - research and development: human, technological and financial resources, protection by and use of patents and copyrights, funding by key customers (internally and externally – e.g. Department of Defense)

■ finance and treasury: ratio analysis, cost of capital, relationship to key providers of funds – including brokers, shareholders, bankers, level of ownership of company by officers of the firm, market valuation of the company's shares and the reasons for this valuation, leverage (comparison to industry), availability of additional equity or debt infusion, day's receivables and payables (and the implications for supplier and customer relationships)

■ management systems: approaches to planning, objective setting, leadership, control and monitoring

● **The competitor's divisions**

■ History (why is it, and how long has it been, part of the company)

■ Relative importance to the corporation (current and historical)

■ Key personnel at the division level (profiles) and the main backers of the division corporately

■ Financial performance

■ Dependency on key accounts, key people (technologists, marketers, etc.), products, regions, financial infusion

■ Portfolio of products and relative emphasis

■ Production: capacity by plant and overall, number of shifts produced per year, on-site warehousing, age and technology of equipment, labor vs capital intensity, union relationships, quality of output (objective measurement and as seen by customers)

■ Marketing: level of personnel, how it is organized (e.g. brand vs market management vs end-user/trade organization), media (expenditures – in total, and by type, agency – current and historical agencies and account personnel (profiles), advertising themes, positioning, consumer vs trade promotion, total discretionary expenditures (percentage of sales, especially during economic downturns and upturns)

■ Selling: number and quality of sales staff (experience, education), training, location of selling offices in relation to key accounts, major territories, approach to remuneration (base vs commission vs bonus), quotas, key people (profiles)

- Other relevant issues, such as those raised for the corporation overall.

- **The competitor's products and product lines**

  - Product, price, promotion, distribution, people, technology, quality, and for each of these, its current position, history and direction, customer and channel perceptions

  - Key accounts, channels, regions and issues covered or suggested by your business planning process

Next, prepare a profile of your own company and divisions using the format you will have employed for competitors' profiles. Compare and contrast your competitive position in the market with those of competitors and develop conclusions and an analysis of implications for your company:

- **Conclusions and implications for your own company**

  - Shifts in bargaining power and emerging threats to your industry and firm

  - Competitors' strengths, weaknesses, dependencies, areas of coverage and lack thereof, areas of vulnerability

  - Resource allocation and deployment

  - Strategic focus, direction, strategies for growth – impact on your company were they successful

Perhaps you are saying to yourself that you can see how this could lead you to a better business position, but that you do not have nearly enough time to do what is suggested here. The following three suggestions could help resolve your dilemma, although each has some detracting features:

- Focus your information gathering and analysis only on the most essential strategic elements that will improve your business position (especially those issues that affect how your customers perceive you in respect of their key purchase criteria). Use the development of shadow marketing plans (see following section) to help you formulate the competitive questions to which you seek answers. However, ignoring short-term tactical competitive issues is likely to limit the usefulness of the competitive intelligence program to some users.

- Consider doing this project once a year instead of on an ongoing basis. This will require less time and may enable you to second individuals to a project team for a short-term concentrated effort.

- Contract out the required work to professional consultants who are experienced at doing projects of this type. This approach could be constrained by budget, but would benefit from the economies of experience that knowledgeable consultants should be able to bring to the project.

4.4 The Shadow Marketing Plan

After competitor profiles have been prepared and the implications of the findings assessed for their impact on your company, you should develop shadow marketing plans for your major competitors' products/services. If you used shadow marketing plans to help formulate the key questions you sought throughout your competitive intelligence program, then this step would involve filling the gaps with the information now available to you.

The format and structure of the shadow marketing plan should be identical to those of the marketing plans you use in your own company to facilitate comparison and to identify the key areas of pressure on your firm and areas of opportunity. The shadow marketing plans could cover the topics listed in table 4.1.*

The shadow marketing plan should be the key tool of the competitor 'shadows', those people employed by your firm whose task it is to monitor and interpret competitive activity for its implications in the context of your own company. They should refer to the plan to determine whether your own objectives are achievable, and what should be changed if they are not (new objectives, strategies or implementation). It should be used in the formulation of contingency plans to address possible competitive threats — for the purpose of risk reduction, a vital part of the successful achievement of any business plan.

*P. Kotler and R. E. Turner, *Marketing Management*, Prentice Hall, p. 287 (modified in the text by the author).

Table 4.1   The shadow marketing plan

Section	Purpose
Executive summary	A brief overview of the competitor's plan for quick review by management
Current marketing situation	Relevant background data on the market, product, distribution, macro-environment and competitor's competition
'SWOTI' analysis	A summary of the competitor's Strengths, Weaknesses, Opportunities, Threats and Issues that the product/service must address
Objectives	A presentation of the competitor's likely product/service objectives, outlining volume, revenue, market share, profit and return on investment objectives
Marketing strategies	A presentation of the broad approach that will be used to address the plan's objectives: identifying (and modifying, if appropriate) target markets, positioning, technology, product, promotion, pricing, distribution, service, relationship management
Implementation	Answers the questions: What will the competitor do? How much will they spend? When will they seek achievement of the objectives? What will be the key milestones? Who will do the work?
Projected income statement	Pro-forma profit-and-loss statement

4.5   Benchmarking Performance Relative to Competitors

After you have completed the shadow marketing plan, you should be in a position to benchmark your company and its offerings in relation to competitors and gain insight from the differences that may exist. The objective of this activity is to establish how your firm stacks up relative to its major competitors in terms of its efficiency and effectiveness. The bases for comparison should be:

- **reality**: measurable differences in every element of the value chain

- **perception**: how your company and its extended product offering (product, technical support, after-sales service and other ancillary services) are perceived by both customers and other key stakeholders, such as suppliers (vital for businesses with rapidly changing technologies), distributors, employees, share owners and bankers.

Figure 4.3 describes the elements of benchmarking leading to strategy development.

• Start the benchmarking process by obtaining income statements for products or product lines which comprise an important percentage of your company's sales and profits. Next to your organization's performance, rule columns to allow you to insert figures for your competitors. Reference your competitive intelligence database, the competitor profiles and the shadow marketing plans to establish competitors' cost structures relative to your own. Indeed, the shadow marketing plans should have concluded with income statements providing this kind of information. Your initial assumption may be that financial information describing your competitors' operations is difficult to establish and that any attempt to develop an income comparison by product is doomed from the outset. That may be so, if your objective is to describe competitors' costs to the nearest penny,

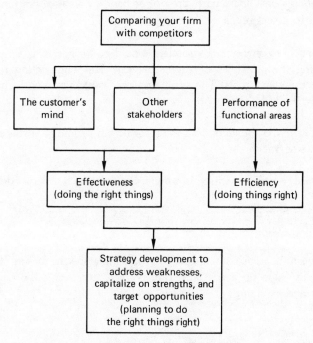

Figure 4.3   Benchmarking

but, if your objective is principally to take remedial action where your costs are significantly out of line, a range of accuracy within a few percentage points should accomplish your requirements (see chapter 5.4 for information regarding the preparation of a competitor's income statement).

- Buy your competitors' products and tear them apart to see what they are providing for their customers. Engineers in Detroit and Tokyo have long done this to examine the cost structure, assembly techniques, contents and quality of competitors' offerings.

  ■ General Motors, for example, has a 'Vehicle Assessment Center' to dismantle and lay out the contents of up to 15 new cars a year for 19,000 engineers, designers and managers to examine.*

  ■ An important factor in Xerox's turnaround has been their reverse engineering of competitive offerings, not just of their products, but also of their services. Xerox buy Kodak photocopiers for detailed analysis. When a machine fails, Xerox call in the Kodak repairman and clock the individual to establish the time taken to diagnose the problem to locate and install spare parts (including how often he/she must defer repairs because spare parts are not at hand), and also, presumably, in order to assess repair quality and durability.†

- Assessments of competitors' products should go further. Reverse engineer them using the principles of value analysis/value engineering to assess their functions and costs. The value engineer could work with marketers to review the following procedures:

  ■ Establish what benefits customers seek from products in this market/ market segment.

  ■ Establish which benefits this competitor's product seeks to deliver.

  ■ Find out how it does this – which features and functions of the product together comprise benefit delivery?

  ■ Establish the approximate cost of producing a specific feature/function module. Build up a cost structure for each by taking the equipment apart and assessing:

---

* *The Toronto Star*, 6 December 1987, p. F2.
† G. Jacobson and J. Hillkirk, *Xerox, American Samurai*, Macmillan, 1986, pp. 230–1.

★ on what machinery it was made, and the implications for unit labor input/productivity, production quality;

★ the costs of labor in the region where the product is made (from the union contract, local Chamber of Commerce), which, together with the above information, should yield unit direct labor costs;

★ plant overhead and indirect labor costs by examining the competitor's organizational structure, number of plant employees per unit item sold and the total number of employees in the plant less the direct labor component (calculated above);

★ the suppliers of the inputs (purchased parts and raw materials), the quality of the inputs and the volume of inputs (from marketing), facilitating determination of the costs of purchased materials used in construction of the product.

■ Complete the cost structure for each feature/function module by adding the elements described above, then arrive at the total product cost by summing the costs of all the feature/function modules and including those costs which have not yet been assigned, such as packaging material costs, non-plant costs (media, sales, transportation, warehousing, etc.) and corporate overhead.

■ Record the costs of each module and total product costs next to a similar analysis of your own products and establish where major differences exist and the reasons for the differences.

■ Establish the implications of changing your own cost structure to be more competitive, of dropping features/functions that add benefits not sought by customers, or adding features/functions to meet currently unmet needs.

This is a sketch of one approach to assessing the relative value of competitors' products. The engineers in your organization should be able to tell you more if you wish to conduct work of this type.

■ Such labors can be very fruitful. For example, Xerox determined that Canon were using a new type of photoreceptor (extruded aluminum) in their photocopiers, an approach Xerox had previously thought would never work. In fact, it proved to be very reliable indeed, and Xerox were prompted to consider using it in their own photocopiers.*

* G. Jacobson and J. Hillkirk, *Xerox, American Samurai*, Macmillan, 1986, pp. 230–1.

4.6   Benchmarking Performance Relative to Excellent Non-competitors

Benchmarking, as described above, seeks to ensure that your firm out-performs the competitor in respect of the main components of value your organization adds to the products you make, or the services you provide. Benchmarking relative to excellent non-competitors takes the process one step further – it seeks to ensure that your company is absolutely the best performer in respect of value-addition, not simply relative to your competitors. After all, your competitors may not be the best at what they do. Often, better firms are to be found in other industries, at least for some of the things you do. For example, if your firm markets adult clothing, you should consider what lessons can be learned from excellent marketers of other products such as consumer packaged goods, an area in which Procter and Gamble, for instance, are a major force. Although your company and theirs operate in entirely different arenas. P & G could serve as an example to be followed in some areas. For instance, P & G have learned how to control their channels of distribution: in an industry characterized by trade 'push', P & G seem to pay less attention to their retailers than to their end-users. Through multi-brand strategies, they pre-empt competition, crowd store shelves and expose their end-users to their message repeatedly and continuously, limiting the need to offer heavy trade 'push' incentives.

Benchmarking against non-competitors should identify the best firms for each of the value-adding steps in your business, without regard to industry. Table 4.2 lists a selection of companies which seem to be particularly strong in adding value to specific aspects of a business.

You could gain a competitive edge by examining each element of your business in relation to those companies which are particularly good in that specific aspect. For example, firms in the courier industry have much to teach others about the logistics and technology of transportation and physical distribution; studying IBM's approach to employee relations (and much else) provides opportunities to improve your own culture, employee selection, training, career path management, performance measurement, reward and punishment mechanisms, and so on.

You can go further. By understanding another company's cost structure, you can establish whether there are opportunities to improve your own efficiency and effectiveness. You may consider other companies to be better or more relevant in selected areas than the ones I have identified. Whichever companies you select, approach them to trade information, and benefit from one another's expertise in specific areas. This twinning of firms and exchange of information about what works for you in your businesses, what it costs you to conduct specific tasks and what you do differently

Table 4.2

Value-adding element:	Examples of firms with particular strength in these areas:
● Design	Honda Motor, Braun, Jaguar, Apple
● Research	Cray Research, AT&T/Bell Labs, Genentech, BASF
● Development	Texas Instruments, Matsushita, Sinclair, International Flavours and Fragrances
● Procurement/purchasing	NCR, Apple, Trump
● Manufacturing and operations	Toyota Motor, Northern Telecom
● Warehousing	L. L. Bean, Canadian Tire
● Transportation and physical distribution	Purolator, Emery
● Sales	RJR Nabisco, Pepsi-Cola/Frito-Lay, Novo
● Marketing	Procter and Gamble, Miller, Labatts, Guinness, Ford, Toshiba
● Human resources and labor relations	IBM, Johnson & Johnson
● Finance and treasury	DuPont, ITT
● Management (planning, organizing, leading, controlling)	DuPont, IBM

from one another and why, have the potential to help both companies. Think hard before approaching a firm for information swapping.

■ When Xerox used this concept, they wished to address a problem in inventory management and order picking, stemming from the handling of partial pallets of parts. They decided that L.L. Bean, a mail order company, were likely to have similar problems, so they approached them to gain understanding about how to automate warehouse operations. On the basis of this information, they developed their own software and, amongst other benefits, cut down on the distance traveled by warehousemen as they collect a few items from many pallets.*

Becoming the best of the best in all aspects of your business makes you a difficult target – not only will you out-perform competitors, but you will have a lead time over their response. Being more efficient and effective in your operations is a worthwhile objective, but only when your customers and potential customers see you to be better at doing some important thing will the financial reward really become apparent.

*G. Jacobson and J. Hillkirk, *Xerox, American Samurai*, Macmillan, 1986, pp. 230–1.

4.7   Benchmarking in the Minds of Customers

Benchmarking your company relative to other companies to become the best in your industry has the implicit assumption that customers will appreciate you for what you really are. However, it is perception that drives product/service purchase and repeat purchase. Reality can and does affect perception, but, on its own, it may not be sufficient to win the sale. For example, does the customer really care that you have the latest management information systems in place, or that your warehouse is extensively automated, as in the example discussed above? Of course not. Customers care only that their requirements should be addressed by your company, and that you help them achieve their objectives. Thus it is critical to understand how your company compares with your major competitors in respect of the main issues that motivate customers' purchase decisions, and those that maintain the vendor/customer relationship. Figure 4.4 provides a framework for assessing the relative competitive value your company delivers, as seen by your customers.

Chapter 2.2 discussed the identification of customers' key purchase criteria and the positioning of your company and competitors in respect of each issue. This is the essence of benchmarking in the minds of customers. Conducting an assessment of this type on an ongoing basis serves to track the evolution of customers' perceptions and provides a basis for rating the 'quality' of your sales (the basis on which the sale is made – price vs non-price criteria) and your organization's improving or worsening long-term prospects.

Expanding the benchmarking process to include middlemen will help ensure that you receive the necessary time, attention and support from your representatives. At this level, your competitors may not be the same ones as those with which you compete in the end-user marketplace. Many middlemen carry complementary lines which, while not competing directly with one another, nevertheless merit different levels of attention from the trade, perhaps because they do not all offer equal profit or other opportunities.

- In one recent assignment, we identified the distributor battle-ground as more important than that of the end-user, because our client was not receiving the support it needed to deliver its programs effectively to the ultimate purchaser. A benchmarking process of the type described here helped identify approaches to improve the response the client received from its distributors. The program went further, and examined the attitudes and perceptions of distributors serving competitors, enabling their

Product or service:

Market segment:

Date of evaluation:

Rating of importance of key vendor and product/service selection/purchase criteria to customers in this segment:[a]   (Scoring: 1 = unimportant; 100 = extremely important)

Normalized value

	Selection/purchase criteria	Rating	(Normalize so that the total of the rating is 100)
1	_____	_____	_____
2	_____	_____	_____
3	_____	_____	_____
4	_____	_____	_____
5	_____	_____	_____

Rate the performance of the major competitors perceived by the customers in respect of each selection criterion: (Scoring: 1% = very poor, 100% = perfect)

	Criterion	Your company	Competitor: A	B	C	D	E
1	_____	_____	—	—	—	—	—
2	_____	_____	—	—	—	—	—
3	_____	_____	—	—	—	—	—
4	_____	_____	—	—	—	—	—
5	_____	_____	—	—	—	—	—

Multiply the normalized value of each selection criterion by the performance of companies in respect of each criterion, and sum to arrive at a 'Competitiveness Benchmark'.

	Criterion	Your company	Competitor: A	B	C	D	E
1	_____	_____	—	—	—	—	—
2	_____	_____	—	—	—	—	—
3	_____	_____	—	—	—	—	—
4	_____	_____	—	—	—	—	—
5	_____	_____	—	—	—	—	—

Competitiveness Benchmark 19 - - ——— — — — —
(a measurement of relative value delivered)

[a] This assessment could be divided into vendor and product/service selection criteria, with each being treated separately. Similarly, selection and support criteria of middlemen could be evaluated separately.

Figure 4.4   Benchmarking in the minds of customers

disaffected, but important, middlemen to be targeted by our client with a view to having them represent this company instead.

- When benchmarking your products relative to those of competitors in the minds of customers, consider the implication of a new product in your market. How will customers receive the new offering? When Canon introduced a new photocopier, Xerox bought ten and gave them to their own customers to find out how they perceived them.* Not a bad way to establish whether your installed base is at risk!

*G. Jacobson and J. Hillkirk, *Xerox, American Samurai*, Macmillan, 1986, pp. 230–1.

5 Analyzing Competitive Intelligence

- Competitors' objectives

- Competitors' employees

- Stakeholders' expectations and changing needs

- Financial and market performance

- Financing structure as a competitive advantage

- Resource availability and deployment

- Industry and competitor capacity utilization

To understand competitors' direction, you need to examine the underlying factors which could cause them to direct their resources in a specific way, and the indications that this is indeed happening.

By the time you have completed the procedures suggested in the previous chapters, you will be ready to analyze the intelligence to assess competitors' strategies and tactics. Your analysis will be driven in part by the questions you formulated at the outset of the intelligence program, perhaps when you developed a shadow marketing plan for competitors. Many of these questions will be of a predictive nature, such as:

- What new products or technologies will competitors introduce in our markets?

- How are they going to change their marketing mix?

- How will they respond to our initiatives in specific areas?

- Are they preparing to wage a price war, and, if so, for how long?

- What will they be doing to gain market share at our expense?

You may also formulate scenarios to engage your competitor in combat and review the implications of these possible game-plans in the light of your analysis. Considerations of this sort will be reviewed in chapter 6.

5.1 Competitors' Objectives

If you are to develop a predictive capability you should understand your competitors' objectives. This could lead to you anticipating and thwarting rational actions they might adopt in pursuit of their objectives.

Asymmetrical objectives – when a competitor has objectives that are fundamentally different from yours – have the potential to transfer market share dramatically one way or the other. For example, many Japanese firms entering foreign markets seek aggressive market penetration, while domestic firms often have short-term profit maximization objectives. Directed by lengthy time horizons that encourage market participation for the very long term, and financially buoyed by a strong home market, Japanese firms often invest for market share growth while domestic firms in many markets are trying to do the impossible – grow market share *and* profits without making competitive investments. The result: predictably, significant market share transfer from the incumbent to the new participant.

Impute your competitors' objectives by examining their past actions and assessing what the drivers for those may have been. Often the implicit objectives and strategies carry more immediate relevance than the statements of executives with the firm, but, nevertheless, these should be examined to shed more light on previous activity, current objectives and emerging competitive developments.

> ■ For example, a competitor monitoring the statements of the owner of a major company in the North American candy market and observing their product changes, would have noticed that the company had an objective of maximizing asset utilization – an objective that led them to make the largest and heaviest candy bars in their category. Because product size and weight are two important purchase criteria, this objective led to market share gains for the firm.

The following is a select listing of objectives which you and your competitors may have:

- market penetration

- market entry

- market development

- vertical or horizontal integration

- risk diversification

- achieving targeted sales, profits, returns on assets or investment.

Consider your objectives and those of your competitors, what the desired performance levels are likely to be, and whether objectives are symmetrical.

5.2 Competitors' Employees

If business is heavily reliant on its employees, then it follows that the future direction of an organization depends on their capabilities and interests. By analyzing competitors' management and culture, you will gain useful perspectives. There are six elements to a thorough probing of an organization's employment:

- management continuity

- the career paths of senior management and changing power balances

- management congruency (the fit between current management and the strategic management roles their positions call for them to play)

- management strengths, weaknesses and capabilities

- the organization's culture as it supports their objectives

- organizational structure in the context of the organization's objectives.

One of the most important factors aiding a determination of organizational direction is management continuity. Companies with managers who have been with the firm and in their current positions for an extended period are more likely to have strategic and market continuity than those where management change is rapid. It stands to reason that if managers have been in their positions long enough to have learned the business, to have formulated plans for change, and to have implemented them (representing a cycle of at least three years, in many industries), they are likely to achieve more than managers in organizations where frequent turnover means that change is often articulated but rarely implemented.

> ■ Take the example of CBS, a company driven, in large measure, by William Paley since 1926 – when he became President. He was named Chairman in 1948. His continuous management and the frequent turnover of some of his immediate subordinates meant that understanding CBS required knowledge about William Paley. Obviously, not all companies have such strong leadership, but an understanding of key management should nevertheless yield important clues about the future of the firm. Examination of the paths to power can also provide an indication of the shifting direction and emphasis of the company.

The personnel/time grid in figure 5.1 may provide insight about your competitors' management continuity and shifting paths to power. List the titles of competitors' key management personnel at the corporate, divisional and product line levels down the left hand column, then note the names of the incumbents of these positions in the years when they were first assigned to these positions. If the individual entered that job as a result of an internal promotion from a position not listed, draw a line from the internal promotion bar. If the entry was from outside the company, pull down an arrow from the relevant bar.

Once you have completed the chart, you should be able to examine issues such as whether:

● the senior executives, including the Chairman and President, have been in their positions long enough to develop new strategies and follow them through

● senior executive continuity is maintained through internal promotions

● the 'path to power' has changed recently – from the financial stream to marketing, for example

● some departments, such as the Planning Department, are fully integrated

TITLE \ YEAR	19 70	71	72	73	74	75	76	77	78	79	80	81	82	83	84	85	86	87	88	89
Entry from outside																				
Internal promotion																				
Chairman																				
President																				
Chief Financial Officer																				
V-P Planning																				
V-P Marketing																				
V-P Manufacturing																				
V-P Sales, etc...																				
Divisional staff:																				
Product line staff:																				

Figure 5.1   Personnel/time grid

in the company (the tenure of the senior executives and their promotion paths are indications)

- morale is likely to be high as a result of many internal promotions at all levels without reassignment of staff that may have lost power struggles.

  - **Woods Gordon Management Consultants** did such an analysis for a major multinational company a client was considering acquiring. In the course of an evaluation to assess the company as both a competitor and a potential acquisition candidate, we found a firm where internal promotion to senior executive levels was rare and where senior executive turnover was rapid. We were concerned about both the depth of senior executive experience and the morale of the rank and file. We identified areas of weakness that our client could address as a competitor and should remedy as an owner. This company has since been bought, and our client was prepared to address key issues: management has been consolidated in the acquiring firm, and staff have been integrated – with the career paths they were previously lacking. Preparation such as this has made the acquisition extraordinarily successful.

Personnel/time charts can be completed using published sources, such as a series of annual industry directories, Dun and Bradstreet reports, annual reports, organization charts available from specialist suppliers that develop them, and Securities and Exchange Commission filings. Information of this sort may be supplemented by interviewing representatives of trade associations, financial analysts, human resource/executive placement professionals, members of the trade, major accounts and, in industries such as aerospace – where one program's subcontractors are another's competitors – directly from the competition itself. At lower than executive levels, the information about which employees are staffing specific assignments becomes more sparse, and interviews will be required to ferret out the information. Chart the incumbents at many levels in the company, paying special attention to those positions which are likely to yield its future executives. In addition, if you frequently bid against a competitor, find out who comprises the bidding teams against which you compete, and if any changes occur, assess their importance. Essentially you are building an organizational chart and watching how it changes over time. In many cases it will be difficult to complete the chart rapidly – you may need to fill in the blanks over an extended period.

By completing this chart you will have identified the key individuals who drive your competitor. To understand these people in depth (where permitted by law — refer to The Data Protection Act of 1984 in the UK, for example), it is helpful to develop profiles that examine their:

- career paths and significant accomplishments/defeats

- orientation towards others and their environment: are you dealing with a 'jungle fighter', craftsman, statesman or gamesman (one who 'plays' life and job like a game)?

- aggression (include a consideration of the sports they play and how they play them)

- organization skills

- leadership capabilities – including the basis for their leadership: whether their authority stems from their actions, presence (charisma), vision of appointment (support by superiors in the organization)

- social consciousness (including a review of the charitable work they have done and the clubs to which they belong)

- intellectual blindsides, fallback positions and zones of comfort (usually executives are most comfortable with the activities they undertook before their rise to prominent positions: these are the areas on which they often focus when building their business)

- management style and its congruency with the company's competitive position and market attractiveness (a manager with a humanistic, creative orientation may well succeed more in a 'star' business than in a 'harvest/divest' operation, where a hard-nosed attitude is often required, for example)

- performance and response under pressure.

  ■ In a recent assessment of a competitor in an advanced technology industry, our client was experiencing particularly intense competition in one area of its business it expected to dominate because the niche was narrow, its expertise well known and its support and company name predominant. Yet this 'upstart' competitor was seizing a considerable volume of business from the client, and was well positioned now to succeed in a major contract. When we examined the competitor, we found that the President's background was in the niche area under consideration and, furthermore, working in it was his spare-time hobby. We concluded that he would expend considerable effort to develop his company in this sector, something that has subsequently occurred.

5.3 Stakeholders' Expectations and Changing Needs

A stakeholder may be defined as an individual, organization or interest group that stands to benefit from an organization's success and could be damaged by its failure. Each stakeholder exerts a pressure on the company to perform in a specific way. Competitors respond to this influence by altering direction, or they risk the alienation of an interested party upon which the organization depends. Thus, it is important to analyze what the expectations of stakeholders are, the extent to which competitors meet their expectations, and stakeholders' changing needs that could cause a competitor to respond in a specific way.

Key stakeholders include:

- employees – unionized and non-unionized;

- management – executive, middle and junior;

- the Board of Directors;

- suppliers – equipment (plant and office) and consumables (raw material, packaging, etc);

- customers;

- middlemen – dealers, distributors and agents;

- stockholders – owners, institutional investors and individual investors;

- bankers;

- government;

- special interest groups, social critics and society at large.

Each of these will be considered in the following subsections (except for management stakeholders, discussed in the previous section).

Employees

Employees are major stakeholders of the company and their expectations of the firm could influence the company's strategic direction. For example, Silicon Valley companies used to be able to team up individual employees in a 'skunk works' that would work as a group for extended hours until the project was complete. Today, candidates for such projects often expect their work to provide for a more balanced life and some companies thus find it difficult to set up intense activity projects.

A general assessment of the changing culture of a competitor's company, and employee expectations of their work and their firm should include examination of expectations of:

● financial reward and remuneration structure

● career advancement

● hours of work, vacation time and fringe benefits

● intellectual growth

● social, affiliation and recognition needs

● the company's strategic direction for products, markets and technology

● management competence

● company risk: acceptance or aversion.

An understanding of issues such as these can be developed over a period of time by interviewing employees of the competitor as the opportunity arises – at trade shows, conferences and seminars – and perhaps by interviewing recently hired ex-employees of competitors, although the expectations and needs of this sample may not be representative of the remaining staff. Conversations could lead to an understanding of the employee satisfaction or lack thereof, and the extent to which competitors' companies are responding to employees' concerns. This is particularly important for employees in 'mission-critical' assignments, which vary according to the industry. For example, in advanced technology industries driven by technological innovation, it is vital that the expectations and changing needs of bright designers are addressed if firms are to retain the required expertise to ensure their long-term success. By understanding the key employee stakeholder issues in the competitor's company, you can explore issues such as:

- whether employees are seeking a different direction for their company from that management is currently providing (if they are, the firm's strategic direction could soon change);

- how aggressive the company will be in the job market;

- whether your company would have more to offer new recruits (from your competitor or from the open market);

- the outlook for growth in your competitor's sales and profits;

- their anticipated product, market and technology thrusts.

Unionized Stakeholders

Unions have, by virtue of concentration of bargaining power, important influence over an organization's efficiency and, as blockers in some cases, over the implementation of long-term strategy. Many of their concerns are aired during contract negotiations, and can be captured by reviewing the local press where the competitor is a major employer or by talking with shop stewards in your own firm, an especially useful approach if you have a common union where information is shared. The union's contract with the competitor can be obtained and examined for possible constraints that it imposes on your competitor's options, thus providing you with a potential opportunity if your company is not similarly constrained. In addition, the contract will provide one element of the cost structure of your competitor's operations, helping you to build their overall income statement.

The Board of Directors

The Board of Directors is a key driver of organizational direction, and its changing composition yields clues as to its expectations and underlying assumptions. Chart the members of the Board, their titles, ages, histories and backgrounds, and number of years on the Board, in a manner similar to that you employed when charting the competitor's management team.

- An examination of the Board can yield interesting insight. When General Electric named Jack Welch Chairman, a chart of the Board of Directors and their backgrounds would have revealed that Welch was appointed to the Board at the age of 44, making him a 'Young Turk' in a sea of aging warriors (the previous Chairman was 62 at the time of Welch's appointment). By understanding his background and competence, it might have been anticipated that Welch would shake the corporation to its roots. Welch has been called 'Neutron Jack', because, some say, like the neutron bomb, he leaves buildings standing, but the people inside have gone! He is a chemical engineer who joined the plastics division and eventually headed it. It is not surprising, therefore, that he has favored this area while restructuring and cutting investment in other divisions. (GE invested about a $1 billion in the plastics division between 1985 and 1988.)

- In another case, a goods producing company not noted for its expertise in distribution channel management or consumer promotion named an executive of a well-known manufacturer of baby boomer apparel to its Board. Monitoring this change would have shown that the Board's direction was changing, that marketing was to receive greater emphasis and that the retail channels of distribution were to merit priority attention.

Suppliers

Suppliers of equipment and consumables often have an important role to play in shaping their customer's destiny. Manufacturers of IBM-compatible personal computers ('clones') know that an early release, at a competitive price and in sufficient volume, of the microchips that are at the heart of IBM's p.c.s is vital to their continued competitiveness. It is their suppliers, companies like Intel, Motorola and Fujitsu, that increasingly determine their success. Because suppliers of key equipment, ingredients and materials can affect a product's success and the company's performance and direction, an understanding of suppliers' perceptions of their customers is vital to an analysis of a competitor.

It is important to differentiate between suppliers that are fundamental to a competitor's success and those that are ancillary. As in the microcomputer example above, some companies supply the heart of competitors' businesses, and a detailed understanding of such a relationship is critical to an examination of a company's future competitiveness. In such cases, you should understand the degree of supplier and customer concentration, and which industry segment is more profitable and where the bargaining power lies – who stands most to lose if the purchase relationship were changed overnight? Where the products or capabilities (such as technology, security of supply or other strategic issues) of a few suppliers are central to the operation of a business, competitors may well be planning backward integration. If this is the case in your industry, you may want to 'lock up' the key suppliers before your competitors have a chance to do this, perhaps by purchasing them, investing in them or signing long-term supply agreements. You might also consider whether your competitors are particularly vulnerable to the disruption of supply from a specific company, and whether you can manipulate such a situation to the advantage of your firm.

Even in less strategic situations, information learned from a supplier can be of important help in analyzing the competitor's:

- plant capacity and production volumes

- packaging methods

- changes in packaging, raw materials, equipment, information handling, warehousing and other issues affecting factory door cost, effectiveness and efficiency

- relationships with suppliers

- speed and terms of payment.

Other information elements to be captured in the competitive intelligence system were described in chapter 4.1.

This sort of information could result in immediate tactical as well as long-term strategic advantage, and will almost certainly yield hypotheses that you will wish to verify. For example, if you found that a competitor was behind in payments to suppliers and that it suspected the cause of this was a cash flow problem stemming from over-production, you might anticipate that the company would work down its inventory levels, perhaps through price cutting of finished goods. You would then wish to confirm how many days' inventory was held by the competitor and its channels to establish if and when price cutting would be likely. Information from suppliers should be integrated with your assessment of competitors' cost structures (discussed later in this section), showing some of the costs which are inputs to their operation.

Customers

Because of their obvious importance as stakeholders in an organization, customers should receive priority analysis by any competitor intent on seizing market share. Examination of the expectations, satisfaction and changing needs of a competitor's customers requires:

- an understanding of the competitor's customer base

- astute segmentation of the market

- market research and hands-on knowledge of customers' attitudes, perceptions and current and emerging needs

- an assessment of what it would take to convert customers from dealing with the competitor to having an ongoing relationship with your company.

Any understanding of customers must start with an answer to the question 'Which customers?' This requires that the customer lists of your competitors be built up over time.

Knowledge of a competitor's customer list can be used in other powerful ways. For example, capital intensive businesses participating in industries with overcapacity may wish to target sales volume from competitors' marginal operations, causing the competitor to shut down plants because the sales volume stripped from its plants makes further operation uneconomic. The challenge could be to obtain the closed plant and keep it shuttered, or to purchase the operation with no intention of running it, and, in this way, avoid the entry of a new competitor into your markets.

At every call on a customer, a salesperson should be recording with which company the prospect currently does business (this could be accomplished along the lines suggested in figure 5.2). This information could also be sought, in part, through a concentrated telemarketing program, or, more thoroughly, via a research program based on a combination of telephone interviews and personal contact. The research could seek to identify the names of key contacts, their purchase criteria and competitors' positioning, their level of satisfaction with current vendors, their expectations of vendors and the extent to which these are being addressed, their evolving needs and the immediate prospects for the goods or services your market, as well as selected additional competitor intelligence. Once the customer list

Date of contact: _____

Completed by: _____

Date of next contact: _____

Company: _____   Telephone: _____

Address: _____

_____

Contact: _____   Title: _____

Purchase decision-forming unit: Purchase decision-forming criteria:

	1	2	3	4
Initiator _____	_____			
Influencer _____	_____			
Influencer _____	_____			
Influencer _____	_____			
Decider _____	_____			
Purchaser _____	_____			
User _____	_____			

Purchase decision-making process:

_____

_____

Current supplier: _____ Sales volume (19__): _____ (19__) _____

Alternative supplier: _____ Sales volume (19__): _____ (19__) _____

History of relationship with current supplier: _____

Three main reasons why company continues to buy from major supplier:

Areas of weak competitive performance:

Potential to supply this firm:

as a second source: good ☐   slim ☐   none ☐   Reason _____

as a main supplier: good ☐   slim ☐   none ☐   Reason _____

As available, secure: price lists ☐   product brochures ☐   manuals ☐

Name(s) of competitors' contacts _____ Frequency of contact: _____

Establish: Products bought (volume) _____

Percentage-off list _____

Special requirements: Product ☐   Service ☐
Describe on attached sheet
                        Inventory Management ☐   Other ☐

Figure 5.2   Call report – competitor information

is obtained (and developed over time), it should be segmented into categories of buyers to determine their expectations and changing needs.

Market segmentation is an old concept, but it is not often accomplished well, bound as it is by traditional ways of looking at or serving the market.

■ For example, I have recently concluded an assignment for a client marketing consumables to a fragmented industry. It had historically segmented its market on the basis of the industries being supplied and the sizes of firms. Our research of its customer base and those of its competitors revealed that segmentation would best be carried out on the basis of price-sensitive vs service-sensitive customers. The client is presently categorizing its customers and prospects (competitors' customers) in this way, and plans to offer products and services of a type and in a manner (relevant distribution channels, pricing structure, level of service) that recognizes and tracks these differences in need and tailors the offering and its delivery to the targeted segment.

By understanding the expectations and emerging needs of key segments, and establishing how they are changing, you will be in a position to determine the market forces propelling your competitors in a specific direction, and the threats that they may be facing in their business. This assessment can help you establish your competitors':

- technology focus

- product development programs

- likely thrusts and alignments in distribution channels

- pricing strategies

- positioning in the minds of customers

- after-sales support and customer relationship management strategies

- strengths and weaknesses as perceived by market participants.

Market research should be complementary to a hands-on understanding of customers and potential customers' needs and their changing nature, not a substitute for it. Managers who are desk-bound, and do not see live middlemen, specifiers, purchasers or end-users, will not fully appreciate the nature of the relationship between customers and their suppliers.

All too often, management considers a relationship to be a positive reception by a customer that stems from entertaining, being 'nice' or being considered trustworthy. Management with this orientation fails to recognize that its company's needs are addressed when it makes the sale, but the customer's needs are only *starting* to be satisfied at the time of purchase. A vendor makes a sale, but a customer buys an expectation of need fulfilment. These needs are satisfied over an extended period, during which the buyer expects the supplier to support the product/service in such a way that it accomplishes its intended purpose — this is the buyer's expectation of a relationship. Companies that recognize the impact of relationship marketing may be more difficult to undermine than those that have yet to appreciate its importance.

To win business from competitors not driven by relationship marketing, alternative suppliers should understand which customers' expectations of relationships are not being satisfied by current vendors and position themselves in the minds of potential customers as viable, long-term alternatives to the incumbent. The development of a relationship management strategy to encourage switching is most likely to be successful if buyers' costs of switching are modest, have a rapid payback, or can be eased by the new supplier. The buyers may consider it important that their supplier have good personal characteristics, but this is not usually a sufficient reason to change, unless the product, price, installation/start-up, ongoing support, service provision and other factors are very similar from vendor to vendor; unless immediate and long-term switching costs are low; or unless they have been very disappointed by their current vendor. The interruption of the relationship between competitors and their customers thus requires an understanding of the level of investment the buyer has in the relationship and what it will take to interrupt those elements

- financial investment — capital equipment cost, cost of operations, cost of training, spares inventory, new business procedures (such as new computer systems)

- technological investment — the relationship between research and development teams of the vendor and customer, who have integrated new product development responsibilities and shared information of a proprietary nature

- operational investment — including computer-to-computer information transfer, knowledge of one another's operations that facilitates on-time, scheduled delivery of product of expected quality in the required quantity: in general, the avoidance of surprises

- psychological dependencies — such as the friendships that have developed between individuals working for suppliers and customers.

By understanding issues such as these, a company can begin to target specific customers or categories of customers to induce switching. Converting customers will require that positive differentiation of product, service (pre- and post-sale) and company be demonstrated and that customers' investments in competitors be overcome. Reducing switching costs could include:

- quantifying switching costs and offering a cash inducement to change

- providing on-site training

- developing new computer systems to replace those installed by competitors

- agreeing to penalty clauses for non-performance

- providing demonstration units

- having contingency inventory available if needed

- setting up emergency repair or problem resolution teams

- breaking up a high risk purchase into several lower risk elements, with decision points regarding vendor performance at interim steps: pricing could be divided into modest increments for specific elements of the product / service, rather than on a one-price basis for the entire offering

- developing an offering which is substantially interchangeable with that of the competitor

- targeting all members of the customers' purchase decision-making units, understanding their vendor and product selection and support criteria, and addressing these issues by instructing senior staff to execute a relationship development program

- providing assurance that your product / service and organization perform at high levels, by offering references, case studies and on-site inspection of other installations, if possible.

Middlemen

Expectations of middlemen, including dealers, distributors and agents, affect your competitors in three ways:

- the relative emphasis they place on trade-push vs consumer-pull strategies

- the extent to which they plan to act as partners of the trade, or whether they see any potential in seeking alternative approaches to distribution

- the channel strategies they adopt to serve specific classes of customers.

While it is important to research the attitudes and needs of middlemen in your specific industry, many middlemen feel that their suppliers:

- do not provide sufficient pre- and post-sales support in their markets

- do not afford them sufficient margin

- do not involve them in their strategic planning process, nor in the outputs of that plan

- do not help them to sell, often because they do not offer product knowledge sessions for new recruits, nor do they provide sufficient product literature, brochures, videos or demonstrator units.

In short, many middlemen consider that their suppliers act in their own self-interest rather than as strategic partners. Find out if this is the case in your market and what the impact could be on a competitor. Questions to consider include:

- Are relationships in need of improvement, bad but salvageable, or bad and deteriorating?

- Will the competitor recommit to its current channels?

- Can it afford to offer more margin?

- Will it re-align distribution against you and other competitors, cutting some middlemen and supporting core channel participants more vigorously?

- Will it go direct to all its end-users or will it serve only its major end-users directly?

Stockholders

An assessment of the expectations of a competitor's stockholders, owners, institutional investors and individual investors, can suggest whether the competitor will become much more aggressive in its markets, open or close plants, diversify or consolidate, and much more. Financial analysts can help you assess stockholders' expectations and they may indicate some of the corrective action they would take if they were in charge of your competitors.

Bankers

Bankers have the potential to constrain the growth of competitors, and have a limited impact on their strategic direction. Bankers are interested in ensuring that growth is controlled and that their investment is not at risk. Whether or not a competitor will be able to secure the funding needed for operations, capital equipment and expansion will depend heavily on the bank's perception of the individuals and their financial projections. The extend to which its loans are secure may also affect its interest in any new proposals from the borrowing organization. Assess whether the bank will be recommending more financial caution to the competitor, or would be amenable to expansion under the current or revised capital structure (perhaps involving the issue of more equity). This will require analysis of the company's financial statements. For example, in relation to industry averages, investigate debt-to-equity ratios, aging of receivables, payables and inventory, liquidity ratios (acid test and current test), time interest earned, gross margins and trends in these ratios. This should help determine the probable expectations of the bank or banks and the impact on your competitor.

Government

Government is a stakeholder in your competitors, but principally for the negative power it can wield, rather than the positive forces it can use to support a competitor (except where government is a customer). Few competitors seek actively to manage the expectations of government. This blind-side has weakened chemicals producers, oil companies, financial institutions, airlines, companies in the tobacco industry and others. Consider what different constituencies within government may expect from your industry and specific companies. Understand what impact this may have on your competitor's product/market strategy, or on any aspect of its operations.

Special Interest Groups

Special interest groups, social critics, newspaper reporters and society at large have a stake in your enterprise and those of your competitors, particularly when the product is used in situations where safety is a key concern, or where the manufacturing of the product affects or has the potential to affect the environment. The temptation in many companies is to pay little attention to these stakeholders. This can dramatically affect product success (GM's rear engined Corvair was discontinued primarily because this sector was aroused) and, in some cases, impact the growth or viability of firms, externalizing costs such as those incurred in pollution control or worker safety, because their suppliers and bankers often would prefer to not be associated with them. Examine the special interests at work in your industry, and understand how your competitors might respond to these forces.

5.4   Financial and Market Performance

Will your competitors increase their prices? Will they seek new channels of distribution? Will they introduce upscale offerings? Are they producing at lower costs than your firm? Will they shut down plants or try to sell them? The answers to questions such as these may lie in a thorough examination of their financial and market performance.

Before conducting any evaluation you should establish the objectives of your competitors (as discussed in chapter 5.1). Do they measure success by revenues, by pre- or after-tax income, by return on investment, by market share growth or other criteria? This assessment can be made from published statements of key executives, interviews with company personnel or analysts who monitor the industry. To accomplish this analysis you will need to:

- review the competitor's profit or loss by product, product line or division

- understand the investment your competitor has made in your industry

- chart market share performance over time.

Developing a Competitor's Income Statement

Most measurements of success will require that you develop an income/ profit-and-loss statement for the products, product lines or divisions with which you compete. (If you compete with the entire company, you can often obtain the audited financial statements from public sources, such as federal and state authorities and the agencies regulating securities and stock exchanges. If this is the case, you may still want to complete a product or product line analysis, because this could show how the competitor will focus its resources over the short and long term.)

Develop a pro-forma income statement using the framework presented in figure 5.3 (or an appropriately modified form). You may doubt that financial information of the type discussed here exists, but it does – certainly to the level of accuracy that would make a competitive difference. Do not attempt to develop an 'exact' assessment of your competitor's costs – this would prove too expensive and time-consuming. Rather, seek information accurate to within 5–10 per cent. This should be sufficient to alert you to areas where you should be improving your own financial performance, and to highlight the financial pressures which could drive a competitor's future direction.

Where accurate information is not available, identify a range of estimate, carrying the calculations through as minimum and maximum points of the range. That is, you may have a final solution which indicates that your competitor's unit costs are somewhere between y and z – this could well be sufficient to guide your strategic and tactical response. If it is not, return to the areas which created the broad range of estimate, and attempt to narrow the range by refining the estimate.

You could employ the following stages in assessing your competitor's cost structure:

- Start by estimating your competitor's total sales volume for the products/product lines with which your company competes. This may be accomplished in a variety of ways and should be cross-checked using more than one method in order to verify estimates based on:

  - information obtained directly from the company's published financial statements or annual report

  - information reported in the trade or general press

  - interviews with financial analysts

  - discussions with common suppliers of equipment and consumables, especially packaging material. Equipment suppliers can help you develop an understanding of your competitor's production capacity and level of utilization. Because everything your competitor ships

Product:	Year:
Market Segment:	Sales volume estimate (units)

	Per Unit	Sources of Information
Sales price	___	Competitor's price list
Less: Discounts	___	Interviews with customers
Net sales	___	Subtract
Less: Cost of goods sold	___	Add from elements below:

- materials . . . . ___   Raw material suppliers
- packaging . . . . ___   Packaging material suppliers
- direct labor . . . . ___   Labor contract, industrial development agencies for
- indirect labor . . . . ___   labor rates, equipment suppliers for productivity, manning

Transportation and warehousing . . . . ___ Your physical distribution department

Gross Margin . . . . ___ Subtract

Less: Consumer advertising and promotion . . . . ___ Your advertising agency, databases, publications

Trade promotion . . . . ___ Your salesforce

Marketing and other allocations: . . . . ___

- research and development . . . .   R&D headcount from financial filings, R&D department
for estimates of number by product line, rates from
industry surveys, divide by sales volume estimate

- installation . . . . ___   Observe installation, assess time, #, level or conduct
research with customers – hourly rate from
chambers of commerce, similar agencies, surveys

- after-sales support . . . . ___   After-sales service from market research to
assess elements, build up cost as above

- product trial . . . . ___   Trial costs determined from estimates of frequency,
trial units, staff employed – field research

- invoicing . . . . ___   Invoicing from estimates of your own costs,
understanding variances – ask finance department

- customer training . . . . ___   Customer training as per trial costs

Contribution . . . . ___

Less: Direct sales force . . . . ___ Direct sales force from sales dept. middlemen

Overhead allocations . . . . ___ Overhead allocations: determine level from
annual reports, work with finance to allocate

Income before financing charges . . . . ___

Less: Carrying costs: raw materials, ... ___ Determine competitor's cost of capital, day's
work in process, finished product,   inventory from annual reports, suppliers
spare parts

Accounts receivable financing . . . . ___ Estimates of outstanding receivables by
segment, supported by financials

Payment terms and discounts . . . . ___ Market research

Net income . . . . ___ Subtract

Figure 5.3   Competitor's income statement

is packed or crated in something, knowledge of your competitor's packaging requirements can yield their annual shipments

■ examination of plans of your competitor's plants, available through local and state planning authorities or the transportation and highways department

■ direct observation of the competitor's plant, including counting the number of cars in the parking lots, by time of day to assess the level of manpower and by shift (which can be grossed up to production volume by knowing the manufacturing process). In addition, the movement of transport trailers and/or rail cars bringing inputs and removing finished goods should be examined to develop or sharpen estimates of production volumes.

● Establish your competitor's prices per unit, typically from its price lists.

● Identify unit discounts by interviewing its customers and finding out what they pay for its product, or by reviewing contract awards.

● Subtract unit discounts from sales price to establish a net price and confirm this by dividing total sales revenue by units sold.

● Develop an estimate of the cost of goods sold, by working with your manufacturing and procurement personnel to assess the unit costs of materials, packaging, and direct and indirect labor. Information regarding materials and packaging can be obtained from common suppliers, while an estimate of labor costs per unit can be built up from knowledge of level of manpower, productivity of equipment and labor rates. Manpower levels in total can be established from published sources, such as credit agency reports and various directories, or via observation at the plant. Manpower per production line can be determined from equipment suppliers, while data on labor rates are available from union contracts, recruitment advertisements, salary surveys done by employment agencies or figures published by local industrial development organizations, such as Chambers of Commerce in the US. Fringe benefits should be estimated and added to the rates – discuss this with employees in your company who are responsible for remuneration and benefit packages.

● Chart the locations of your competitor's plants and warehouses and the distances between them. Also assess average distance to market from each site, by finding out the level of sales to each region or type of customer from each warehouse location. Establish who owns the trucking and warehousing facilities, and the probable operating or in/out and storage costs involved. Interviews with your physical distribution personnel, common carriers and public warehousing facilities in the same areas as your competitors will help in developing this assessment.

- Subtract above costs from net sales for gross margin.

- Assess consumer advertising and promotion costs by asking your advertising agency to help with the assessment. They should be able to establish the media expenditures of your competitors by brand or product category. Make sure that all such costs are included, not just spending on television and print media. Include co-operative advertising, outdoor and highly targeted media, and couponing in this assessment. If you do not have an ad agency, various databases and publications can assist your examination of competitors' expenditures – your library should provide more detail. Then convert total expenditures to unit costs.

- Expenditures on trade promotion can be estimated by asking your salesforce to report competitive trade activity, subscribing to industry monitoring reports (such as Nielsen's in the US and Canadian grocery trade) or employing third-party shoppers to track off-price discounts offered by retailers, displays and special deals for which the manufacturer may have paid. Unit costs can be developed by establishing the supplier's approximate investment in each of these trade promotions, by brand and then converted to unit costs.

- Marketing and other allocations can be estimated by finding out your competitor's investment in areas such as research and development, installation, after-sales support, product trial, invoicing and training, and identifying how these costs may be allocated to specific products.

  - R & D costs can be determined in total from annual reports and financial filings with regulatory authorities. Allocation to specific products or product categories could depend on headcount by area of investment or other approaches, such as percentage of sales or profits – interview your cost accountants for direction. Contact your R & D personnel to establish how well they know (or could know) your competitor's R & D efforts and manpower or budget allocations. Instruct them to gather information as indicated by your cost accountants.

■ Installation costs can be determined by buying a competitor's product and timing and tracking the installation activity. Alternatively, research with customers could help quantify the duration of the installation, number and seniority of people involved in the task and other relevant costs associated with labor, supplies and overhead. Labor rates can be determined from Chambers of Commerce in the area or through employee surveys undertaken by many employment agencies. Include fringe benefits as discussed above.

■ After-sales support costs should be determined by interviewing customers to gather information about the components of after-sales service provided by your competitors, and then expenditures on each aspect of support should be determined.

■ Product trial costs can be established by finding out the extent to which trial is employed in your competitor's marketing strategy, and then assessing the costs per trial occasion. Much of this information could come from your salesforce.

■ Invoicing costs could be similar to your own, but look for differences that could signal that costs vary, such as having an outside agency issue invoices, or having a centralized operation for a major corporation that would benefit from scale economies.

■ Customer training costs can be determined as for product trial costs (see above). Customers can be interviewed to find out the extent of training they have received at different stages of the purchase/ adoption process, and then the scale of the training operation can be inferred. If the trainers employ specialized equipment or have dedicated facilities, the nature of these and their associated costs should be determined, and a per-unit charge developed.

● Totaling the above costs and subtracting from the gross margin yields contribution per unit. This is a very important estimate. Compare it with your own contribution and understand the fixed costs of your operations and those of your competitors. What volume do you need to cover your fixed costs? What volume do competitors need to break even? What are the implications for their operations and your own? Are production facilities sized appropriately for individual companies and the industry overall? If not, how can they be changed? How can individual firms reduce their break-even points?

- Establish how many salespeople the competitor has in the field and at head office and approximately how much they are paid. Information such as this becomes available over time, either directly from new recruits or from interviews during hiring programs, or from employee surveys. Add fringe benefits and other charges salespeople attract, such as automobile and entertainment costs: aggregate and divide by the annual sales volume to establish a unit cost.

- Overhead allocations on a brand or product category basis can be arbitrary and are difficult to establish outside the firm from publicly available information. The total overhead is usually known from annual reports or financial filings. Work with cost accountants in your company to review the alternative ways competitors may have allocated these charges, which would result in a range of unit costs being developed which are applicable to overhead.

- Subtract these costs from contribution to obtain income before financing charges.

- Establish the inventory your competitors carry for raw materials, work in process, finished goods and spare parts by interviewing suppliers and analyzing financial statements. Assess your competitor's cost of capital and determine the carrying cost of inventory.

- Apply the cost of capital you have developed to your competitor's outstanding receivables, which, in turn, can be assessed from sources such as financial statements, creditors and Dun and Bradstreet reports.

- Determine payment terms and discounts that customers typically deduct from their invoice. Interviews with customers should help this assessment. In some industries, terms of 2/10 days, net 30, apply, allowing customers to deduct 2 per cent from the value of the invoice if they pay in 10 days, but must pay the net invoice price within 30 days. Your challenge would be to assess what percentage of the invoiced value of products sold do indeed have a deduction.

- Subtract these costs to arrive at net income for the brand/product category.

This provides a view of the competitor's income by product, product line or division. However, revenue or income maximization may not be the company's sole objective. Some firms measure success by Return on Investment (ROI) or other criteria, including market share. These issues are discussed in the following two subsections.

Analyzing a Competitor's Return on Investment

If ROI maximization is the competitor's objective, the income statement described above will only provide the return-on-sales component of ROI measurement. You will need to determine the competitor's balance sheet or develop an assessment of its investment in the industry from other sources. It is not realistic to attempt to disaggregate the competitor's balance sheet by division or product line, because of the complexity and limited value of this task. The key issues to examine are the inventory levels (raw materials, packaging materials, work in process and finished goods) and current investment in property and equipment. Of the two, inventory levels are the hardest to estimate.

Ways of assessing inventory levels include:

- Reviewing industry ratios (usually available from several sources, including government statistical agencies such as the US Federal Trade Commission and Securities and Exchange Commission, and private organizations, such as Dunn and Bradstreet, and Robert Morris Associates in the US), comparing the ratios of your own firm to these and understanding which factors drive any differences in performance between your company and the industry. For example, plant centralization may enable you to have lower raw material inventory per unit of output, while lengthy distance to a market comprising a few demanding customers may increase your finished-goods inventory holding requirements. Once you understand why your performance compares as it does to the industry, and have attempted to scale elements of the differences, establish competitor's inventory levels by understanding how they differ from your operation.

- Interviewing individuals who have toured the competitor's operation, such as common suppliers, to determine the volume of or approximate square footage covered by various elements of inventory.

- Interviewing suppliers to understand a competitor's purchasing cycle and determine the approximate frequency and size of orders. Observing the plant for incoming production inputs, and finished product and scrap/by-product shipments continuously between the periods of minimal and peak demand (often just before and just after the fiscal year end, respectively) can also provide clues, but this is time consuming and may only serve to confirm what is available from other sources.

An assessment of the investment a competitor has in property and equipment should follow. This can be estimated as follows:

- **Land:** gather information from the deeds-transfer or similar local registry office.

- **Buildings:** establish date and size of construction from plans filed with municipal authorities, and obtain average costs of construction prevailing at the time from Chambers of Commerce or private real estate organizations that monitor such costs. Depreciate at the rates prevailing under taxation law.

- **Equipment:** list the major items of equipment your competitor has in its plant(s), and the approximate year of purchase. This information could come from equipment suppliers, supplemented, in the US, from a Uniform Commercial Code (UCC) filing made to state authorities which identifies equipment – and often the purchase price – against which the competitor has secured a loan. Dun and Bradstreet credit reports usually provide some UCC information. Depreciate the equipment at the applicable rates.

Other investment in the industry could be roughly developed by assigning current assets less inventories on the basis of percentage of sales splits between divisions or product lines where you have the balance sheet for the overall company. If it is a small, narrowly focused company which does not file a published financial statement, develop an estimate of the balance sheet from public sources, such as those noted above, and credit reports.

You should now be ready to undertake a DuPont Analysis, as described in figure 5.4. According to this chart:

$$ROI = \text{Return on sales} \times \text{Asset turnover}$$

$$= \frac{\text{Net Income}}{\text{Sales}} \times \frac{\text{Sales}}{\text{Investment}}$$

Each of the items in the numerator and denominator can be further broken

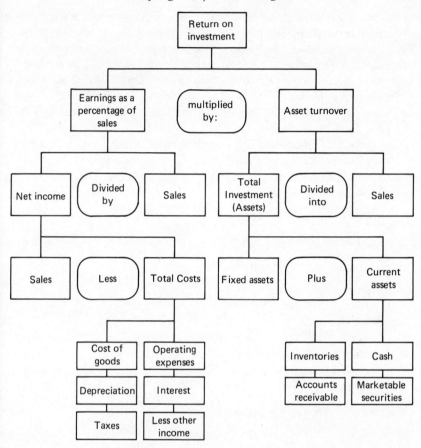

Figure 5.4   DuPont analysis

down, as described in figure 5.4. For example, Net Income = Sales — Total Costs, and Total Costs comprise cost of goods, depreciation, taxes, operating expenses and interest, less other income.

This should enable you to establish the financial strengths and weaknesses of your competitor's performance. Does it trace its ROI to high returns on sales or high asset turnover? Which is the weaker? If you wished to make its financial position in your industry even worse, where would you focus — on reducing its margins, on causing it to develop unprofitable lines of business or undesirable market segments, or forcing it to choose between investing more in your industry and withdrawing? What could it be likely to do to improve its financial performance? Could it prune unprofitable product lines? Could it seek to upgrade asset management? With increasing costs associated with new product development, could it be focusing its resources in fewer areas or spreading its risks around in several areas via 'strategic alliances' with others eager to do the same? Could it be amenable to a 'swap' arrangement, whereby it could trade unproductive plants and, perhaps, associated customers to make asset utilization more effective? Could it consolidate its operations? Could it sell off under-utilized plant (if so, would you want to buy it?)? Could it sell and lease back its land, buildings and even its equipment? Should you do the same or not?

Other financial ratios could help you determine the competitor's probable risk acceptance or avoidance in the coming year, based upon its overall financial health. Ratios which could aid the assessment include:

- **Liquidity / activity ratios**

  - $Current\ ratio = \dfrac{Current\ assets}{Current\ liabilities}$

    How strong is the competitor? – Are its pockets deep? Could industry changes or specific pressures you might initiate put it out of business?

  - $Quick\ ratio = \dfrac{Cash\ and\ near\ cash + accounts\ receivables}{Total\ current\ liabilities}$

  - $Day's\ receivables = \dfrac{Accounts\ receivables}{Net\ sales\ on\ account} \times 365$

  - $Day's\ inventory = \dfrac{Inventory}{Cost\ of\ goods\ sold} \times 365$

    Could the competitor discount inventory?

  - $Day's\ payables = \dfrac{Payables}{Cost\ of\ goods\ sold} \times 365$

    Could it have bad trade relationships? Should you verify if this is the case? How could you exploit this if true?

  - $Financing\ operations = \dfrac{Sales}{Working\ capital}$

- **Stability ratios**

  ■ $\dfrac{Current\ liabilities}{Assets}$

  Could the competitor seek more long-term debt?

  ■ $\dfrac{Long\text{-}term\ debt}{Assets}$

  Does the competitor need equity injection?

  ■ $\dfrac{Debt}{Assets}$

  Is the competitor over-levered/geared? Could it be bankrupted?

  ■ $\dfrac{Sales}{Assets}$

  How does this compare to your company's performance? Is the competitor managing its assets more productively?

- **Profitability ratios**

  ■ Usual measures of profitability, such as profit/sales, operating profit/net sales, net profits/total assets, net profit/average equity

  ■ $\dfrac{General\ selling\ and\ administrative\ expenses}{Net\ sales}$

  Examine how this compares with your company's performance. Is it a rude lesson or a pleasant surprise?

  ■ $Break\text{-}even\ analysis = \dfrac{Fixed\ costs}{Contribution\ margin}$

  Can the competitor break even at a lower dollar level than your firm or is the reverse the case? Does this give you a competitive advantage in the case of an economic downturn? Does it make the competitor eager to gain volume throughput to cover fixed costs, and make it even more price competitive?

- **Coverage Ratios**

  ■ $Times\ interest\ earned = \dfrac{Earnings\ before\ tax\ and\ interest}{Interest}$

  ■ $Interest\ service\ ratio = \dfrac{Cash\ flow\ from\ operations + Tax + Interest}{Interest}$

  ■ $Current\ service\ ratio = \dfrac{Cash\ flow\ from\ operations}{Current\ debt + lease\ obligations}$

  Can it service more debt or is it already stretched?

- **Growth ratios**

  ■ $\dfrac{Sales\ growth}{Asset\ growth}$

  If assets have been growing faster than sales, can the competitor sustain such investment? Will it? (Other competitive intelligence input would be beneficial here, such as commitments of senior executive officers.)

  ■ $Growth\ factor\ (GF) =$

  $$\frac{Net\ income}{Net\ sales} \times \left(1 - \frac{Dividends\ (preferred + common)}{Net\ income} \right) \times$$

  $$\left(1 + \frac{(Total\ liabilities)}{Total\ net\ worth} \right)$$

  $$Sustainable\ growth\ rate = \frac{GF}{\dfrac{(Total\ assets)}{Net\ sales} - GF} \times 100\%$$

  The sustainable growth rate is the level of sales growth which a competitor can develop from internal sources of financing without revising or jeopardizing its capital structure. Check your company's. Examine that of your competitor. Does the relative structure of your capital place limitations on stable growth? Is this a source of competitive strength or weakness?

Tracking of Market Share Performance

In some companies sales or profits are the most important measures of success. Yet they fail to see whether the future is being mortgaged for the present, whether more market opportunities exist than the company is addressing or if the market has expanded faster than sales. Issues such as these require that market share be examined at least as closely as financial measurements and that competitive market share performance receive close attention. This requires knowledge of:

- the size of the market and specific market segments, and the outlook for both

- the competitor's sales in a given period

- your own sales levels.

A detailed map of the market is a vital element in the analysis of competitors and the development of a winning competitive strategy. While companies obviously understand their own levels of sales, few have a reliable, ongoing and timely measurement of total industry shipments by application or product line, or demand/consumption by market segment. Most companies rely on government shipment statistics to which they add imports and subtract exports to arrive at 'apparent domestic consumption', or demand. While this is useful information, more is needed. The outlook for the market, segment analysis and competitors' market shares should be assessed, to develop a map of the industry, such as that described in figure 5.5. To accomplish this, perhaps your industry could consider sharing information through an industry association or reputable consulting firm. (Individual firms' sales could be aggregated for industry shipments, with or without revealing the sales of individual companies.) Alternatively, you may consider other approaches, such as market research, to estimate demand by market segment, the market share each major supplier represents and the outlook for demand by segment. Although this could prove quite expensive, this information could prove vital for your strategy development, because it would enable you to identify specific segments for penetration

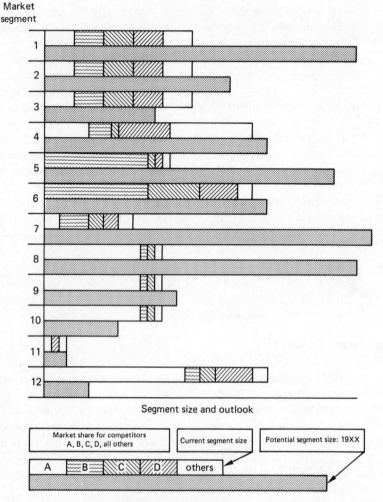

Figure 5.5   Market map

or defense, to monitor your performance and that of competitors and take corrective action as necessary.

The market map can be a powerful predictor of competitive direction. For example, if competitor A in figure 5.5 developed this diagram, it might anticipate that competitor B would focus on customer needs and shifting patterns of demand in segment 1, while seeking to gain share at the expense of competitors in segment 2. B would be likely to seek share growth very aggressively in segment 3 or decide to ignore this segment altogether, focusing instead on other opportunities, such as that in segment 7. To counter, A might decide to target B head-on in selected markets where the opportunities look interesting, such as in segments 1 and 7, yield share in segment 3, while gaining a beachhead in segment 5.

The market map enables hypotheses to be developed and checked with other competitive information that has been obtained. The map could be prepared in several ways, depending upon the approaches adopted for market segmentation. Indeed, more than one market map may be appropriate. The more creative the method of segmenting the market, the easier it could prove to develop winning competitive strategies.

Market segmentation could be based on:

- **Region**

- **Demography**

  - industrial markets: type of customer, size of customer, industry, application

  - consumer markets: age, income, education, sex, family size, stage of life, occupation, religion, race, nationality, social class

- **Psychographics**

  - industrial markets: benefits sought, price-sensitive vs service-sensitive customers, purchase process and decision sponsors/approvers/influencers, usage rates, order frequency, loyalty, single vs multiple sources of supply, new buy vs modified rebuy vs routine repurchase

  - consumer markets: lifestyle, usage rate, purchase preparedness, attitude and priorities

You may identify yet other approaches which could be adopted feasibly in your industry. Whichever method you use, recognize that market segments should be large enough to make aggregation sensible; they should be accessible for physical distribution, sales calls and media; and they should offer reasonable expectation of significant profit. The objective of segmentation is to homogenize needs and thereby bring together like customers. The underlying idea is that it will be more profitable to reach aggregated customers with communication, products and services, and to produce specifically for them. This remains true in many markets, but you may find that the application of technology in your production, selling, distribution and media departments allows customers to be treated uniquely and still very profitably. The 'custom' market segment could thus be one that you should consider adding to your list of segmentation approaches.

In addition to the market map, you should track market share developments over time (plot market share on the vertical axis, time on the horizontal), to see where competitors are gaining share and where they are being defeated. Look behind the trend lines for reasons for the performance. Has management changed? Have new products been introduced targeting a specific segment? And so on.

5.5 Financing Structure as a Competitive Advantage

Knowledge of the capital structure of a company can be an important source of competitive advantage and an indicator of the company's strategic orientation. For example, many Japanese firms benefit by the equity investment of financial institutions that could often count as debt on a North American or European balance sheet. This provides some firms with a stable financial base and an ongoing source of funds and makes the banks essential partners in the growth of the enterprise. This stability helps increase the time horizon according to which these firms plan, and, excluding the risk premium that equity investment should, but often does not, command, could lower the firm's cost of capital – an important enabler of investment in areas competitors may consider marginal. All else being equal a firm with a low cost of capital has a unique opportunity for market dominance. Few companies accord their capital structure the strategic relevance it does indeed have. The challenge for many is to reduce the capital cost below their competitors' levels, so that high hurdle rates of return will not serve as barriers to market penetration.

■ For years Japanese firms have been following what Westerners have often regarded as 'kamikaze' strategies – entry into markets of modest size that may not expand much and already suffer from too much competition. A case in point has been Fujitsu's entry into automated teller machines in the US when market conditions suggested that a new entrant could face an uphill battle for significant sales volume. Fujitsu's major bankers are Dai-Ichi Kangyo, Industrial Bank and Kyowa, which together also owned 12.4 per cent of the outstanding shares of the firm at approximately the time of entry into the market. A study of Fujitsu might have revealed that this investment interest would lower Fujitsu's cost of capital and that assured financial support would remove short-term concerns associated with US market entry at what was an apparently inappropriate time.

Many textbooks on capital budgeting, investments and managerial finance provide instruction on the measurement of capital costs. The reader is referred to these texts for a more detailed consideration of the assessment of cost of capital than would be possible here.

5.6 Resource Availability and Deployment

A company's history of the resources it has had available and how it has put them to use can provide important clues regarding the direction it could follow in the future. Analyze competitors' resource availability and deployment in respect of:

- **People**: how many, where, what level, what education (key executives), in which divisions, which functional areas

- **Money**: from where (investment source – debt, equity, parent contribution or whatever), to where (dividend policy, royalty or license remissions, investment policy), applications of funds to equipment, salaries and benefits, acquisition expenditures

- **Time**: urgency of management and execution – how long does it take to introduce a new product, what implications does this have for exploiting a 'window of opportunity', is this timing a competitive strength or weakness (are they more or less able to respond to marketplace requirements than your company)?

Perhaps the most effective technique for understanding competitors' resources and how they are likely to apply them, is to play a 'war game'. Identify one person who will represent each major competitor and one who will represent an important customer in each major market segment. You be the arbiter, director and provider of environmental information. Provide each participant with detailed background information retrieved from your information system and have each play the role of the person he or she is assigned to emulate. First ask those representing competitors to tell you their strategies for product development and market positioning. Ask 'customers' in the targeted segments to say whether the competitors will be successful and why or why not. Then present your own strategies for market participation and screen your intended direction against each competitive capability, while competitors indicate how they would address your change in strategy. Modify your strategies if necessary to gain a competitive edge, then ask customers in targeted segments how your new strategy would be received and what they would like to see done differently. Through an iterative process such as this, you could increase your understanding and that of others in your firm not only of competitors, but of how you can succeed in spite of competitive challenge.

Your analysis of the competitor's resources and resource application should first evaluate the competitor's parent company and then focus on the strategic business unit and product or product line.

For both evaluations consider:

● What is the portfolio of products and markets in which the competitor participates? This provides an indication of the sources of cash generation and the uses to which the cash is put. Refer to figure 5.6.

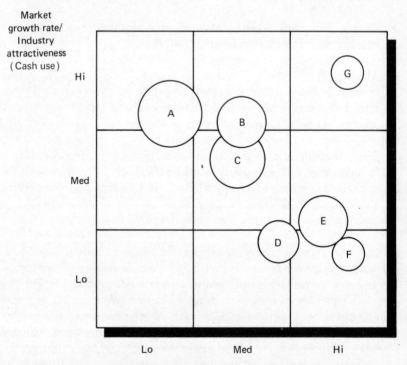

Figure 5.6   Portfolio of products and markets

Here, products or business units such as D, E and F provide the cash that this competitor consumes in A, B and C. G may provide the firm with a little cash, or may consume a modest amount. Given that the size of the circle is proportionate to the sales the firm derives from the business area, this competitor appears to be generating less funds from its product/market position than it is consuming. It could continue to milk D, E and F unless it has ongoing access to deep pockets of investors, affiliated companies or other sources of equity or debt. This firm might seek to move B and/or C into an improved competitive position/high market share area, and may be prepared to concede ground in area A, perhaps even selling this division to consolidate its strength in the opportunities that remain. A matrix such as this (based on the GE model) helps you to understand the attention and level of resources the competitor could invest in the product line with which you compete.

An alternative matrix based on an Arthur D. Little approach, relating the product/industry life cycle and competitive position, is presented in figure 5.7 – where a company is profiled which has a solid position in growth markets and is apparently willing to seek rejuvenation in market segments where it is already strong or where it believes reasonable potential may exist.

• Are the strategic business units or product lines with which you are competing being managed for growth, selective investment, cash harvesting or divestiture? Where the firm has a strong competitive position in an attractive, fast-growing market, the firm is likely to manage them for growth. Where the competitor has a weak market position in an unattractive market that is not growing, there is a potential for divestiture. Selective investment will occur when the company has a product in an attractive market but with a modest market position, while cash generation will stem from a strong position in a slow growth market. However, not all firms are being managed by portfolio analysis techniques, such as those described above. Determine whether your competitor has exhibited signs of using these approaches in the past, such as exiting unattractive businesses, or investing heavily in market segments touted for strong growth. If it has, you may have an opportunity selectively to magnify its portfolio techniques, *and make its predictions of poor market conditions come true!* For example, if a competitor does not invest in a market segment because it believes it to be unattractive, this may represent an important opportunity for your company to gain sales, because it is unlikely to provide the resources necessary to retain business.

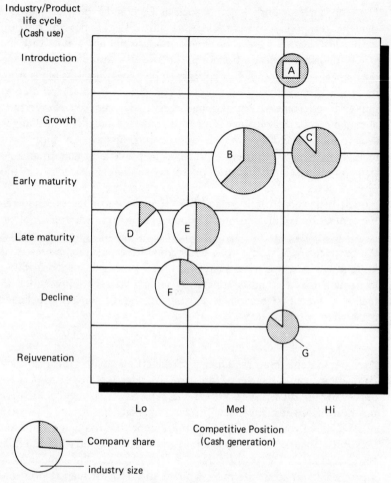

Figure 5.7   Product life cycle/competitive position map

- How is the competitor's marketing effort focused – by region, product or product line (discussed above)?

- What is the one factor that contributes most to its success (for instance: wide distribution, technological superiority, perceived product uniqueness, uniformity of product quality, price competitiveness), and how has it focused its resources to achieve this position? How does this differ from the manner in which you have focused your resources? Is this a strength or a weakness, an opportunity or a threat? Expand your conclusions by recording all relevant strengths and weaknesses in each

Conceive/design/develop	Strengths	Weaknesses	Threats	Opportunities

Focus of research and development:
  Technology
  Product
  Market
Resources invested:
  People – number, level
  Financial resources
  Percentage of sales
  External funding
Outputs:
  Productivity/proficiency
  Patents, royalty/licensing agreements
  Science/business orientation
  Economies of scale, scope
  Reputation and reasons				

Production and quality management				

Facilities:
  Proximity to labor, market
  Size of plants
  Geographic dispersion of facilities
  Integration with other operations: scale and scope
  Capital-to-labor ratios per unit of output
Quality of labor
Cost of labor
Age of workforce and turnover
Age of plant
Unionization and labor relations
Incoming quality assurance on inputs
Quality control in process and final assurance				

Sales, marketing and distribution				

Sales:
  Number, skills
  Location
  Territorial coverage
  Industry focus
  Fixed-to-variable salary structure
  Effectiveness
Marketing:
  Number, skills
  Organization
  Product positioning
  Support for product claims
  Consistency with purchase criteria
  Consistency with purchase process
  Consistency with competitive environment
  Consistency with regulatory/social/legislative environment
  Expenditure on media
  Media selection, creative
Distribution:
  Channels
  Number, dispersion, quality, type, strengths of middlemen
  Margin by stage of distribution
  Alignment of strategies
  Warehousing locations, in relation to market
  Transportation
  Order size, shipment, return and other policies				

Finance Cost of funds, availability, structure, strategy Management Planning, organizing, leading, controlling				

Figure 5.8 Competitive analysis using the value chain

step in the value chain (figure 5.8): conceive/design/develop; production and quality management; sales, marketing and distribution; finance and management. Then assess the nature of the opportunities and threats each area of capability would represent for your own firm. A chart that could be prepared to summarize your findings is shown as figure 5.8. (You may wish to supplement this chart with issues that are particularly important to your firm and your industry.) Identify factors which have a positive or negative implication for your firm by a ' + ' or ' − ' sign, and code each with a number. Then expand your assessment in greater detail by referring to the code in attached pages.

- What is likely to change over the near- intermediate-term time horizon that could affect its financial resource availability and the allocation of these funds to products or markets?

- Is the competitor committed to improving its market share, financial performance or expanding market participation? What will it do to achieve this?

- Are your competitor's capabilities congruent with its articulated or apparent strategic direction? Is its positioning and that of its middlemen consistent? If not, does this represent an opportunity to exploit?

- Is its strategy defensive, aggressive or geared to preserving the status quo?

- If you were the competitor, what would you be doing differently next month, next year, three and more years from now?

- If you were the competitor, where would you consider the competitor's company to be most vulnerable?

- Knowing what you know about the weaknesses of your own firm, and imagining for a moment that you work for the competitor, where and how would you attack your own company? What are you doing to defend your company against this eventuality?

Markets are becoming increasingly difficult and expensive to develop. The research and development costs of new products are becoming too large for all but the major firms to afford, and even they are finding new ways to reduce the investment. For example, a new automobile can cost a manufacturer $1.25 billion to develop, so Ford is beginning to produce 'world' cars for international markets, so that the expenditures can be amortized over a larger volume and do not need to be incurred more than once. 'Strategic alliances' are being employed by many high-technology firms to ensure that they participate in a portfolio of technologies and do not 'bet the company' on just one high-risk venture. To reduce the costs of growing sales through internal generation and investment, companies often find it cheaper to acquire products, technologies, markets or other elements of value, such as distribution. Thus, an examination of a competitor's acquisition history can yield valuable clues as to its future direction and the level of resources it will invest in acquisitions.

One way of doing this, is to chart a company's acquisition history over the previous ten-year period. Figure 5.9 presents a useful approach. The competitor profiled has consistently bought firms to serve the same types of markets or customers, and similar or related operations, technology and expertise. It is diversifying its product line, building on its current positioning and beginning to broaden it.

The areas in which acquisitions are made should be viewed in the context of the company's growth and its reliance on acquisitions to bridge revenue or profit targets. Different charts could be developed to track internally developed growth, and that achieved from acquisitions over time. Another useful way of establishing the direction of acquisitions is to take a ratio of the acquired company's assets to those of the acquirer before the acquisition – see figure 5.10. The company shown here seems to make acquisitions every 2–3 years and is making progressively larger purchases, both as a percentage of assets and significantly larger purchases in absolute terms.

A similar chart could be developed to reflect divestment policy and, when both acquisitions and divestitures are correlated to the portfolio matrices discussed previously, patterns emerge which highlight the competitor's perceptions of the future, or areas of weakness/synergy requirements; the level of resources it is committing to develop its vision; and what it is giving up as it strives for a superior portfolio of technologies, products and markets. Ask yourself what this means for your business. What will happen to your company and your product lines if it is successful in achieving what it is doing?

5.7 Industry and Competitor Capacity Utilization

Industry overcapacity, particularly in capital intensive businesses, is an important driver of industry profitability. Selected actions and strategies of a firm can be predicted with reasonable accuracy if its unutilized

	Same	Related /Similar	New
Products	1979 ● Blodgett Ind	1982 ● Acme Corp.	1984 ● Carman Co. 1986 ● Celebrity Inc. 1989 ● Cradenza Co.
Positioning		1979 ● Blodgett Ind 1982 ● Acme Corp. 1984 ● Carman Co. 1986 ● Celebrity Inc.	1989 ● Cradenza Co.
Markets/ Customers	1979 ● Blodgett Ind 1982 ● Acme Corp. 1984 ● Carman Co. 1986 ● Celebrity Inc.	1989 ● Cradenza Co.	
Distribution	1979 ● Blodgett Ind 1989 ● Cradenza Co.	1982 ● Acme Corp. 1984 ● Carman Co. 1986 ● Celebrity Inc.	
Operations	1979 ● Blodgett Ind	1982 ● Acme Corp. 1984 ● Carman Co. 1986 ● Celebrity Inc. 1989 ● Cradenza Co.	
Expertise		1979 ● Blodgett Ind 1982 ● Acme Corp. 1984 ● Carman Co. 1986 ● Celebrity Inc. 1989 ● Cradenza Co.	
Technology		1979 ● Blodgett Ind 1982 ● Acme Corp. 1984 ● Carman Co. 1986 ● Celebrity Inc. 1989 ● Cradenza Co.	

Figure 5.9   Acquisitions history

capacity is known and tracked over time. Their competitors' many plants and the difficulties associated with gathering the required information deter some companies from attempting such tracking; but although on-site assessments are often needed to ferret out the data, generally only a few major plants need to be tracked and this can be done at modest cost if sales or other calls staff gather the data while they are in the vicinity of the competitor's plants.

When competitors are operating far below capacity for an extended

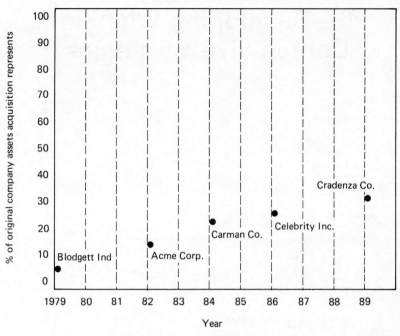

Figure 5.10 Value of acquisitions

period, they will either resize their operations and close plants, acquire a business for its product volume and consolidate operations, or sell off what is, in all likelihood, a money-losing division. When they are operating undercapacity for a short time, they will start to discount prices, offer additional merchandise 'free' with the current products, find new ways to add value, or discount their products. When at full capacity, it is likely that rational competitors will take the opportunity to upgrade their margins, become more selective about current and new business opportunities and begin to consider adding more capacity. In all cases, the results are reasonably predictable, and an informed firm has a chance to ensure that sales are profitable in spite of the conditions faced by competitors. An aggressive firm can act to weaken a competitor in distress further by targeting key accounts and forcing it to reduce its prices to an even lower level, ideally in areas where it is not in widespread competition with the aggressor.

6 Developing Winning Competitive Strategies

- Choosing the competitive arena

- Waging a business war

- Planning to win tomorrow's war

- Towards long-term dominance

- Steps to take when you have read this book – a checklist

The previous chapters have shown how to analyze competitors so that you understand their capabilities, strategies, areas of vulnerability and the potential threats that they represent. In so doing, these chapters have presented many of the core concepts you could use to develop your own strategies for resource allocation and competitive focus. Indeed, if you have employed the preceding principles to analyze a competitor, you are likely to have assessed your enemy more thoroughly than your own company. Thus, use of the approaches described before could have already led you to enhance your competitive strategy, at both the business unit and product level. This chapter provides more detail, considering how your resources can be maximized by a strategy that makes the most of your strengths and exploits the weaknesses of competitors. Military analogies can be usefully employed in making the right business decisions, and so frequent reference is made to the principles of war.

In today's competitive climate, business is war. In the preparation and conduct of war, intelligence is an essential part of the development of military strategy. On the business battlefield, competitive intelligence is a core ingredient in winning. The business leader is a general and directs the campaign to win on the battlefield in the mind of the customer. Capture of territory is measured by market share. The capture of the right territory is reflected by profit. Defeating the competitor – transferring market share from its control to yours – requires selection of the right battlefield and employment of the appropriate strategies and tactics.

6.1 Choosing the Competitive Arena

Selecting the right competitive arena, the battlefield on which you will compete, is vital to gaining market share. In order to choose an appropriate battleground you might refer to the market map described in figure 5.5, which required research of the potential battlefield arenas – describing segments as they are now and as they could be 3–5 years hence – and competitors' shares of today's available business. Once you understand alternative segmentation methods and the purchase and patronage criteria of key decision-makers in each segment, you are ready to select a battlefield to target. You can choose to pursue strategies for growth of sales and profits, maintenance of market position and redeployment of resources from apparently unattractive segments to other opportunities.

The criteria for market segment selection include:

● market segment size

● market segment rate of growth and outlook

● number of competitors

● stage of competitive development (early dominance by the segment developer, subsequent supplier proliferation as the market segment grows, then consolidation in a maturing market, and finally concentration as the market begins to decline)

● level of technology employed

● profitability of the segment (current and projected)

● positioning of the suppliers in the minds of customers

● capabilities of competitors that give them the 'high ground' – a maintainable stance or a tenuous position.

Markets evolve. In the course of their evolution, the level and intensity

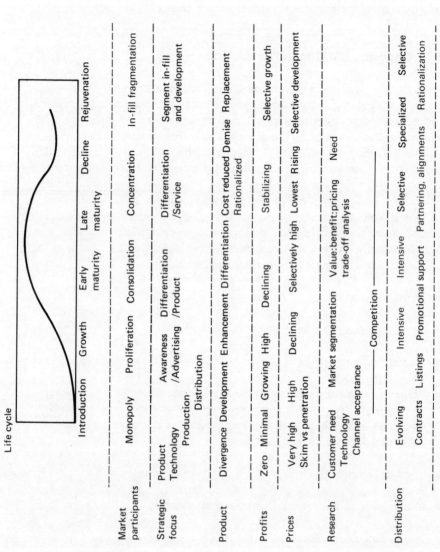

Life cycle

	Introduction	Growth	Early maturity	Late maturity	Decline	Rejuvenation
Market participants	Monopoly	Proliferation	Consolidation	Concentration		In-fill fragmentation
Strategic focus	Awareness /Advertising Production Distribution	Differentiation /Product	Differentiation /Product	Differentiation /Service		Segment in-fill and development
Product	Divergence Development	Enhancement	Differentiation	Differentiation Cost reduced Rationalized	Demise	Replacement
Profits	Zero Minimal	Growing High	Declining	Stabilizing		Selective growth
Prices	Very high Skim vs penetration	High Declining	Selectively high	Lowest	Rising	Selective development
Research	Customer need Technology Channel acceptance	Market segmentation		Value:benefit:pricing trade-off analysis	Need	
		——————— Competition ———————				
Distribution	Evolving Contracts	Intensive Listings	Intensive Promotional support	Selective	Selective Specialized Partnering, alignments	Selective Rationalization

Figure 6.1 Evolution of the battleground

of competition changes which, in turn, affects the 'rules' for succeeding. Refer to figure 6.1. It suggests that the number of firms participating in a market or market segment changes from one – the firm that initially developed the opportunity – to many, as the market grows. This has been the case in the markets for photocopiers, automobiles, cameras, personal computers, robotics and many more. When markets mature, consolidation occurs and market power becomes concentrated among fewer companies – as in the household appliances market, for example. As markets begin to be rejuvenated, companies proliferate in segments where customers' needs were incompletely met. Sometimes the innovators are the same firms which had consolidated before. More often, new, small suppliers emerge to capture opportunities that, in the initial stages of development, are too small to interest the larger firms. This is the case in many service industries, including retailing, where start-ups frequently segment markets and address highly targeted needs more effectively than do mass merchandisers.

Choosing the right strategy to follow, therefore, involves more than just choosing the right battleground – it demands an understanding of the concentration, deployment and movement of the competitor's resources. Thus, truths that apply in war can be used to equal effect in the Battle of Business.

6.2 Waging a Business War

Attack, defense, flanking maneuvers, decoys, alliances and guerrilla assaults can each be used to defeat an enemy at a particular intersection of time and market conditions. It is not appropriate for companies to adopt just one of these stances for the conduct of their entire business campaign – they are besieged by many enemies with different positions in specific product/market segments, and individual strategies are required to defeat each one. It is thus simplistic to suggest that a single rule of strategic combat exists: it does not. However, general guidelines can help firms to position themselves appropriately against the enemy. For example, market share leaders must protect share, and thus should simultaneously follow a defense strategy and *themselves* attack before their competitors do. The number-two company in a market or market segment should be offensive against the leader and seek to gain ownership of territory that is now superior or could prove better in the long run. It should do this by focusing on competitors with a weaker market position rather than by launching an uphill battle against a stronger company. The number-three in a market should conduct flanking maneuvers, looking for high market share in a specific market segment, then chip away at the share positions held by the

*war
strats
+
tactics*

leaders. Smaller companies should seek to provide what the bigger firms cannot or will not provide. They should follow the strategy of a raider, developing an opportunity and being prepared to redeploy if the segment grows sufficiently large or profitable to warrant consideration by the majors.

Military principles drawn from the lessons of battles waged since the dawn of time may be examined for the truths they reveal for business. Fourteen such axioms are discussed below:

Conduct Reconnaissance

Battles are usually won before they are fought. Using information about the scale, structure and deployment of the enemy's forces, a commander can plan the winning strategy. In the business context, information yields the insight from which business victory can be developed – information such as market size, growth rate, market shares, emerging and growing market segments, key product- and firm-selection and patronage criteria, customers' perceptions of competitors' products and the actions competitors are beginning to undertake to improve customers' perceptions and their own competitive positioning.

Good information does not often come at low cost. Senior executives may acknowledge this, yet rarely commit the resources they need to make information provide their real strategic edge. Many prefer to invest in plant and equipment or other tangibles, even though they may not know if such investment will make a material difference to their customers. Sustained tracking of customers' satisfaction with your performance and that of competitors, and of what can be done to improve your position, is as vital to today's executive as a map was to Napoleon. Without it, a victory becomes a matter of chance – as if two soldiers were firing muskets at one another in the dark.

Avoid a Frontal Assault

Consider two enemies about to engage in hand-to-hand combat. One side has 1000 warriors. The other, 500. Which side do you think will win? Unless your forces are qualitatively and quantitatively superior (people, technology, products, distribution, service) and have deeper pockets, it is foolish and perhaps suicidal to attack a competitor directly at its points of strength. Consider the graveyards in the computer industry for those that have tried to attack IBM head-on. Big companies have made serious errors of judgement. They include RCA, GE, Xerox and Univac. And others have yet to learn the lessons of their predecessors. They will.

Superior companies can gain by attacking weaker firms – but even they need to ensure that their strengths have the potential to overwhelm those of the entrenched defender at the point of attack.

One strategy for defeating an enemy that is more or less equally matched is to ensure that it competes on the territory you 'own', where you have the 'high ground', where you are entrenched and cannot be easily dislodged. Frequently, you do not have to do much to ensure this: for some reason, competitors, like moths to the flame, seem drawn to attack you at your point of strength rather than building on their own position.

> ■ For example, RCA may have had similar overall resources to IBM at a time when they could have developed a communications computer, but instead they attacked IBM head-on. (Northern Telecom built the computer RCA did not and, in so doing, out-flanked computer manufacturers and the much larger AT&T.) Did IBM's success magnetize the minds of the RCA executives, causing their strategic pathfinders to point in the same direction? Did IBM encourage so many competitors to attack them head-on so that they could defeat them all at once, without waging separate wars on different battlefields?

Concentrate Strength at an Enemy's Points of Weakness

To return to our example of the two enemies fighting for control of a battlefield: if the side with 500 warriors attacks a weakly defended area, perhaps on the enemy's flank, it can defeat a portion of the troops, and then progressively repeat this strategy until the enemy is defeated. This could best be accomplished where the enemy is over-extended.

Opportunities for such an approach exist in virtually every industry where over-eager managers have extended the limited resources of their companies into too many regions, too many market segments, too many product lines ... Employ the principle of 'divide and conquer' to develop market share, perhaps slowly, but inexorably.

Seek out Uncontested Territory

Although it is harder to find now than ever, uncontested territory still exists in many markets. 'Company-think' sometimes causes a competitor's camp to develop the prejudice that a specific market is too small to be profitable, or that it is too much nuisance to target, or that technological advantage cannot be economically achieved, and so on.

■ The 'Big 3' automakers in North America are now less big
   than they could have been because they initially chose not to
   compete in the small-car segment. Their 'company-think'
   suggested that 'small cars are less profitable than large cars,
   and we don't know how to make small cars, so we will avoid
   this segment.' The Japanese automakers staked out their claim,
   and are expanding their bridgehead far beyond. In fact, the
   Japanese did with cars what they had previously done with
   motorcycles. Their strategy could have been predicted had the
   'Big 3' been watching.

Finding an uncontested market may require identifying novel niches, such
as those discussed under the heading Tracking of Market Share Performance,
in chapter 5.4.

Cut the Enemy's Lines of Supply

Armies with vital lines of supply can be choked if they do not receive the
replacement troops, equipment and armaments, fuel, ammunition, medical
supplies, food and water needed to keep the military machine progressing.
In business, companies are often dependent upon a few key suppliers which
may operate at a physical, financial and emotional distance from their
customers. This creates a point of vulnerability. What would happen to
the manufacturers of IBM-compatible personal computers if they could not
obtain the chips they need to power their machines? What if IBM were
to impact their lines of supply, perhaps resulting in late availability, limited
numbers or increased costs of new chips to the compatibles?

Weaken the Enemy through Harassment

Sometimes executives confuse the deployment of a guerrilla strategy with
the absence of strategy. Managers will advocate an apparently illogical
action to 'keep the competitors off-balance'. For example, they may suggest
deliberately under-bidding a contract to cause the competitor to reconsider
its future bidding strategy (actually, this would be a decoy strategy).
Actions such as this can serve to undermine the profitability of an entire
industry. Rather, guerrilla action should seek to force the competitor to
divert and/or waste resources to enable the company to gain a foothold
or expand its market position. Guerrilla approaches are invariably tactical,
limited in scope and enable rapid withdrawal without much cost. Examples
include the use of legal action, regardless of the foundation of the claim
in law, to tie up the competitor's executives and waste their managerial

time and talent, and sometimes to buy time for a competitive response. A major razor and blade company did this when a new entrant began to test a disposable razor and seek out acquisition candidates to market its product. A distributor of beer did this to protect the battleground in Alaska, where it was entrenched, when a European firm indicated it would build a brewery.

A more strategic use of guerilla warfare is illustrated by companies that undermine a competitor's overall profitability by targeting the competitor's high-volume segments with low priced product, which causes the competitor to reduce price across its entire volume, whereas the guerrilla has only to supply a modest volume at the low price. A marketer of vodka attempted to attack the industry leader in this way (and only lost when the leader underbid the price of the upstart entrant with a low priced flanker brand of its own).

Operate below 'Radar Range'

Your competitors are constantly scanning the environment looking for signals that your company is about to do something differently. Perhaps they have become used to dealing with the 'old' you. They may be concerned about what you might become and are monitoring your company and the things you do for signs of change. (If you are watching them, you can be sure they are watching you. Even as you read this passage, your enemy is probably doing likewise!) If you are seeking to dethrone the incumbent, do not tell it in advance. Couch your moves in secrecy.

Establish security on all internal information. You could classify the information you have. IBM has four levels of information security – 'for internal IBM use only', which applies to telephone directories, 'IBM confidential' for maintenance manuals, 'restricted confidential' for product designs and business plans, with the highest level being 'registered confidential', which applies to the most sensitive material. (The Hitachi scandal involved an attempt to procure 'IBM confidential' material and that cost Hitachi around $300 million, so you can imagine the value the firm places on its more sensitive information!) Refer to chapter 3.12 for more information on keeping your secrets secret.

Operating below radar range suggests that stealth is required to ensure that competitors are caught unprepared. They will eventually respond, but the lag between your move and theirs gives you time to solidify your position.

Mask the Intention – Create a Diversion

Great battles are preceded by great subterfuge. The objective is to lead the enemy astray. Make your competitors think you will land your invasion forces somewhere else. Make them believe you will attack where you will not, perhaps by sending the generals, troops and selected armaments to the inoperative front. Develop an initial thrust in an area that will not be contested for a lengthy period – just long enough to delay the enemy from focusing on your real intention. Principles such as these have long been used by the military. They apply equally in the business environment.

Companies could launch a product targeting a minor market segment, to divert attention from their main thrust. Or they could concentrate their salesforce to focus on a given region or type of customer in a blitz, planning to attack ground zero as soon as the competitor begins to realign its own forces. Or they could communicate specific intentions to their competitors through disinformation.

Thus, in addition to protecting against unauthorized access to information, or minimizing inadvertent leakage, ensure that what you do communicate to the market is managed. Develop an information plan, and perhaps a disinformation plan, which would include a targeting of information recipients (such as financial analysts, customers, middlemen, suppliers and competitors), identifying the information (or disinformation) you wish to convey to them and describing who is authorized to conduct your communication. When you do indeed communicate with the competitor, seek to steer it away from the areas in which you intend to commit your resources.

Use communication to stake your claim to a specific position in the minds of targeted customers, while ceding other positions to competitors – in effect creating a situation analogous to that following from the principle of hegemony, whereby countries would tacitly divide the world into 'spheres of influence' in which each would be the predominant, unchallenged power. Then, ensure that competitors appreciate that you will defend the territory you control at all costs. As T. C. Schelling said in a book on warfare: 'The strategy of threat is not so much to inflict maximum damage on an adversary as to convince him that an attack will be costly.'*

Exercise Control over the Territory already Governed

Wars are not easily waged on several fronts. It is almost impossible to fight when the home front is in turmoil. If your core customers are defecting to a competitor, you will not easily gain control of another market position. It is essential that you control what you already have. The strategies for

---

*T. C. Schelling, *Strategy, Tactics and Non-Zero-Sum Theory*, reported in A. Mensch, *The Theory of Games*, p. 476.

ensuring this are many, and will depend upon the specifics of the situation you face. Virtually all elegantly defensive approaches to entrenchment require that relationships be managed. The reason is simple. When your customers buy, your needs are satisfied. After all, you have supplied the product or service and have been paid for it. However, for your customers the transaction is only beginning. They will scale your performance over the entire period of consumption against their expectations at the time of purchase and on this basis will decide whether to buy from you again, make referrals of your firm to others, approve you as a sole supplier, and so on. Success therefore requires that the customer relationship be managed by the supplier throughout the course of product or service consumption. This is discussed further in chapter 6.3.

Territory already governed should also be secured at the dealer, distributor or retailer level, in addition to that of the customer. If Company A gains share of shelf or additional support with specific middlemen, Company B can find access to its customers cut off or seriously eroded. This can be a powerful competitive strategy and particularly effective against off-shore suppliers or smaller companies seeking to gain a market presence or improve market position. It may force competitors to seek out alternative distribution which should be more costly and less effective, if you have already 'locked up' the most efficient and effective middlemen.

Deploy Overwhelming Technology

Armies with superior technology have often out-performed the enemy laboring with inferior equipment. To illustrate:

- The nineteenth-century Germans experienced much success on the battlefield thanks to their Krupp-made field artillery, which could lob heavier shells further than the enemy's, thereby providing a protective shield for their soldiers.

- Certain white South Africans celebrate the Day of the Covenant as the time their ancestors were victorious over attacking Zulu tribesmen. An unsurprising victory – the Zulus were armed with spears, the Afrikaners with rifles.

- The Second World War was won in the Far East when technology obviously triumphed in the form of the atom bomb.

But overwhelming technology need not be the most advanced; it must simply be what is needed to defeat the enemy. For instance, the Iraqis recently succeeded with chemical weapons based on 70-year-old technology used in the trenches of the First World War.

In business, application of better technology can give your firm the 'cutting edge' and provide important benefits to the customers that competitors cannot or will not deliver. Computers, for example, were used first for cost reduction, then for management reporting and control. Today, they are applied in areas that are strategic to the market success of firms, helping to address the customer's key purchase criteria and increase barriers to switching. After all, if your design, research and development, purchasing and operations are integrated electronically with those of your suppliers, would you be prepared to invest the time and funds necessary to switch to a competitor if the service and value you otherwise received met your requirements?

Progressively Encircle the Enemy

Few firms have the necessary resources to surround all their enemies in all markets. By addressing virtually all customer needs in all market segments, IBM have come close to achieving this; but even they have gaps in the product line, most notably at the very high end (vs Cray), at the very low (in the at-home market), and at places in-between (in portable p.c.s and, until recently, in mini-computers vs DEC's VAX line).

To surround an enemy successfully requires that you identify a source of the market share you wish to transfer. Usually a single competitor, or group of competitors that are sufficiently similar to be regarded as one, should be selected, and engagement should occur along a narrow front. Having achieved market share transfer from the initial campaign, the incremental visibility and success stemming from the product line or benefit package can be broadened still further to preclude the competition. As Von Clausewitz, the philosopher of war, said: 'The fruits of power used at the right time against the right adversary bring more power.'* Invariably, the fruits of power are deployed from the 'high ground'. In business, this means having highly visible control of an attractive, profitable or 'sexy' market segment. For example, owning Lamborghini may give Chrysler an enhanced image in the sports car market segment. The challenge is to deploy high-ground advantage against competitors who are within shooting range, and not to pursue those too distant to be hurt by your position. Surround positions in close proximity and work at cutting the enemy off from its customers and suppliers.

*K. Von Clausewitz, *On War* (originally *Vom Kriege*, 1832), Penguin Books, 1968.

In almost every industry, 'kamikaze' warriors lurk, waiting to unleash themselves against a rational-economic adversary. They may seek to buy market share, hoping that they can increase prices later. Or they may act out of desperation, bravado, from political imperatives or other motives. Whatever the case, root them out before they weaken your industry. Target their customers aggressively for market share transfer. Ensure that they have enough problems to work on so that they will not easily focus on your customers in your markets. If you believe such companies exist in a foreign market and intend to target your country, consider entering their home market with the single-minded objective of undermining their domestic profitability to erode their ability to finance an off-shore campaign.

Attack yourself

In the battle for North Africa in the Second World War, both Montgomery and Rommel used men to monitor the campaigns and history of the enemy and predict what it would do. In business, such an approach can yield useful information (see the 'war game', discussed in chapter 5.6).

How you act on this information is critical. Have the courage to attack yourself through innovation. Have more than one product line from which the customer can choose. Even consider having more than one company. Approaches such as these may not be as 'neat' as those you currently employ, but it is preferable for you to offer customers choices than for your competitors to step in.

- When Ford introduced the Probe, they had intended it as a front-wheel drive replacement for the Mustang. Instead, they had the courage to let both compete side by side in the dealers' showrooms and let customers decide which they preferred. The Mustang and the Probe have both done surprisingly well.

Consider whether there are opportunities to attack yourself or to improve your performance in the following areas:

- **Product**: can you make a product that offers customers benefits of enhanced speed, weight, size, intelligence, integration with customers' current products, visual appeal ... ?

- **Price:** can you out-perform competitors by offering better terms, extended terms, interest rates, rebates, bulk or volume incentives, repeat-purchase incentives, first-purchase incentives, specific customer incentives, specific product incentives, time-of-purchase incentives ... ?

- **Promotion**: are there ways to cut through the competitive clutter that you have yet to employ? Could public relations be more effectively used?

- **Distribution**: are channels consistent with the strategies you wish to follow, are they controllable, have you investigated channel alternatives, are you represented internationally, should you adopt a more intensive or selective distribution posture?

- **Target market**: are you segmenting the market effectively, are you segmenting in multiple ways, such as to reflect (if relevant in your industry) the custom segment, the graying (aged) market, segments within the baby-boom market and the post-boomers, working women, small business, the service sector ... ? Perhaps you say that you do already know about segmenting in this manner. Are you acting on your findings?

Attack the Enemy before it becomes Entrenched

When the enemy attacks, its likely approach will be to establish a beach-head, consolidate, and move out from the new encampment. The strategy of the defender must be to counter-attack before the enemy becomes entrenched in its new beach-head. In business, companies that begin to supply new products to your customers or potential customers must be neutralized before they become a significant factor in the market. This includes small attackers, especially if they have radical innovation in product, service, delivery or positioning that could win them market share.

Counter-attack can take many forms, such as imitating and developing a superior offering of the type just introduced, repositioning the competition as suppliers of an inappropriate solution, or even buying the upstart. Companies that have attacked and won have usually done so in full view of the enemy, while they watched and convinced themselves that the new approach was wrong. This happened when American Airlines introduced the Sabre reservation system, when Ford announced that their vehicles would be 'shaped by the wind' and when Merrill Lynch developed the Cash Management Account. In each case, there were losers that had to play 'catch-up' once these spectacular innovations were already entrenched – by then it was too late.

Have Strong Allies

Wars are not usually fought on the same battleground between many enemies. More commonly, antagonists align themselves into a small number of camps and then groupings of forces from different locations attack one another. So, too, in business, few firms can afford to attack competitors on many fronts. 'Strategic alliances' are becoming more common as companies seek to participate in a portfolio of high risk/high reward opportunities, without underwriting the total investment, which can be immense. They are beginning to co-operate with their competitors to mutual benefit. However, in this case, if the technology materializes as feasible technically and commercially, the reward is a shared one.

In addition to forming alliances with competitors, the business strategist could seek alternative groupings of firms to concentrate on a specific competitor. Consider aligning middlemen and customers into a strategic 'battle group', where there would be a high degree of integration of objectives, strategies and operations to achieve the goals of each component of the group. This will require suppliers to select those middlemen they wish to develop and identify those customers that they will work with to achieve market dominance. They could then integrate design, research, development and many aspects of operations with the customer to achieve product/system superiority and thereby an assured stream of demand. For example, on an exclusive basis, could a concrete company work with a construction firm to revolutionize building methods? Could a packaging firm aid Wimpy to keep their food warmer longer in bio-degradable packaging? Could a plastics company work with a car assembler to produce orthopedically correct seating for an aging population? In situations such as these, the future success of both supplier and customer is reciprocal, and the commitment to one another increases to mutual advantage, leading to the development of a true relationship. This is discussed further in chapter 6.4.

6.3 Planning to Win Tomorrow's War

The military principles referred to above provide a basis for achieving competitive superiority; but approaches such as these need to be weaved into a detailed plan to defeat the enemy. If tomorrow's war is to be won, strategists should first understand why they are not more successful in today's battles and then plan to address these issues.

For many firms, sales and profitability are being depressed by many of the factors discussed in chapter 1.2, but especially by two factors:

- maturing markets: the slowing of population, economic and market growth rates

- the declining differentiation of companies, products and services.

This section considers the implications of maturing markets for business strategy and what should be done about declining differentiation.

Maturing Markets

Winning the war has been complicated by the impact that economic instability, fluctuating interest rates and saturating primary demand have had on market growth.

Some industries have a bleaker outlook than others. Where industries are in long-term decline, strategists should consider if they wish to participate there any longer or strike out into new battlefields, like Singer did when they left the sewing machine business they pioneered to concentrate on aerospace.

Dramatic changes in strategic direction should stem from a review of the ultimate attractiveness of the battleground and the likelihood of dominating it. If the control you will win will be of scorched earth, do you want it? If you can only win with massive injection of capital and time, will a victory be Pyrrhic?

Re-examine the key to your battle plans: the firm's mission and objectives. (The mission statement of a firm describes the ultimate philosophical purpose or qualitative description of 'what we are – how our customers perceive us, and what we want to become – what we will be if we are to satisfy the needs of all our stakeholders'.) The mission statement should plot the philosophical path to victory, leading to definition of clear objectives to serve as a goal, gauge progress and rally the troops. Then, specific business unit and product line strategies should be developed and the details of implementation (timing, responsibility, tasks, budget) delineated. Care should be taken to ensure that all strategies for all functional areas are consistent with the overall corporate strategy. For example, are the objectives and strategies of the human resource function, the training department, the site location and real-estate development group, the production, engineering and maintenance departments, the order desk and the pricing department all tied in directly to corporate strategy? If soldiers in each of these platoons are fighting for the same cause, the enemy will be vanquished in record time. Repeated communication of simple, stretch, yet attainable goals (whether in groups, in meetings, in person, in print, in videos or elsewhere) can help avert internecine warfare.

One of five different generic objectives may be appropriate if you are to increase the net present value of your firm in a maturing market (the first objective may be used in conjunction with one of the other four):

- Increase the total market volume, or slow the market's rate of decline.

- Increase the sales volume of your firm or maintain sales at present levels.

- Maintain your current market share.

- Improve your cash flow.

- Withdraw from the market.

An objective of influencing market volume (either increasing total industry sales, or slowing its rate of decline) is especially relevant to firms which have a dominant or significant market position. If your firm is in this category, you may want to identify the factors causing declines in industry shipments and try to reverse the trend. Trade associations can perform an important role here.

If you plan to increase your sales volume, or maintain it at its present level in a declining market, you will be seeking to increase domestic market share or build sales internationally, whether through export or direct investment. As should be obvious by now, market share growth is contingent upon competitor analysis. As emphasized throughout this book, this stems from competitive intelligence and the development of winning strategies based on the insight it provides. However, the rationale for investment in a mature market may be less clear. Like the commitment of resources to the trenches in the First World War, is the motive for investment the lack of a suitable alternative ('in the absence of a suitable direction, we redoubled our efforts') or does it stem from vanity?

The single most important reason for considering investing in your declining market is that you seek to obtain long-term industry dominance and benefit from the higher profits that are often associated with such control. Basically, you are betting that you can increase present value more by investing, rather than cashing in, the investment you have already made. If your competitors perceive that you are committed to remaining in the industry and will seek to control the battlefield, they may decide to exit or otherwise yield, rather than engage in a costly attempt to increase their own participation. If they do indeed divest, and significantly below the depreciated value of the assets, the purchaser could become a 'new' low-cost producer, which is a desirable position to hold in mature markets because of their price competitive nature. Accordingly, it is important that excess capacity is retired, rather than sold to a new entrant. Your firm could consider being the 'acquirer and retirer'.

If you believe that realistically the best you can do is to maintain market share and accept declining sales levels in your maturing markets, then you should keep your spending and pricing at levels that are similar to those of major competition. Close monitoring of competitive activity is therefore most important. Offensive and defensive strategies can still be employed. Be offensive through segmentation (with investment being directed to market niches which seem to offer the most profitable potential – not necessarily the ones on which the firm has historically focused, like diet sodas and coolers in the beverage market) and defensive by emulating competitors and ensuring that they do not open differentiation gaps in key areas of profitability – as has happened in the 'Cola Wars' between Coke and Pepsi.

Other than the one-time approaches to improving cash flow (such as upgrading inventory management, accelerating receivables and so on), cash flow is usually improved by trading market share for cash: essentially, recovering prior investment by trading away the market position you now own. In much the same way as there is domestic discontent when countries trade captured territory in an attempt to secure peace, the culture of many companies resists harvesting of business units. Everyone wants to be involved in expansion, few in the travails of contraction. The managerial, technical and marketing skills required for harvesting are quite different from those needed for growing a business. For example, many managers of harvested businesses cut discretionary costs indiscriminately across the board, or selectively reduce spending by reflecting on percentages (per unit, per cent of sales) or by making reference to historical trends. A shrewd few evaluate cut-backs independently, based on the merits of each and the impact on short- and long-term prospects – to increase net present value. Thus, the selection and training of managers and staff for harvested businesses is important if the entity is not to demoralize troops elsewhere in the company. Employees need to be reassured that positions remain for them in the corporation, even if divestiture does subsequently occur.

Reflect on the impact of competition and the economic environment on your competitors. What if you do not leave? Will they? Can you speed up their exit? Money can still be made by being the last iceman (a supplier of ice for refrigeration – made largely superfluous in an age of electric refrigerators).

Rather than leave the market entirely, you may be able to withdraw and redeploy in a more profitable manner. Consider all your assets, not just your plant, equipment, buildings and other physical infrastructure. Include those such as your firm's personal contacts, reputation, service, technology, technical support and distribution network. For example, if your firm has long manufactured a product which is being gradually displaced in the market by a substitute, perhaps you can capitalize on your distribution strengths and become a distributor for a manufacturer of such products. In so doing, you would be offering your customers an even broader product choice, and helping to entrench your firm as the supplier of a benefit, rather than a product.

If, after careful analysis, you believe that the outlook for your industry in general and your firm in particular is indeed bleak, then you may choose to exit. Note that the first firm to sell out usually receives a better price than the stampeding hordes who try to retreat next. Therefore, move quickly to complete your analysis and exit strategy before competitors, too, become aware of the hopelessness of the situation.

Declining Differentiation

One of the by-products of market maturity is the declining differentiation of companies, products and services. This stems from a proliferation of competition — both direct and indirect (substitute products or systems), the dissemination of learning and experience within an industry, and the application of similar resources to like strategies. Such a situation is described by the cube of figure 6.2, where company, product and service differentiation has declined over time, and the organization, with little in the way of recognized points of difference relative to its competitors, must compete

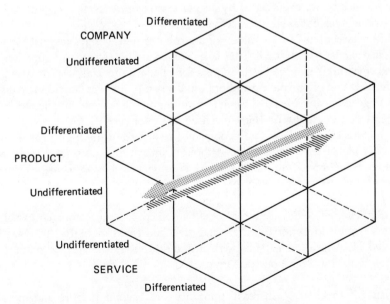

Figure 6.2 Declining differentiation

with price as its major weapon. Declining profitability is often the result of such a scenario, but this need not be so.

Opportunities to reverse the trend in all three dimensions and create meaningful differentiation in the minds of customers are discussed in the following subsections.

Company differentiation   Before differentiating a company, an organization should understand how differentiation can aid the product/service positioning. For example, Mars/Effem Foods, the enormous candy bar and food company, have a fundamentally different corporate culture, but the organization have resisted the temptation to trumpet their high standards of ethics and their egalitarian nature (everyone dresses in white coats, all employees are called 'associates', managers and staff sit at desks of similar size in mammoth open-plan offices). Mars clearly appreciate that this has little to do with selling more to consumers, and that buyers who have visited the company would be well aware of their differences, anyway.

For your company to be perceived as unique, or at least as very different from competitors, it should be able to make a statement of relevance to the key vendor selection and support criteria. All else being equal, significant size and, to a lesser extent, fast rate of growth become important bases for differentiation, just as large or mobile armies tend to do best in battle. Buyers seek the reassurance that dealing with the largest and fastest growing companies bring, exemplified by an old saying in the computer industry: 'No one ever got fired for specifying IBM.'

Purchasers tend to associate good attributes with companies that have a scale similar to their own. Thus large companies buy from large suppliers, and small firms may be better targets for smaller organizations. Increasing centralization of purchasing authority in the hands of fewer decision-makers in large companies makes it even more important for the supplier to be seen to be operating on the same scale as the buyer.

In consumer markets, large companies also occupy the high ground in the minds of their purchasers. Although small restaurants may serve a better hamburger, for example, many consumers still visit a major chain because it offers a less risky purchase – the size, cleanliness and product quality at least will be uniform, if not particularly exciting in some cases.

Rather than compete on the same battlefield as large companies, small firms would do better to emphasize their battlefield mobility: flexibility, speed, customization, personal service and responsiveness – areas in which large firms are often poor performers.

Product differentiation   In reality, products are becoming more and more alike. It is hard to find a meaningful basis for differentiation of product attributes in mature markets like those for alcoholic beverages, automobiles, carbonated beverages, chemicals, grocery products, machine tools, and many other industrial and consumer goods categories. There are thus two alternative paths of pursuit: the search for a real product difference and the quest for differentiation of perception.

Real product differences should be researched and developed based upon objective market research investigating the needs of customers. Sometimes marketers follow the 'eureka principle' whereby they stumble across a product difference in the lab and then promote the meaningless attribute as though the customer really cared. If you do not recall a major firm launching a deodorant containing vitamin E, then you are one of millions who did not find that claim to superiority believable or relevant, even though it may have been true. Although product differences may be hard to identify, they can be found. Go through a creative development process and research the opportunities.

■   I recently concluded an assignment where a major company wished to compete on a new battleground in a high technology industry. Together with a five-person team from the client, we developed objectives for the process, screening criteria, brainstormed 274 different concepts that would address the objectives, screened them against the criteria, evaluated 12 in overview, examined 4 in depth and identified 1 significant opportunity for which we developed a detailed feasibility assessment and market entry plan. The company has commercialized this with success.

However, because it is not always possible to find fundamental points of product difference in industries which have been through lengthy experience curves and have entrenched patterns of buyer behavior (although some continue to try, such as RJR Nabisco's smokeless cigarette), many firms would do better to differentiate their offerings on the basis of image. Most companies are still addressing the first-tier needs of Maslow's need hierarchy, shown in figure 6.3. Some, such as beer companies, have migrated to the second level because they have had the insight to recognize that first-level needs are saturated. Here the basic idea is that an appeal to the peer group will influence the individual to buy the product. One footwear company has approached the third level, inviting buyers to 'UBU', essentially to live their lives in an integrated way, presumably while wearing its products.

However, few companies have seriously sought to address the high ground represented by the third-level needs of Maslow's hierarchy. Yet

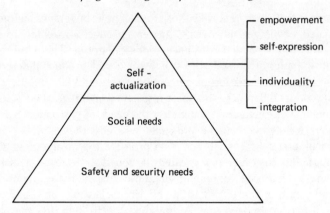

Figure 6.3   Maslow's hierarchy and image differentiation

this may be the highest margin opportunity because it is an 'uncontested territory' in most market segments. (Would BMW or Mont Blanc disagree?) As such, there may be a potential for companies in most mature markets to find creative ways to differentiate on the basis of empowerment, self-expression, individuality or integration (a way of saying that individuals balance the various forces and demands for time in their lives in a 'well rounded' manner). This is an important issue. Give it consideration.

Service differentiation   As markets have matured, as product differentiation has decreased, and as customers increase their familiarity with the use and performance of their suppliers' products, the title of the buyer has probably changed. Perhaps the 'technical specialist' introduced your type of products to his or her organization, but the shift has now been made to a generalist purchaser fulfilling that role. Firms dealing principally with or through purchasing agents will continue to experience pricing pressure, because this is perhaps the main *raison d'être* of generalist purchasers – to squeeze yet more money out of their suppliers. For many, the challenge is to weaken the influence of this person, or at least, reduce the focus on price – unless their company is the low-cost producer in their industry.

One way of shifting emphasis away from price is to move your target from the purchasing agent to senior executives in charge of operations and to focus on service differentiation. Offering benefits such as rapid delivery, consistent quality, inventory management and assured availability can help secure the favor of operations and build value into the relationship, going beyond the value of the physical product alone.

Service differentiation requires that the key attributes of service be established through research and that the organization be rededicated to the delivery of superior service. Ask your staff how they consider their company's performance in respect of the service it delivers and you will have a benchmark from which attitudes are likely to need to be moved. Many companies believe they are doing a good job of providing excellent service to their customers. To find out whether or not this is true, carry out the following quick check and see how good your service really is:

- Try to reach one of your managers by calling in the main line. The likelihood is that he/she is in a meeting, your call will be answered by a machine, or someone will pick up the phone who does not know where he/she is.

- Call your switchboard at 8:00 a.m. and 5:30 p.m. Is your call answered? Who answers the call (security personnel, someone who happens to be passing the telephone, or a professional receptionist who takes a message)? What response do you get?

- Examine how many telephone numbers you have in the phone book. Are they arranged as your divisions are defined, or are they organized according to the needs of the caller? That is, is it obvious who to call?

- Phone your switchboard and ask for technical, operating or price information about your products. Time the delays, record the number of parties to whom you are referred, note wrong advice or a cool reception.

- Query how your organization handles complaints. Does it actively encourage them or does it perpetually seek to explain away annoying consumers? Does it have a way to ensure that the problems are addressed? Does it consider complaints as a useful source of new ideas? Does it have a toll-free inbound calling number or does it ask consumers to find out how to complain and then pay for their call themselves?

- Take a look at the invoices you send to your customers. Do they recognize the buyers' importance and thank them for their business, or do they ask for all references to quote your file number and emphasize your payment terms?

- Examine the service strategy you have written into your business plan. Can you find it? If not, this is something that should be added.

By accepting payment, you have already satisfied your immediate need.

The temptation, therefore, is to keep the money and turn a deaf ear to distraught customers. The traditional wisdom has been that you cannot possibly control the many interactions the customer has with your firm. Well, you can. Set customer satisfaction objectives, develop service strategy, implement it, then track your performance in the minds of customers.

To do this effectively over the long term, a supplier should move from an orientation focused on making the transaction to one which values the relationship.

- The customer's strategies should be known and the supplier must work towards achievement of the customer's objectives, integrating research, development and operations, where indicated.

- A relationship management plan should be developed, with specific responsibilities identified for each individual making contact with a person in the customer's firm. Guidelines should be set for those personnel who interact most with the customer, especially those who form part of the selling, ordering, shipping, installation, billing, maintenance and servicing continuum.

- Salesforce compensation programs should be revised, with emphasis placed on repeat sales and customer retention, in addition to new sales.

- Ongoing and consistent service should receive more attention than may currently be the case. (For example, do you have a quality assurance program for service provision, just as you do for the production of goods?)

- Staff should receive the best training in the industry, with only high performers being recruited and retained. Expectations of employees and their responses to your customers should be examined. Employees' priorities need to be defined and the most suitable staff must be selected and fostered, with a heavy emphasis on recruiting and training, including the recruiting and training of the right recruiters and trainers!

- A feedback channel should be implemented to facilitate complaints from customers (if you are serving their needs as you should be, the staff supporting this channel, such as retired executives of your company, or a toll-free line, or both, may be as busy as the Maytag repair man).

- Rapid response teams should be formed to address rush customer concerns immediately.

- Customers should be given the office and home telephone numbers of their key account team.

- Information technology (electronic data interchange – EDI) should be applied to ease the customer's ordering procedures, reduce paperwork and speed shipment as required.

- Barriers to switching to alternative suppliers should be removed, but reasons to switch reduced.

6.4 · Towards Long-term Dominance

Service differentiation is the key battleground on which tomorrow's wars will be fought. In the past two decades, the economies of industrialized countries have moved the strategic orientation of companies from market development to market share growth – a competitor orientation. This has resulted in companies seeking one another's customers. Many companies are now recognizing the huge costs associated with developing new customers, and that retention and development of current customers can be much more profitable.

While customer retention can help increase sales over the long term, customer selection is required if profits are to be increased. Thus, companies will be expected to identify and reject those customers they do not wish to serve, and then address the needs of the remaining customers very well indeed. This will require:

- understanding:

  ■ customers' strategy for servicing their customers

  ■ customers' expectations of their vendors

  ■ the positioning of the company in respect of these expectations and

  ■ how competitors are positioned

- examining your current customers to establish which are profitable, which are not and have a poor outlook, and which are not but have good prospects

- investing heavily with each targeted customer to improve your position, and integrate strategies and aspects of operations to help customers achieve their strategic objectives.

Improving positioning should, in addition, involve:

- verbally reviewing customers' strategies or seeing their plans, perhaps in a formal presentation

- mapping all points of contact between your customers and your firm

- establishing the expectations of individuals in respect of product, service and your company, in general

The supplier should examine how these goals could be exceeded, and go beyond customer satisfaction to achieve customer happiness. This, in turn, could require changes to a company's:

- culture and 'way of thinking' about its customers and the scale of its business

- communications − overt (advertising and promotion) and implicit (manner of dress, speech, conduct)

- customer service (discussed in the previous section)

- supplier and distributor selection to ensure that the customers' needs are well served. The competitive alignment of a chain of value-adders which are each ultimately dependent upon the business of the same customers could be called 'strategic integration'. This is likely to work best where supply and primary demand is highly concentrated and offers the potential for superior system performance compared to competitors that perform as individual companies.

If your firm is to dominate the competitive battleground of the 1990s, it will have to develop one or more differential capabilities that set it apart from competitors and make it difficult or costly for competitors to emulate. Differential capabilities may be defined as the ability of one firm to out-perform others in the industry, based upon specific or sets of capabilities that can be exploited in the mind of the customer. Differential capabilities thus stem from an understanding of the critical factors which drive success in an industry, which, in turn, are based upon customers' key purchase criteria.

Systematic provision of superior service and strategic integration, discussed above, are two differential capabilities. Others include:

- **the objectives of a company** – for example, if market penetration is considered the main objective for one firm, which has often been the case for foreign entrants into a domestic economy, then another company, seeking to maximize profits, may find itself at a competitive disadvantage

- **access to more resources** (time, money, expertise, knowledge, labor)

- **greater efficiency**, stemming from:

    - scale or scope economies

    - learning curve experience

    - vertical or horizontal integration

    - financing cost structure

    - location in relation to raw materials, labor and suppliers, and markets

    - labor relationships and costs

    - capital vs labor intensiveness, including a consideration of an appropriate level of automation

    - the sharing of resources between divisions or product lines that enables improved cost effectiveness in areas such as marketing, the sales force, procurement, warehousing, transportation, distribution channels, manufacturing facilities, order processing, quality control/ testing, maintenance/repair, buyer financing, product or process technology, and research and development

- **improved effectiveness**, including resource deployment issues such as relative product/market emphasis as discussed in chapter 5.6 and investment in company vs product vs service differentiation

- **doing all the little things a little better** – after all, a 1 per cent real (compared to competitors) improvement per year in all aspects of your operations and in customer satisfaction will lead to an 11 per cent advantage in a decade.

6.5 Steps to Take when you have Read this Book – a Checklist

Having read the foregoing material, you may consider competitive intelligence a daunting task and the rewards unproven. You may be wondering whether the rewards justify what appears to be an immense amount of effort. Prove the benefits to yourself by starting with specific divisions in selected product lines and regions, and then extending the program. The following points are intended to help you to minimize your initial investment and get fast results.

1 Describe the rationale for conducting a competitive intelligence program and the potential benefits. Seek commitment to the concept of competitive intelligence rather than employing a cost:benefit quantification. Confine your intelligence operations to a narrow front, until the benefits can be demonstrated conclusively. Secure management approval and commitment.

2 Survey the potential users of the intelligence within your company to understand their information needs.

3 Take inventory of the competitive information that exists on file in the various areas of your company, and identify the types of information individuals routinely capture as part of the formal or informal conduct of their jobs.

4 Identify individuals to serve on a competitive intelligence committee.

5 Schedule an initial committee meeting to establish which competitors to monitor, which to analyze, and to secure agreement on methodology, timing, responsibilities and budget. Discuss customers' key purchase criteria and their implications for competitive information gathering.

6 Assign specific competitors to individuals for them to 'shadow' in order to develop a shadow marketing plan. In the light of this plan, your knowledge of critical success factors in the industry, and your own capabilities, identify competitive questions to which an answer is needed.

7   Establish a format for information storage and retrieval. Use a manual system at first. Insert available information.

8   Interview internal staff. Insert their responses into the system. Record all sources for subsequent follow-up.

9   Search for published competitor information: background information on the competitor and its staff. Search for articles in trade, business, popular and local press. Monitor key publications on an ongoing basis. Review patent filings, financial analysts' reports and other publicly available printed information.

10 Prepare competitor profiles. Each committee member should prepare one.

11 Commission competitive market research with customers, potential customers and middlemen.

12 Commission or conduct interviews with knowledgeable third parties about your competition.

13 Organize the information in your storage and retrieval system and analyze competitors' strategies. Provide reports of profiles and strategies to users.

14 Modify your own strategic or marketing plans. Each product or business line strategy and sub-strategy (product, price, promotion, distribution, target market) should reflect your deliberations.

15 Monitor the competition on an ongoing basis for tactical as well as strategic advantage, using internal and external sources. Conduct data searches of published information quarterly, and interviews and competitive market research semi-annually or annually in a manner consistent with historical practice. Compare with prior results for trends.

16 The committee should meet quarterly to discuss new developments and to examine shadows' reports on their analysis. Quarterly updates of competitor profiles should be prepared and circulated. Strategic analyses should be undertaken annually, before the business planning cycle.

Bibliography

The following material will be useful to those who wish to read more about issues related to or stemming from the subject matter presented in this book.

Biblin, D. L., Daniels, L. M. and Gibber, B., *How to Find Information about Companies*, Washington Researchers Ltd, 1983.

'Business Sharpens its Spying Techniques', *Business Week*, 4 August 1975.

Casey, W. L., Jr, Marthinsen, J. E. and Moss, L. S., *Entrepreneurship, Productivity and the Freedom of Information Act*, Lexington Books, 1983.

Daniels, L. M., *Business Information Sources*, University of California Press, Berkeley, 1976.

Flax, S., 'How to Snoop on your Competitors', *Fortune*, 14 May 1984, 29–33. Freemantle, B., *The Steal: Counterfeiting and Industrial Espionage*, Michael Joseph, 1986.

Gordon, I. H., 'Why you should be Fine Tuning your Competitive Intelligence Network', *Industrial Management*, April 1982, 42–4.

Gordon, I. H., 'Competitive Intelligence, A Key to Marketplace Survival', *Industrial Management*, November 1982, 69–74.

Gordon, I. H., 'Strategies for the Eighties', *Sales and Marketing Management in Canada*, June 1983, 8–19.

Gordon, I. H., 'The War of the Marketplace', *Executive*, June 1984, 30–2.

Gordon, I. H., 'Exit Marketing Concept, Enter Competitive Concept', *Business Quarterly*, Summer 1986, 28–32.

Greene, R. M., Jr, *Business Intelligence and Espionage*, Dow Jones-Irwin Inc., 1966.

Hershey, R., 'Commercial Intelligence on a Shoestring', *Harvard Business Review*, September–October 1980, 22–30.

How to Find Information about Japanese Companies and Industries, Washington Researchers Ltd, 1984.

Lesko, M., *Information U.S.A.*, Penguin Books, 1983.

Miller, M., *Where to Go for What*, Prentice Hall, 1981.

Montgomery, D. B. and Weinberg, C. B., 'Toward Strategic Intelligence Systems', *Journal of Marketing*, 43, Fall 1979, 41–52.

Murray, J. A., 'Intelligence Systems of the MNCS', *Columbia Journal of World Business*, September–October 1972, 63–71.

Newman, M. M. and Underwood, L. A., *European Markets: A Guide to Company and Industry Information Sources*, Washington Researchers Ltd, 1983.

Pearce, F. T., 'Business Intelligence Systems: The Need, Development, and Integration', *Industrial Marketing Management*, 5, 1976, 115–38.

Porter, M. E., *Competitive Strategy*, The Free Press, 1980.

Porter, M. E., *Competitive Advantage*, The Free Press, 1985.

Rogers, D., *Waging Business Warfare*, Charles Scribners', 1987.

Sammon, L. W., Kurland, M. A. and Spitalnik, R., *Business Competitor Intelligence*, John Wiley & Sons, 1984.

Slee-Smith, P. I., *Industrial Intelligence and Espionage*, Business Books Limited, 1970.

Todd, A., *Finding Facts Fast*, 10 Speed Press, 1979.

Wall, Jerry L., 'What the Competition is Doing: Your Need to Know', *Harvard Business Review*, November–December 1974.

Technical Information about Data Searches

Catheryne, S. and Marcinko, T., 'Sci-Mate: A Menu-Driven Universal Online Searcher and Personal Data Manager', *Online*, September 1983, 112–16.

Jagiellowicz, J. and Gordon, I. H., 'Now On-line Information can Give you a Competitive Edge: a primer on using your desk-top computer to mine rich information deposits', *Sales and Marketing Management in Canada*, June 1986.

Kayback, S. M., 'Online Patent Searching: The Realities', *Online*, July 1983, 22–31.

Wagers, R., 'Effective Searching in Database Abstracts', *Online*, September 1983, 60–77.

Walton, K. R., 'Experience at Exxon in Training End-Users to Search Technical Databases Online', *Online*, September 1983, 42–50.

Appendices

Appendix 1   Understanding your own Company

- General

- Markets

- Advertising and Promotion

- Pricing

- Distribution

- Product Development and Manufacturing

- Competition

- Sales Staff

- Customer Service

- Purchasing

- Finance, Accounting and Treasury

- Personnel

In addition to the usual elements considered as part of the business planning process, answers to questions such as the following could give you a deeper understanding of your own company and identify areas where you should improve organizational efficiency and effectiveness, thereby laying the foundation for competitive advantage.

A1.1   General

- Why was our company formed?

- What specific opportunities did the founder(s) have in mind at the outset?

- Do we still have a similar focus to the original intent for our firm? If so, why have we not changed product or market direction – what are the forces that have held us on our first path? If not, why are we no longer following the 'grand vision' – what has happened to make us change our minds about our direction?

- What is the current ownership structure of our firm? How has that changed over the years, and what has that meant in terms of the company's direction and investor expectations of the firm?

- What is the history of our entry into, and exit from, specific industries, companies or investments? Why have we done what we have? If the reasons are in large measure attributable to executive preference, do we still have the same executives in place? If so, does this serve as a barrier to entry into potentially lucrative opportunities, or a barrier to exit from poor performers?

- What is the sales and profit history of the company, by product and by business unit? What are the reasons behind the solid profit areas, and the weak ones?

A1.2   Markets

- What is the sales and profit performance of the company by market area, channel of distribution, size of city, type of customer (industry, size of company, amount of purchase, frequency of repeat purchase, nature of purchase decision, demography)?

- Considering market size, growth rate and level of competition, which areas offer greatest long-term potential? Are these the ones on which the company currently concentrates?

- What are the company's objectives with regard to segments such as those described above? If the company has none, why not? Does the firm have a co-ordinated and coherent planning process? What is the attitude to planning? And to implementation of the plan?

A1.3   Advertising and Promotion

- What is the annual expenditure for advertising, consumer promotion, trade promotion and public relations? Why have expenditures been allocated in this way?

- Who determines the advertising and promotion budget?

- Which media are used for advertising and what percentage of the advertising budget is spent on each? What is our 'share of voice' in each media channel – including mass circulation, regional and financial newspapers; mass, specialty and trade magazines; local and national radio and television; Yellow Pages; and outdoor?

- How is our investment in advertising and promotion established? (percentage of sales or profits, what we can afford, related to what we spent last year, related to what our competitors are spending, what we need to spend to accomplish our objectives, or other).

- What do we believe the relationship between advertising/promotion and sales to be?

A1.4   Pricing

- How do we determine the selling price of our products: cost plus a mark-up? pricing to competition? what the market will bear? other?

- Is price the major determinant of demand? If so, is this a symptom of a larger problem, such as not being sufficiently differentiated from competitors?

- How often do price increases occur? Are price increases large and infrequent, or small and frequent? Are increases related to competitors' pricing actions or are they independent? Are increases across the board, or selective by product, product line or customer type, size or importance to the company?

- Are prices to the end-user determined by the distribution channel? If so, do they take the same margins on our products as they (or competitive middlemen) do on competitors' offerings? Do we receive adequate support from the channels?

- What is our discount policy re current customers, new customers, large accounts, 'strategic' accounts, etc.?

A1.5   Distribution

- What percentage of our volume moves through the various distribution channels?

- How do our customers prefer to be served? Do our products require more personal attention, service or knowledge than our distribution methods provide? Should we be more or less selective in our distribution policy, or do we currently have the right balance? Can we ship in larger or smaller volume? Should our sales staff carry spare parts or inventory on their sales calls?

- Do we have a genuine 'partnership' with our distributors? (Consider issues such as sales support, co-operative advertising, order-shipping-billing cycle, quality of staff, communication, packaging, pricing, promotional material.)

- What is our profitability by channel? Do the least profitable channels consume proportionately more time of ours than they should?

- How are the channels rewarded? Is this consistent with our sales objectives?

- When last did we change our middlemen? Should we do so more or less frequently?

A1.6   Product Development and Manufacturing

- How does our company's product line differ from that which we had five years ago? What is the percentage of our sales today from products which did not exist five years ago? If this figure is very modest, do we have a sufficiently large or effective product development or acquisition capability? If our policy was to not invest in areas such as this, how does the profitability of the company compare with those firms that have made such an investment and were similar in size and nature five years ago? That is, is such a policy appropriate?

- How many products have been added to the line and how many deleted? What percentage of our sales, profits and management time and attention is taken up by the slowest selling 5 per cent of our products? Do we have a sufficiently aggressive product elimination program?

- Are we working on any radical, breakthrough technology, or is the development work principally on product extensions and enhancements?

- Do we patent what we develop? Do we monitor competitors' patents? Do we understand competitors' development programs that could redefine our industry?

- Do we produce private-label or generic products for retailers, or for other manufacturers?

- Why do we have our own manufacturing facility? Why do others not make the products we market? Alternatively, why do we not make the products that smaller companies market?

- Why do we not licence our technology to others, to make it the industry standard?

- What is the real plant capacity? That is, what is the absolute maximum production that could feasibly be obtained from the plant without incurring expenditures that would increase the unit cost more than a few percentage points? What percentage of this production is the plant currently producing? How has this changed over the last five years?

- Is production seasonal? What happens to unused capacity in the off-peak periods?

- Could the same plant produce other products fairly readily, without much additional capital or operating costs?

- Does the plant plan and control production effectively? Are costs properly allocated to production? Do 'rush' orders constitute an unrealistically high percentage of total production?

- What percentage of delivery dates are not met and what is the reason for the delays? How does our reputation for on-time delivery compare with competitors?

- What percentage of our products are returned to us for replacement or rework? What percentage of our inputs wind up as effluent, wastage or scrap? (These figures should be available: if not, why not?) Why are these figures as high as they are? Do we not have an adequate approach to quality performance in all areas of our company? Or is quality the responsibility solely of the quality control department? If the latter, do they have sufficient resources and clout at least to hold back inadequate products from the market?

- Which are the bottlenecks in the plant and what is being done to eliminate them?

- What is the percentage of downtime in the operations, and what is being done to improve this?

- Are capital budgeting and expenditure priorities related to product/ market strategy and focus?

A1.7 Competition

(A preliminary assessment – primarily of response to competition, defining which are the key firms to watch and where your company is positioned.)

- What is the history of the major issues that have shaped our industry? Where have we been positioned on each issue? If we have not led the charge on each one, where have we been positioned? Follow, resist, oppose, or analyze then decide? Which company has done most to shape the current form of the industry? Which has done most to improve the industry's profitability? Which has served to worsen the overall profitability of the industry?

- Why do we have the market share we do? Why do competitors have the shares they do?

- What has accounted for any recent changes in market share?

- What are the long-term trends in market share and what are the reasons behind these?

- How have we traditionally responded to competitive innovation? Does our response differ if the innovation is of a technology, packaging, design, production, promotion, price or distribution nature? Is this posture consistent with our position in the industry? If we are the industry leader, do we exercise leadership? If we are not, do we follow appropriately?

- What are the key opportunities and threats in our industry over the next five years and where is each competitor positioned? How are we positioned on these issues? Are our views symmetric with those of competitors?

- What are the core strengths of the company? Are we building on these? For example, do we have sufficient products moving through our channels of distribution, if this is a core strength? Were we a competitor, which would be the areas of weakness we would target in our own firm?

A1.8 Sales Staff

- How many people are there in the sales force? What are the revenues and profits per sales person?

- How are the sales force's territories delineated? How does this compare with actual sales and sales potential in those territories? Are quotas established for salesmen, key accounts, geographic regions, channels of distribution ... ?

- What is the age and experience of the sales team? What is the rate of turnover of our sales staff? Who is responsible for this rate of turnover – the sales staff leaving, or the managers 'dehiring' salesmen? Could the rate of turnover be improved by more equitable compensation, more training of the management team, more careful hiring practices, more teamwork, responsibility, recognition ... ?

- Are the most capable and energetic sales people on our key accounts?

- How does the 'quality' of our sales group compare with that of our major competitors? How do we define 'quality'? Is this the way that customers define it? Do we have a sufficiently comprehensive training program to upgrade the technical and sales skills of the sales force? Is the performance of sales staff monitored closely? Do managers make sales calls with the field representatives?

- How is the sales force remunerated? Is this consistent with the professionalism of our firm? Does it serve to motivate the sales force sufficiently?

- Do sales staff submit call reports? Do these reports, or others, offer opportunities to record competitive information?

A1.9 Customer Service

- Is there a customer service function in our company? Is the orientation to customer service confined to this one area in the firm, or is it more widespread?

- Has customer service received the recognition it deserves? Does management recognize that keeping the customers we have may be at least as important as generating new ones? Have we done all we can to offer our customers an opportunity to air and resolve their grievances?

- Do competent people staff the customer service department? Are they thoroughly trained in handling customer enquiries and problems?

A1.10 Purchasing

- Does the firm have supply agreements with strategic vendors?

- Do we get the support from those suppliers who most directly affect our ability to produce a state-of-the-art product and be first-to-market with it? If not, what are we doing to resolve and solidify key supplier relationships?

- Do we have second sources for the products and services we need?

- Do we focus on suppliers' prices without paying sufficient attention to their other capabilities, particularly those that will make a meaningful difference in the marketplace?

- Do we have procedures for examining the quality of incoming goods? If they are defective, do we have a standard way of charging suppliers for defects?

A1.11 Finance, Accounting and Treasury

- Do managers receive financial statements showing sales, cost and profit performance monthly – actuals, comparisons to budget, comparisons to prior year equivalent period?

- Are funds obtained at competitive rates? What level of risk do we assume in our procurement of funds? Do we reward staff who speculate and succeed, while punishing those who speculate and fail?

- Do we publish or circulate our views internally regarding interest rates, currency exchange rates, inflation rates and key economic issues?

- Do our actions and those of our competitors (e.g. short-term to long-term debt ratios) suggest that we have a symmetric view of the future economy?

- What is the quality of our relationships with our bankers, brokers and others in the financial community? Do they consider us to be a high priority – particularly compared to our major competitors? Do they go out of their way to help us (e.g. returning unused collateral if our financial position has improved since it was first pledged)?

- Do we have financial policies for both payables and receivables that are consistent with our marketing strategies? (e.g. do we have credit terms with strategic accounts? Does our desire to defer payment affect our relationship with key suppliers who affect our ability to keep at the 'cutting edge' of our business?)

- Do we understand our cost of capital?

- Does capital budgeting reflect our business priorities and strategies? How often are capital budgets prepared? How are capital requirements to be financed – what percentage will be from internal sources, what from external? Do we have a plan to raise external capital – covering sources, amount, timing?

A1.12　Personnel

- Does the reward system for the company compensate in a manner consistent with strategic objectives?

- Is there a role model in the company (e.g. founder or current President)? Is our organization driven?

- Is the organization unionized? What is the quality of the relationship between the firm and its unionized employees? And with non-unionized employees, including management? What are the benefits for these critical stakeholders to ensure that the firm is the most competitive in the industry?

- How successfully does the company compete for quality labor at all levels? Are the best and the brightest joining the company? If not, why not?

- Is the company structured consistently along product, market or other lines? Is this structure supportive of a desire to be 'market oriented' and 'competitively superior'?

- How do our labor rates compare with competitors?

- Are performance objectives developed and weighted in accordance with business priorities, clearly stated and measurable? Do we have both informal and formal reviews of employee performance to assess progress in achievement of objectives?

- Do we have career plans for employees? If so, have these been developed jointly with employees or are they imposed?

- Do we have a personnel manual committing the company to following specific policies?

- Do we have a profitability improvement program that shares savings or rewards with employees?

- Does everybody's view truly count?

- What is the concentration of expertise in the company? If 5 per cent of the key people left, would it ruin the firm? If so, is a review of the organization's succession planning warranted?

- Has management recognized the critical importance of training (in-house and at external workshops and seminars) in the achievement of a superior competitive position? Do planned budgetary expenditures reflect this?

Appendix 2   Data Sources: United States

- Directories and Indexes

- Focused Information Sources

- Statistics

- Industry-specific Information from Government

- Technical Information

- Personnel

- Databases

- Selected Firms with Financial Analysts on Wall Street, by Industry

A2.1   Directories and Indexes

Directories

- *Directory of Directories* (Gale Research)
  A directory of other directories which you may need to reference data sources.

- *Moody's Industrial Manual* (Moody's Investor Services)

- *The Million Dollar Directory* (Dun's Marketing Services, Dun and Bradstreet)
  Also available on-line through Dialog

- *The Directory of Corporate Affiliations* (National Register Publishing)

- *Who Owns Whom – North America* (Dun and Bradstreet)

- *Standard and Poor's Register of Corporations, Directors and Executives* (Standard and Poor's Corp.)

- *Standard Corporation Descriptions* (Standard and Poor's Corp.)

- *Standard Directory of Advertisers* (National Register Publishing)

- *Thomas' Register of American Manufacturers* (Thomas Publishing)

Directories of Trade Associations

- *The Encyclopedia of Associations* (Gale Research Company, Book Tower, Detroit, Michigan 48226. Tel: 313-961-2242)

- *National Trade and Professional Associations in the U.S.* (Columbia Books, 777 Fourteenth St. NW, Washington, DC 20005. Tel: 202-737-3777)

Use these reference books to locate relevant trade associations and their representatives. Conduct telephone or personal interviews with their personnel.

Indexes

- *Applied Science and Technology Index* (H. W. Wilson Co, 950 University Ave, Bronx, New York 10452)
  Covers most subjects in applied science, including automation, chemistry, construction, engineering, machinery, physics and transportation.

- *Business Peroidicals Index* (H. W. Wilson Co, New York)
  Information about your competitors indexed from US and international periodicals and newspapers. Includes index of book reviews.

- *Guide to Special Issues and Indexes of Periodicals* (Special Libraries Association, New York)
  Listing of periodicals giving date and titles of special articles.

- *F & S Index* (Predicasts Inc., 11001 Cedar Ave, Cleveland, Ohio 44106)

Information indexed from US and international periodicals and newspapers.

- *Standard Periodical Directory* (Oxbridge Communications)
  Covers over 70,000 magazines, journals, newsletters and directories in the US and Canada.

- *The New York Times Index* (The New York Times Company, 229 West 43rd Street, New York, NY 10036)

- *The Wall Street Journal*

- *Ulrich's International Periodicals Directory* (R. R. Bowker, 205 East 42nd St, New York, NY 10017)
  Guide to periodicals classified by subject heading.

A2.2   Focused Information Sources

Clipping Services

- *The Literary Market Place: the directory of American book publishing* (R. R. Bowker)

- Electronic clipping services from database vendors, such as Dialog

- Other clipping services from the Yellow Pages of your local telephone directory

Credit Reporting Services

- Dun and Bradstreet (99 Church Street, New York, NY 10007. Tel: (212) 285-7274)
  Provides information about a company, its offices, history, size of plant, upkeep of premises, sales, payables and financial condition.

- TRW (PO Box 5300, Orange, CA 92667. Tel: (714) 937-2700)
  Information about a company's payment practices and banking.

Other financial information may be obtained from the publications of the following companies, or by calling them directly:

- Moody's Investor Services (New York Tel: (212) 553-0300)

- Standard and Poor's Corp. (New York Tel: (212) 248-2579)

Filings with Securities and Exchange Commission

- Disclosure Inc. (5161 River Road, Bethesda, MD Tel: (301) 591-1300) Also available on-line

Freedom of Information Act

- FOI Services Inc. (12315 Wilkins Ave., Rockville, MD. Tel: (301) 881-0410)

For general information on the FOI Act:

- FOI Clearinghouse (Washington, DC Tel: (202) 785-3704)

Marketing Information

Data for specific industries, such as food products:

- A. C. Nielsen Company

- SAMI

'Off-the-shelf' studies may be identified by referencing:

- *Directory of U.S. and Canadian Marketing Surveys and Services* (Charles H. Kline and Co, Fairfield, New Jersey)

- *FINDEX* (FIND/SVP, 500 Fifth Ave., New York, NY 10036)

- *International Directory of Published Market Research* (British Overseas Trade Board, London)

Two of the larger publishers of multi-client or off-the-shelf reports are:

- Predicasts

- Frost and Sullivan

Consulting Firms such as Woods Gordon Management Consultants (PO Box 251, Royal Trust Tower, Toronto Dominion Center, Toronto, Ontario, Canada M5K 1J7. Tel: 416-947-7398) specialize in assisting clients gain a competitive advantage through research and strategy development for individual clients on a custom basis. In addition, they may have conducted multi-client studies that you may be seeking or will identify and obtain relevant ones for you.

Conversations between Executives and Financial Analysts

The Wall Street Transcripts captures the verbatim responses of senior executives to speeches, and to questions posed by financial analysts – a very useful source to guide predictions of companies' actions.

- *The Wall Street Transcripts* (120 Wall Street, New York, NY 10005)

A2.3   Statistics

- *Statistical Abstract of the U.S.* (Bureau of the Census, Department of Commerce)
  Broad coverage of general statistics, and a good source for locating other statistical information sources which are referenced in the book.

- *U.S. Industrial Outlook* (Bureau of Industrial Economics, Department of Commerce)
  Statistics and projections for major industries, with names, titles and telephone numbers of government experts in specific industries.

- *Census of Manufactures* (Bureau of the Census, Department of Commerce)
  Quantity and value of materials consumed and products shipped.

- *Current Industrial Reports* (Bureau of the Census, Department of Commerce)
  Production, inventory and other statistics.

- *U.S. Foreign Trade Statistics* (Department of Commerce, 14th and Constitution Ave., Washington, DC 20230. Tel: (202) 377-2185)
  Import and export statistics by commodity and by country.

Industry specific statistics can be obtained by referencing:

- *Bureau of the Census Catalog* (US Department of Commerce, available from: Data User Services Division, Customer Services, Bureau of the Census, Washington, DC 20233. Tel: 301-763-4100)

A2.4 Industry-specific Information from Government

- Foods, cosmetics and pharmaceuticals
  Freedom of Information Office, FDA, Department of Health and Human Services, 5600 Fishers Lane, Rockville, MD 20857. Tel: (301) 443-6310

- Banks
  Comptroller of the Currency, Department of the Treasury, 490 L'Enfant Plaza East, Washington, DC 20219. Tel: (202) 447-1800

- Common carriers, including telephone companies
  Common Carrier Bureau, FCC, 1919 M St. NW, Washington, DC 20554. Tel: (202) 632-6910

Other individuals and agencies may be found by referencing:

- *The U.S. Government Manual* (available from: Superintendent of Documents, US Government Printing Office, Washington DC 20402. Tel: 202-783-3238)

- *U.S. Industrial Outlook* (from the Superintendent of Documents at the above address)

State Information

Sources of state information and state industrial directories available from:

- Chamber of Commerce of the United States, 1615 H Street NW, Washington, DC 20006

- Names and addresses of private and public agencies which furnish information about their states.

- Directories published by state.

A2.5   Technical Information

- National Technical Information Service (NTIS) (Springfield, VA)
  On-line search capability

- *Applied Science and Technology Index* (H. W. Wilson Co., 950 University
  Ave., Bronx, NY 10452
  Index covers periodicals in the field of engineering, applied science,
  and industry.

Patents and Trademarks

- *Trade Names Directory* (editor Ellen Crowley)
  Lists over 100,000 trade names.

- Patent Office (Department of Commerce, 2021 Jefferson Davis Highway,
  Arlington, VA 22202. Tel: Patents – (703) 557-2276. Trademarks –
  (703) 557-3281)

A2.6   Personnel

- *Who's Who in America* (Marquis Who's Who Inc., 200 East Ohio Street,
  Chicago, Ill. 60611)

- *Who's Who of American Women* (Marquis)

- *Who's Who in Finance and Industry* (Marquis)

- *Current Biography* (monthly) (H. W. Wilson Company, 950 University
  Avenue, Bronx, NY 10452)

- Selected data on individuals may be obtained on-line. See next section.

A2.7   Databases

The following are major database vendors in the US:

- BRS – Bibliographic Retrieval Systems, 1200 Route 7, Latham, New
  York 12110. Tel: 518-783-1161

- Dialog Information Services, Inc., 3460 Hillview Ave., Palo Alto, California 94304. Tel: 800-227-1927

- Mead Data Central, 9443 Springboro Pike, PO Box 933, Dayton, Ohio 45401. Tel: 513-865-6800

Write to them and ask for a catalog of the databases they make available through their systems. Other database vendors may be identified by referencing catalogs or directories such as:

- *The Computer Data and Database Sourcebook*, Matthew Lesko (Avon Press, 1984)

- *The Directory of Online Databases* (Cuadra/Elsevier, 52 Vanderbilt Ave., New York, NY 10017. Tel: 212-370-5520)

Dialog have perhaps the largest selection of databases on their system. Some of the more useful databases for company information which are available through Dialog are:

- *ABI/Inform*
  Summaries of articles from major business and management journals.

- *Adtrack*
  Descriptions of advertisements from 150 US consumer magazines.

- *Biography Master Index*
  Index to biographical information from source publications.

- *Commerce Business Daily*
  For companies doing business with the US government, this captures requests for proposal and contract awards among other information.

- *Disclosure*
  Information filed by publicly traded companies with the Securities and Exchange Commission. The SEC 10K report is particularly useful, and provides more information than is typically available in many companies' annual reports.

- *Harvard Business Review*
  Full text of HBR articles, which often have company references. (Incidentally, the Harvard Business School cases can frequently provide

insight into competitive strategies and individuals, if any have been prepared on your competitors. A directory is available from Harvard).

- *Find / SVP Reports and Studies Index*
  Summaries of industry and market research reports that are available from specified vendors.

- *Investext*
  Full text of reports from financial analysts on Wall St.

- *Marquis Who's Who*
  Biographies of approximately 75,000 people.

- *National Newspaper Index*
  Index to the *Wall St. Journal, New York Times, Christian Science Monitor, Los Angeles Times, Washington Post.*

- *PTS / Promt*
  Summaries of articles from trade and industry sources. Good source of quantitative information such as market share.

- *PTS U.S. forecasts*
  Provides outlooks of US industries from published data sources such as trade journals, business and financial publications.

- *Thomas' Register On-line*
  Detailed listing of companies and their products.

- *Trinet Establishment Database*
  Directory of establishments, with address, employees and other information.

- *UPI News*
  Current information carried on the United Press International newswire.

A2.8 Selected Firms with Financial Anaylsts on Wall Street, by Industry

Industry	Firm	Industry	Firm
Advertising agencies	County Securities USA Drexel Burnham Lambert		Goldman Sachs & Co. Prudential-Bache Securities

Industry	Firm	Industry	Firm
	L. F. Rothschild & Co.		First Boston
	Wertheim Schroder & Co.		E. F. Hutton & Co.
			Jesup & Lamont Securities
			Merrill Lynch
Aerospace	Cowen & Co.		Montgomery Securities
	Dean Witter Reynolds		Morgan Stanley & Co.
	Donaldson, Lufkin & Jenrette		Paine Webber
			Prudential-Bache Securities
	Drexel Burnham Lambert		Salomon Brothers
	First Boston		Smith Barney, Harris Upham & Co.
	Goldman Sachs & Co.		
	E. F. Hutton	Banks	First Boston
	Paine Webber		Goldman, Sachs & Co.
	Prudential-Bache Securities		Merrill Lynch
	Salomon Brothers		Montgomery Securities
Airlines	Dean Witter Reynolds		Morgan Stanley & Co.
	First Boston		Paine Webber
	Goldman Sachs & Co.		Prudential-Bache Securities
	Salomon Brothers		Salomon Brothers
	Shearson Lehman Brothers		Smith Barney, Harris Upham & Co.
	Wertheim Schroder & Co.		
Autos and auto parts	Donaldson, Lufkin & Jenrette	Beverages	First Boston
			E. F. Hutton & Co.
	Drexel Burnham Lambert		Kidder, Peabody & Co.

Industry	Firm	Industry	Firm
	Merrill Lynch Montgomery Securities Oppenheimer & Co. Prudential- Bache Securities L. F. Rothschild & Co. Salomon Brothers Smith Barney, Harris Upham & Co.	Building	Smith Barney, Harris Upham & Co. Donaldson, Lufkin & Jenrette Drexel Burnham Lambert First Boston Kidder, Peabody & Co. Merrill Lynch Prudential- Bache Securities Salomon Brothers Smith Barney, Harris Upham & Co. Wertheim Schroder & Co.
Biotechnology	Cable, Howse & Ragen Hambrecht & Quist E. F. Hutton & Co. Kidder, Peabody & Co. Paine Webber Prudential- Bache Securities	Chemicals	Anantha Raman & Co. Dean Witter Reynolds Drexel Burnham Lambert First Boston E. F. Hutton & Co. Merrill Lynch Morgan Stanley & Co. Prudential- Bache Securities Salomon Brothers Shearson Lehman Brothers
Broadcasting	Cyrus J. Lawrence Inc. Donaldson, Lufkin & Jenrette Drexel Burnham Lambert First Boston Goldman, Sachs & Co. Kidder, Peabody & Co.		

Industry	Firm	Industry	Firm
	Smith Barney, Harris Upham & Co.		Merrill Lynch Morgan Stanley & Co. Salomon Brothers
Chemicals / Specialty	Drexel Burnham Lambert First Boston Kidder, Peabody & Co. Merrill Lynch Oppenheimer & Co. Prudential- Bache Securities	Defense electronics	Smith Barney, Harris Upham & Co. Wertheim Schroder & Co. Cowen & Co. Donaldson, Lufkin & Jenrette
Coal	Dean Witter Reynolds Donaldson, Lufkin & Jenrette Kidder, Peabody & Co. Merrill Lynch Salomon Brothers		Drexel Burnham Lambert Goldman, Sachs & Co. E. F. Hutton & Co. Merrill Lynch Oppenheimer & Co. Smith Barney, Harris Upham & Co.
Containers	First Boston Merrill Lynch Paine Webber Prescott, Ball & Turben	Drugs	Cowen & Co. Donaldson, Lufkin & Jenrette
Cosmetics	Donaldson, Lufkin & Jenrette Drexel Burnham Lambert First Boston Goldman, Sachs & Co. E. F. Hutton & Co.		Eberstadt Fleming & Co. First Boston Goldman, Sachs & Co. Merrill Lynch Morgan Stanley & Co. Paine Webber

Industry	Firm	Industry	Firm
	Sanford C. Bernstein & Co.		Montgomery Securities
			Prudential- Bache Securities
	Smith Barney, Harris Upham & Co.		Smith Barney, Harris Upham & Co.
Electrical/ Connectors	Donaldson, Lufkin & Jenrette		
	Drexel Burnham Lambert	Engineering construction	Drexel Burnham Lambert
	Merrill Lynch		First Boston
	Prudential- Bache Securities		Kidder, Peabody & Co.
Electrical/ Consumer	Donaldson, Lufkin & Jenrette	Financial services	Drexel Burnham Lambert
	First Boston		First Boston
	Merrill Lynch		Paine Webber
	Salomon Brothers		Prudential- Bache Securities
Electrical/ Equipment	Dean Witter Reynolds		Salomon Brothers
	Drexel Burnham Lambert		Wertheim Schroder & Co.
	First Boston		
	Goldman, Sachs & Co.	Food	Donaldson, Lufkin & Jenrette
	Kidder, Peabody & Co.		Drexel Burnham Lambert
	Merrill Lynch		First Boston
	Salomon Brothers		Goldman, Sachs & Co.
Electronics	Cowen & Co.		Merrill Lynch
	Drexel Burnham Lambert		Paine Webber
	First Boston		Prudential- Bache Securities
	Merrill Lynch		

Industry	Firm	Industry	Firm
	Smith Barney, Harris Upham & Co. Wertheim Schroder & Co.	Household products	Donaldson, Lufkin & Jenrette Drexel Burnham Lambert First Boston Goldman, Sachs & Co. Kidder, Peabody & Co. Salomon Brothers
Hospital management	First Boston Merrill Lynch Morgan Stanley & Co. Paine Webber Salomon Brothers Sanford C. Bernstein & Co. Smith Barney, Harris Upham & Co.	Information technology/ Mainframes	Bear, Stearns & Co. Cowen & Co. Dean Witter Reynolds Drexel Burnham Lambert Eberstadt Fleming & Co. First Boston Kidder, Peabody & Co. Merrill Lynch Morgan Stanley & Co. Shearson Lehman Brothers Wertheim Schroder & Co.
Hospital supply	Cowen & Co. Donaldson, Lufkin & Jenrette Drexel Burnham Lambert First Boston Goldman, Sachs & Co. Merrill Lynch Paine Webber Salomon Brothers Sanford C. Bernstein & Co. Smith Barney, Harris Upham & Co.	Information technology/ Office equipment	Cowen & Co. Eberstadt Fleming & Co. Goldman, Sachs & Co. Kidder, Peabody & Co.

Industry	Firm	Industry	Firm
	Morgan Stanley & Co. Paine Webber Salomon Brothers Sanford C. Bernstein & Co. Wertheim Schroder & Co.		Oppenheimer & Co. Paine Webber Prudential-Bache Securities Salomon Brothers Smith Barney, Harris Upham & Co.
Information technology / Software and data services	Donaldson, Lufkin & Jenrette Goldman, Sachs & Co. Hambrecht & Quist E. F. Hutton & Co. Merrill Lynch Montgomery Securities Morgan Stanley & Co. Prudential-Bache Securities Smith Barney, Harris Upham & Co.	Leisure time	Goldman, Sachs & Co. Merrill Lynch Paine Webber Shearson Lehman Brothers Smith Barney, Harris Upham & Co. Wertheim Schroder & Co.
Insurance	Conning & Co. Dean Witter Reynolds First Boston Goldman, Sachs & Co. Merrill Lynch Morgan Stanley & Co.	Lodging and restaurants	Drexel Burnham Lambert First Boston Goldman, Sachs & Co. E. F. Hutton & Co. Merrill Lynch Montgomery Securities Smith Barney, Harris Upham & Co. Wertheim Schroder & Co.

Industry	Firm	Industry	Firm
Machinery	Donaldson, Lufkin & Jenrette		First Boston
	Drexel Burnham Lambert		Goldman, Sachs & Co.
	First Boston		Kidder, Peabody & Co.
	Goldman, Sachs & Co.		Merrill Lynch
	Morgan Stanley & Co.		Oppenheimer & Co.
	Paine Webber		Prudential-Bache Securities
	Prudential-Bache Securities		Shearson Lehman Brothers
	Salomon Brothers		Smith Barney, Harris Upham & Co.
	Shearson Lehman Brothers	Oil/Domestic	Bryan Jacoboski
	Wertheim Schroder & Co.		Cyrus J. Lawrence Inc.
			Dean Witter Reynolds
Natural gas	Dean Witter Reynolds		Donaldson, Lufkin & Jenrette
	Donaldson, Lufkin & Jenrette		Drexel Burnham Lambert
	Drexel Burnham Lambert		First Boston
	First Boston		Goldman, Sachs & Co.
	E. F. Hutton & Co.		Kidder, Peabody & Co.
	Kidder, Peabody & Co.		Merrill Lynch
	Merrill Lynch		Morgan Stanley & Co.
	Prudential-Bache Securities		Paine Webber
	Shearson Lehman Brothers		Salomon Brothers
			Smith Barney, Harris Upham & Co.
Nonferrous metals	Dean Witter Reynolds	Oil/Exploration	Donaldson,

Industry	Firm	Industry	Firm
	Lufkin & Jenrette		Wertheim Schroder & Co.
	First Boston		
	Goldman, Sachs & Co.		
	Kidder, Peabody & Co.	Paper and forest products	Cyrus J. Lawrence Inc.
	Morgan Stanley & Co.		First Boston
	Smith Barney, Harris Upham & Co.		Goldman, Sachs & Co.
			Kidder, Peabody & Co.
			Merrill Lynch
Oil / International	Cyrus J. Lawrence Inc.		Morgan Stanley & Co.
	First Boston		Oppenheimer & Co.
	Goldman, Sachs & Co.		Paine Webber
	Kidder, Peabody & Co.		Prudential-Bache Securities
	Merrill Lynch		Salomon Brothers
	Morgan Stanley & Co.		Smith Barney, Harris Upham & Co.
	Nomura Securities International		
	Paine Webber		
	Salomon Brothers	Photography	Dean Witter Reynolds
			Donaldson, Lufkin & Jenrette
Oil services and equipment	First Boston		E. F. Hutton & Co.
	Paine Webber		Merrill Lynch
	Prudential-Bache Securities		Morgan Stanley & Co.
	Salomon Brothers		Smith Barney, Harris Upham & Co.
	Sanford C. Bernstein & Co.		Wertheim Schroder & Co.
	Smith Barney, Harris Upham & Co.		

Industry	Firm	Industry	Firm
Pollution control	Dean Witter Reynolds Donaldson, Lufkin & Jenrette Kidder, Peabody & Co. Merrill Lynch Prudential-Bache Securities Smith Barney, Harris Upham & Co.		Paine Webber Salomon Brothers Wertheim Schroder & Co.
		Retailing	Cyrus J. Lawrence Inc. Donaldson, Lufkin & Jenrette Drexel Burnham Lambert First Boston Goldman, Sachs & Co. Merrill Lynch Morgan Stanley & Co. Paine Webber
Publishing	Cyrus J. Lawrence Inc. Drexel Burnham Lambert First Boston Kidder, Peabody & Co. Merrill Lynch Paine Webber Smith Barney, Harris Upham & Co.		
		Savings and loans	Dean Witter Reynolds Montgomery Securities Prudential-Bache Securities Sanford C. Bernstein & Co. Shearson Lehman Brothers
Railroads	Dean Witter Reynolds Donaldson, Lufkin & Jenrette First Boston Goldman, Sachs & Co. E. F. Hutton & Co. Kidder, Peabody & Co. Merrill Lynch Morgan Stanley & Co.	Steel	First Boston Kidder, Peabody & Co. Merrill Lynch Oppenheimer & Co. Paine Webber Salomon Brothers

Industry	Firm	Industry	Firm
Telecommuni-cations equipment	Cowen & Co. Donaldson, Lufkin & Jenrette First Boston Goldman, Sachs & Co. Merrill Lynch Morgan Stanley & Co. Prudential-Bache Securities Smith Barney,	Telecommuni-cations services	Harris Upham & Co. Drexel Burnham Lambert First Boston Morgan Stanley & Co. Prudential-Bache Securities Smith Barney, Harris Upham & Co.

A listing of financial analysts may be obtained from:

- Financial Analysts Federation (1633 Broadway, New York, NY 10019. Tel: (212) 957-2860)

- *The Directory of Securities Analysts* (Nelson Publications, 11 Elm Place, Rye, NY 10580. Tel: (914) 967-9100)

Appendix 3   Data Sources: Canada

- Directories

- Trade Indexes

- Business Databases

- Periodicals Indexes

- Statistics

- Financial Information

- Industry-specific information

- Financial Ratios

- Sources of Information about Japanese Companies

- Selected Firms with Financial Analysts on Bay Street, by Industry

A3.1   Directories

- *Canadian Key Business Directory* (annual) (Dun and Bradstreet, Toronto)
  Provides sales figures for top 3 per cent of Canadian companies.
  Companies are arranged alphabetically and by industry.

- *Canadian Book of Corporate Management* (Dun and Bradstreet, Toronto)
  Lists of companies, also people in key positions; includes an index
  by company and personal name.

- *Scott's Directory of Ontario Manufacturers* (annual) (Scott's Directories, Oakville)
  Lists companies geographically, people in key positions, and number of employees. Editions exist for Quebec, Western Canada and Atlantic provinces.

- *Blue Book of Canadian Business* (annual) (Canadian Newspaper Services International, Toronto)
  Contains profiles of leading Canadian companies; history, ranking and data on ownership, officers, etc.

- *Standard and Poor's Register of Corporations, Directories and Executives* (annual) (Standard and Poor's, New York)
  Volume I lists over 36,000 corporations in the US and Canada with addresses, names and titles of principal business affiliation, business address, birth date, educational history and fraternal membership. Volume II lists directors and executives. Six sections compose Volume III and include: SIC index and codes, geographic index, new individual listings, obituaries, and new company additions.

- *Contacts Influential* (Contacts Influential, Toronto)
  Comprehensive directory of business firms. Arranged by business classifications. Information given includes names of key personnel, number of employees, type of location. Includes a market planning section.

- *Directory of Associations in Canada* (Micromedia Ltd, 158 Pearl St., Toronto, Ontario M5H 1L3. Tel: 416-593-5211)

A3.2 Trade Indexes

- *Canadian Trade index* (annual) (Canadian Manufacturers' Assoc., Toronto)
  Lists names and addresses of Canadian companies belonging to the Canadian Manufacturers' Association. It also indicates branches and key personnel. See on-line source in next Section.

- *Fraser's Canadian Trade Directory* (annual) (3 Volumes, Fraser's Canadian Trade Directory Ltd., Toronto)
  Companies are listed alphabetically and by product classification.

Lists trade and brand names and has an alphabetical list of foreign manufacturers.

- *Guide to Canadian Manufacturers* (annual) (Dun and Bradstreet, Toronto)
Provides marketing information on 10,000 top manufacturing locations in Canada; lists company products; purchases of raw materials and capital machinery used in production.

- *Financial Post Corporation Service* (Financial Post, Toronto)
This card file provides up-to-date investment information on Canadian businesses. Two cards are provided for each company. The basic card (yellow) contains a history of the company, the operations, capitalization, stock information, and other financial information. The current information card (white) supplies additional, recent information.

- *Directory of Canadian Scientific and Technical Periodicals: A Guide to Currently Published Titles* (National Science Library, Ottawa)
Includes trade magazines, journals, and research reports from government, industry, universities and other sources.

A3.3 Business Databases

Dialog's catalog provides considerable information about databases, as do catalogs from other vendors, such as Nexis/Lexis. In Canada, the main database suppliers include I. P. Sharp, InfoGlobe, InfoMart, *FPOnline* and Insight.

- *I. P. Sharp Associates* (2 First Canadian Place, Suite 1900, Toronto, Ontario. Tel: 416-364-5361)
Excellent source for demographic indicators, economic indicators and market data for broad product categories.

- *InfoGlobe* (444 Front St West, Toronto, Ontario. Tel: 416-585-5250)
Includes the full text of the *Globe* and *Mail*, Canada's premier daily newspaper (which includes the 'Report on Business', the business section of the paper), the *Canadian Periodical Index*, which indexes the major periodicals in Canada, the Key Government Documents database,

and various databases containing financial statements, annual reports and other financial information.

- *InfoMart Online* (164 Merton Street, Toronto, Ontario M4S 3A8. Tel: 416-489-6640)
  Contains information from *The Ottawa Citizen, The Financial Times* of Canada, *The Montreal Gazette, The Toronto Star, Southam News, The Windsor Star, The Vancouver Sun, Les Affairs,* and the Canadian Press Newswire. Also has US databases for national and regional papers and Dow Jones News. Dow Jones has, in turn, information from *Dow Jones News,* the *Wall Street Journal, Japan Economic Daily* and other sources.

- *FP Online – The Financial Post Information Service* (777 Bay Street, Toronto, Ontario M5W 1A7. Tel: 416-596-2525)
  Includes the full text of the *Financial Post,* including special reports, the 'Financial Post 500', the 'Investor's Guide' and 'Report on the Nation'. *The Financial Post* is a leading business newspaper published daily in Toronto.

- *Insight – Canada Systems Group* (955 Green Valley Crescent, Ottawa, Ontario K2C 3V4. Tel: 613-727-5445)
  Includes information on the names of companies that are incorporated provincially and federally, and financial information on federally incorporated companies. Other databases include intercorporate ownership, trade marks listings, personal and corporate bankruptcies, and an on-line edition of the *Canadian Trade Index* which provides data such as products, companies, addresses, trade marks and executives.

A3.4 Periodicals Indexes

- *Canadian Business Index* formerly *Canadian Business Periodicals Index* (monthly) (Micromedia, 158 Pearl St, Toronto, Ontario M5H 1L3. Tel: 416-593-5211)
  Provides access to over 140 Canadian periodicals and newspapers in business, industry, economics, administrative studies and related fields. Arranged in three sections: (1) subject, (2) personal names, and (3) corporate names. This index can be searched by computer, but is also available in published format.

  ■ In the subject index entries may be found under business subject terms as well as political events or geographical units.

■ The personal name section cites the authors of books and periodical articles and names of chief executives, directors of corporations, trade unions and associations mentioned in the periodical articles. A concise description (i.e. speech, biography, interview, author, obituary) is found under each name (or sometimes the title of the article) followed by the journal citation.

■ The corporate name section includes names of Canadian corporations, trade unions, associations, federal and provincial government. Issued monthly with annual cumulations.

● *Canadian Advertising Rates and Data (CARD)* (monthly) (Maclean Hunter, Toronto)
Identifies Canadian periodicals which may be reviewed for their content regarding specific business information.

A3.5 Statistics

● *Statistics Canada* (Statistics Canada, Central Enquiries Lobby, R. H. Coats Building, Ottawa, Ontario M4T 0T6. Tel: 613-990-8116)
Statistical information on business and industry in Canada, e.g. number of employees, wages, raw materials, and production. Obtain the *Statistics Canada Catalogue*, which identifies publications produced by this government agency. The following is a selected list:

Bibliography of Federal Data Sources, excluding *Statistics Canada*
CANSIM Summary Reference Index
Census of Manufactures
Guide to Federal Government Labour Statistics
Historical Catalogue of Statistics Canada Publications, 1918–1980
Index of Municipal Data
Listing of Supplementary Data
Statistics Canada Daily
The Standard Industrial Classification

● *CANSIM*
A data bank for Statistics Canada, the statistical agency of the Canadian government. Referenced on-line, and manuals are available to describe content. Information available from the address noted above. Available through computer utilities such as I. P. Sharp, referenced previously.

Contains much of the Statistics Canada data that appear in their publications.

- *Market Research Handbook* (annual) (Statistics Canada, Ottawa)
  A compilation of marketing information from various Statistics Canada sources with emphasis on provincial and sub-provincial data. Includes: general economic indicators; government revenue; population characteristics; personal income and expenditure; housing and household facilities; merchandising and services data; some breakdowns by metropolitan area.

- *Canadian Statistical Review* (monthly) (Statistics Canada, Ottawa)
  Summarizes Canadian economic indicators and statistics. Includes seasonally adjusted major indicators and feature articles on general economic conditions and special subjects.

A3.6   Financial Information

- Canadian Financial Information Library (CAN/FIL)
  A microfiche service providing information on 2,000 Canadian corporations. Information includes all relevant documents, reports and correspondence filed with cooperating provincial security commissions and Canadian Stock Exchanges.

- Consumer and Corporate Affairs (Corporations Branch, Ottawa, Ontario K1A 0C9. Tel: 819-997-1142)
  Provides information on all federally chartered companies filing with Consumer and Corporate Affairs.

- Ministry of Consumer and Commercial Relations (Companies Branch, Records Section, 900 Bay Street, second floor, Room M2-49, MacDonald Block, Toronto, Ontario. Tel: 416-963-0510)
  Provides information on all companies provincially chartered in Ontario and filing with Consumer and Commercial Relations.

- Insider Corporate Information Service (Micromedia Ltd, 158 Pearl Street, Toronto, Ontario M5H 1L3. Tel: 416-593-5211)
  This service provides, on microfiche, copies of such corporate documents as annual reports, financial statements, proxy statements, and new releases which are filed by every public company registered with the Ontario Securities Commission. This includes over 800 companies listed

on the Toronto Stock Exchange and approximately 500 unlisted but publicly traded companies. In addition, Insider contains current annual reports of 4,000 public and private Canadian companies required to file annual financial statements with the federal government. Included are those corporations whose gross assets exceed $5 million or whose total annual revenue exceeds $10 million. The reports can be accessed directly as the companies are filed alphabetically or by using the *Canadian Business Index* – Corporate Index.

A3.7   Industry-specific Information

● *Financial Post Survey of Industrials* (annual) (Financial Post, MacLean Hunter, Toronto)
Surveys give information on federally incorporated companies; details of operations, management, financial data, and subsidiaries.

● *Financial Post Survey of Mines & Energy Resources* (annual) (Financial Post, Toronto)
This annual survey presents a comprehensive review of the mining and energy industries in Canada. Companies covered are operating in the areas of petroleum, natural gas, uranium, coal and hydro-electric power. The survey offers information on the business activities, corporate structure, subsidiaries, financial data, capital stock, long-term debt, management and corporate ownership of over 2,300 public corporations. This survey replaces the *Financial Post Surveys of Oils, Mines and Energy Resources,* and should be used with the *Financial Post Survey of Industrials.*

● *Directory of Restaurant and Fast Food Chains in Canada* (Monday Report on Retailers, Toronto)
An alphabetical listing of chain restaurants and fast food outlets in Canada. Provides information on management, finances, and merchandise. An index by location is provided at the back.

● *Directory of Retail Chains in Canada* (Monday Report on Retailers, Toronto)
An alphabetical listing of Canada's retail chains. Includes important data about their management teams, physical plant, financial status and merchandising.

- *Canadian Directory of Shopping Centres* (Monday Report on Retailers, Toronto)
  This three volume set is divided into (a) West, (b) East, (c) supplement. For each shopping centre, detailed information is provided on the rent, percent gross, stores, space available and leasing manager and a list of tenants is also provided.

- *National List of Advertisers* (annual) (MacLean Hunter, Toronto)
  Provides information on the national advertisers in Canadian media including their products, agency,d approximate budget appropriation and media used. Includes a direct mail directory.

Press Clipping Services

The following is a selection of prominent clipping services:

- Bowdens Information Services, Toronto

- Canadian Press Clipping Service, Toronto

- Clip, Inc., Montreal

- Mediascan Canada, Inc., Ottawa

A3.8 Financial Ratios

- *Key Business Ratios in Canada* (annual) (Dun and Bradstreet Canada, Toronto)
  Alphabetically lists key business ratios for Canadian industries. Includes gross margin, current assets to current debt, collection period, etc.

- *Corporation Financial Statistics* (annual) (Statistics Canada, 1965–1977, Ottawa)
  Contains aggregate balance sheet, income and expense, profit and retained earnings information for corporations classified by 182 industries. Since 1969, the previous year's revised data (as well as current year's financial items) are included along with the 15 commonly used key ratios.

A3.9 Sources of Information about Japanese Companies

Refer to sources of Japanese information in Appendix 5. The following are additional potential sources of company-specific information which Canadian firms may obtain:

- Canadian Embassy (3-38 Akasaka 7-chome, Minato-Ku, Tokyo 107, Japan. Tel: (03) 408-2101. Telex: DOMCAN J22218)

- Government of Alberta (17th Floor – New Aoyama Building West 1-1, 1-chome, Minamiaoyama, Minato-ku, Tokyo 107, Japan. Tel: (03) 475-1171. Telex: J28543)

- Government of Ontario (Suite 1219, World Trade Centre Building, 4-1 Hamamatsu-cho 2-chome, Minato-ku, Tokyo 107, Japan. Tel: (03) 436-4355. Telex: J27145)

- Government of Quebec (Suite 501, Sanno Grand Building, 14-2, Nagata-cho 2-chome, Chiyoda-ku, Tokyo 100, Japan. Tel: (03) 581-4618)

- Canadian Chamber of Commerce in Japan (Central PO Box 2089, Tokyo, Japan. Tel: (03) 585-9441)

- The Canada–Japan Trade Council (Canada–Japan Trade Council, 75 Albert St., Suite 903, Ottawa, Ont. K1P 5E7. Tel: (613) 233-4047) Distributes economic information about Japan to Canadian businesses in a monthly newsletter, occasional reports and seminars. Annual membership is $45.00.

- Japanese External Trade Organization (JETRO) (151 Bloor St. W., Suite 700, Toronto, Ontario. Tel: (416) 962-5050) Provides information on Japanese companies, handles trade inquiries and offers a trade consultation service for evaluating the marketability of Canadian goods in Japan. It acts as a trade ombudsman in cases of non-commercial disputes. Has an extensive reference library of over 100 Japanese business magazines and directories in English.

- JETRO (Edmonton Office, Room 812, Royal Bank Building, 10117 Jasper Avenue, Edmonton, Alberta T5J 1W8. Tel: (403) 428-0866)

- JETRO (Vancouver Office, Room 916, Standard Building, 510 West

Hastings Street, Vancouver, British Columbia V6B 1L8. Tel: (604) 684-4174)

- The Canada–Japan Business Co-operation Committee (Canada–Japan Business Co-operation Committee, c/o Aluminum Co. of Canada, 1188 Sherbrooke St. W., Montreal, P. Q. H3A 3G2. Tel: (514) 877-2340) Consists of senior executives from Canadian companies with major trade dealings with Japan. Each year it arranges the Canada–Japan Businessmen's Conference. Membership is by invitation only to companies with current or potential business dealings with Japan. The committee also plays a major role in selecting members of the MITI-funded executive study tour of Japan.

- The Federation of Canadian Manufacturers in Japan (Canadian Manufacturers' Association, Export Forum, 14th Floor, One Yonge Street, Toronto, Ontario M5E 1J9. Tel: (416) 363-7261. Telex: 365-24693)
  Maintains a Tokyo office to help Canadian companies penetrate the Japanese market by acting as a branch of their export department. Charter memberships cost $10,000 for 100 hours of assistance.

A3.10   Selected Firms with Financial Analysts on Bay Street, by Industry

The following is a list of selected firms with prominent financial analysts on Bay Street, Toronto's financial district:

Industry	Firm	Industry	Firm
Breweries & distilleries	Deacon Morgan Merrill Lynch Nesbitt Thomson		Merrill Lynch
		Economics	Burns Fry Merrill Lynch Wood Gundy
Communications & media	Brown, Baldwin, Nisker Capital Group McLeod Young Weir	Financial services	Alfred Bunting Burns Fry Nesbitt Thomson
Consumer products	Deacon Morgan Loewen Ondaatje	Golds	Alfred Bunting

Industry	Firm	Industry	Firm
	Burns Fry	Pipelines	Burns Fry
	Wood Gundy		Nesbitt Thomson
High technology	Dominion		Richardson
	Securities		Greenshields
	McLeod Young	Portfolio	Dominion
	Weir	strategy	Securities
	Richardson		Nesbitt Thomson
	Greenshields		Wood Gundy
Industrial	Loewen	Quantitative	Dominion
products	Ondaatje	analysis	Securities
	McLeod Young		Wood Gundy
	Weir		
	Richardson	Real estate &	Brown, Baldwin
	Greenshields	construction	Nisker
Integrated oils	Alfred Bunting		Merrill Lynch
	First Marathon		Wood Gundy
	Nesbitt Thomson	Special situations	Deacon Morgan
Management	Dominion		Merrill Lynch
companies	Securities		Nesbitt Thomson
	McLeod Young	Steels	McLean
	Weir		McCarthy
	Nesbitt Thomson		McLeod Young
Merchandising	Loewen		Weir
	Ondaatje		Richardson
	McLeod Young		Greenshields
	Weir	Technical	Dominion
	Nesbitt Thomson	research	Securities
Metals &	First Marathon		Gordon Capital
minerals	Merrill Lynch		Merrill Lynch
	McLeod Young	Transportation	McLeod Young
	Weir		Weir
Oil & gas	Alfred Bunting		Richardson
producers	First Marathon		Greenshields
	Nesbitt Thomson		Wood Gundy
Paper & forest	Deacon Morgan	Utilities	Burns Fry
products	McNeil Mantha		Nesbitt Thomson
	Pemberton		Richardson
			Greenshields

Appendix 4   Data Sources: United Kingdom

- General Sources

- Reference Books

- Off-the-shelf Studies

- Databases

- Industry Data

- Trade Associations

- Government Sources

A4.1   General Sources

The following is a list of general and background sources of business information. More detailed sources of published company information may be found in the next section.

- *Sources of UK Marketing Information* (Wills and Tupper, 2nd edition, Ernest Benn, London, 1975)

- *Principal Sources of Marketing Information* (Hull, C., The Financial Times Information and Marketing Intelligence Unit, London, 1976)

- *Statistics Europe: Sources for Social, Economic and Market Research* (4th edition, CBD Research Ltd., Beckenham, 1981)

- *Published Data on European Industrial Markets* (Industrial Aids Ltd, London, 1983)

- *The Marketing Year Book* (annual) (Institute of Marketing, Cookham)

- *The Market Research Society Yearbook* (annual) (Market Research Society, London)

- *International Directory of Published Market Research Organizations* (6th edition, Market Research Society, British Overseas Trade Board, 1982)

Directories and Indexes

The following directories and indexes are among the more frequently used background publications. Other references are listed in the section that follows.

- *Kompass Products and Services* (Vol. 1) and *Company Information* (Vol. 2)

- *Who Owns Whom* (annual) (Dun and Bradstreet, London)

- *Europe's 5000 Largest Companies* (Dun and Bradstreet, London)

- *Extel Handbook of Market Leaders* (semi-annually) (Extel Statistical Services, London)

- *The Hambro Company Guide* (semi-annually) (Extel Statistical Services, London)

- *Jane's Major Companies of Europe* (Jane's Yearbook, London)

A4.2   Reference Books

The following general and industry-specific reference books may be useful, depending upon what it is you are investigating. Many provide additional sources of information to be investigated further.

Many of the following books are published annually – make sure you obtain the most recent offering. (A word of caution: investigate the prices of these books before buying!)

One of the better sources of company information is:

- *European Companies: A Guide to Sources of Information* (CBD Research Limited, Beckenham, Kent, England)

Others include:

- *A−Z of UK Marketing Information Sources and UK Retailing*

- *European Directory of Marketing Information Sources*

- *European Directory of Non-Official Statistical Sources*

- *International Directory of Marketing Information Sources*

- *Sources of Free Business Information*

The following is a selected listing of business reference information that could yield insight into specific industries and companies:

- *Advertisers' Annual*

- *African Economic Handbook*

- *Arab Business Yearbook*

- *Asia's 8500 Largest Companies*

- *Asian Economic Handbook*

- *Bankers' Almanac and Yearbook*

- *Bibliography of British Business Histories*

- *Building Societies Association: Building Societies Yearbook*

- *Business Fact Finder*

- *Business-Line Company Information*

- *Business-Line Finance*

- *Business-Line Management, Marketing and Administration*

- *Business Location Handbook*

- *Caribbean Economic Handbook*

- *Cassell Directory of Publishing*

- *Central American Economic Handbook*

- *China Economic Handbook*

- *China Investment Guide*

- *CICI Directory of UK Information Services and Products*

- *Crawford's Corporate Finance*

- *Crawford's Directory of City Connections*

- *Crawford's Investment Research Index*

- *Databook of Exhibitions, Trade Fairs and Conference Centres – UK and Europe*

- *Datastream Company Handbook*

- *Datastream Japanese Company Accounts Handbook*

- *Denmark's 10,000 Largest Companies*

- *Directory of Directors*

- *Directory of European Retailers*

- *Directory of Management Consultants in the UK*

- *Directory of Unit Trust Management*

- *Dod's Parliamentary Companion*

- *Dun & Bradstreet Billion Dollar Directory: America's Corporate Families*

- *Dun & Bradstreet Million Dollar Directory: Vols 1–4*

- *Dun & Bradstreet Million Dollar Directory: Vol 5 (Top 50,000)*

- *East European Economic Handbook*

- *Economist Business Traveller's Guides: Arabian Peninsula*

- *Economist Business Traveller's Guides: Britain*

- *Economist Business Traveller's Guides: Japan*

- *Economist Business Traveller's Guides: United States*

- *Economist: The World in Figures*

- *Euromarket Directory*

- *European Drinks Marketing Directory*

- *European Marketing Data and Statistics*

- *Europe's 15,000 Largest Companies*

- *Facts on File Directory of Major Public Corporations*

- *Financial Times Industrial Companies: v.1: Electronics*

- *Financial Times Industrial Companies: v.2: Chemicals*

- *Financial Times Industrial Companies: v.3: Engineering*

- *Financial Times Investor's Companion to Top 100 Companies*

- *Financial Times Mining*

- *Financial Times Oil and Gas*

- *Financial Times Who's Who in World Oil and Gas*

- *Financial Times World Hotel Directory*

- *Financial Times World Insurance*

- *Gulf Directory*

- *Gulf Directory of Trade and Finance*

- *Hambro's Corporate Officers Guide*

- *I.C.A.E.W. List of Members and Firms*

- *Industrial Performance Analysis*

- *Innovator's Handbook*

- *Insurance Directory and Yearbook (3 vols)*

- *International Corporate 1000*

- *International Marketing Data and Statistics*

- *International Organizations: a Dictionary and Directory*

- *International Stock Exchange Official Yearbook*

- *International Yearbook and Statesman's Who's Who*

- *Investment Bond Yearbook*

- *Investment Trust Yearbook*

- *Japan Marketing Handbook*

- *Jordan's Top 2000: Britain's Privately Owned Companies*

- *Jordan's 2nd 2000: Britain's Privately Owned Companies*

- *Kelly's Business Directory*

- *Kelly's Post Office London Business Directory*

- *Key British Enterprises: Britain's Top 20,000*

- *Kompass Central London*

- *Kompass UK Volumes 1–4*

- *Laby's Primary Commodity Markets and Models – an International Bibliography*

- *London International Financial Futures Yearbook*

- *Longman Directory of Local Authorities*

- *McCarthy Information – Globally Traded Securities*

- *McCarthy Information – UK Company Almanac*

- *Macmillan Directory of Financial Futures Exchanges*

- *Macmillan International Directory of Business Information Sources*

- *Macmillan Investment Trust Yearbook and Who's Who*

- *Macmillan 10,000 unquoted Companies*

- *Macmillan Top 100,000 Company Ratings*

- *Major Chemical and Petrochemical Companies of Europe*

- *Major Companies of Europe (3 vols)*

- *Major Companies of the Arab World*

- *Major Companies of the Far East (2 vols)*

- *Major Companies of the USA*

- *Major Energy Companies of Western Europe*

- *Major Financial Institutions of Continental Europe*

- *Major Transportation Companies of the Arab World*

- *Merrill Lynch Euromoney Directory*

- *Middle East Economic Handbook*

- *Municipal Yearbook (2 vols)*

- *Norway's 8000 Largest Companies*

- *Pacific Basin Economic Handbook*

- *Personnel Yearbook*

- *Public Relations Yearbook*

- *Retail Directory*

- *Ronay Cellnet Guide Hotels and Restaurants*

- *Scandinavia's 5000 Largest Companies*

- *Solicitors and Barristers Directory & Diary: volume 1 – Diary*

- *Solicitors and Barristers Directory & Diary: volume 2 – Directory*

- *Sources of Unofficial UK Statistics*

- *South American Economic Handbook*

- *Springboard – Directory of Women's Businesses and Organisations in the London Area*

- *Statesman's Yearbook*

- *Statesman's Yearbook World Gazetteer*

- *Stock Exchange Official Yearbook*

- *Sunday Telegraph Business Finance Directory*

- *Sweden's 6000 Largest Companies*

- *Telerate Trader's Directory of Foreign Exchange, Futures and Options Dealers*

- *Times 1000*

- *UK Franchise Directory*

- *UK Hotel Groups Directory*

- *UK's 10,000 Largest Companies*

- *UK Trade Names*

- *Unit Trust Yearbook*

- *USSR Economic Handbook*

- *West European Economic Handbook*

- *Whittaker's Almanac*

- *Who Owns Whom – Australasia & Far East*

- *Who Owns Whom – Continental Europe (2 vols)*

- *Who Owns Whom – North America*

- *Who Owns Whom – UK and Republic of Ireland (2 vols)*

- *Who's Who*

- *Who's Who in Accountancy*

- *Who's Who in Corporate Finance*

- *Who's Who in The City*

- *Who's Who in Venture Capital*

- *Willing's Press Guide*

- *Woodhead Faulkner City Directory*

- *World's Largest Industrial Enterprises 1962–1983*

Publications such as these may be obtained from major booksellers in the UK or from the publishers. The following is a list of firms publishing many of the above books:

- Dun and Bradstreet (26–32 Clifton Street, London EC2P 4LY. Tel: 01-377-4377)

- The Financial Times (Bracken House, 10 Cannon Street, London EC4P 4BY. Tel: 01-248-8000)

- Jordan and Sons Ltd (Jordan House, Brunswick Place, London N1E 6EE. Tel: 01-253-3030)

- Kelly's Directories Ltd (Windsor Court, East Grinstead House, East Grinstead, West Sussex RH19 1XB. Tel: 342-26772)

- Kompass Publishers Ltd (Windsor Court, East Grinstead House, East Grinstead, West Sussex RH19 1XB. Tel: 342-26772)

They may also be obtained by mail order from:

- Parks (244 High Holborn, London WC1V 7DZ)
  Write for their catalog.

A4.3   Off-the-shelf Studies

Four of the largest publishers of off-the-shelf studies are:

- Frost and Sullivan (104–112 Marylebone Lane, London W1M 5FU)

- Jordan and Sons (Jordan House, Brunswick Place, London N1E 6EE)

- Larsen Sweeney Publications Ltd (PO Box 70415, 1007 KK, Amsterdam)

- Predicasts (199 High St., Orpington, Kent BR6 0PF)

These companies can be contacted directly to establish the studies they have available, or assignments may be referenced through catalogs or indexes such as:

- *Marketing Surveys Index* (Marketing Strategies for Industry, 22 Wates Way, Mitcham, Surrey CR4 4HR)

- *Market Research Reports and Industry Surveys* (Science Reference Library, 25 Southampton Buildings, London WC2A 1AW)

- *FINDEX* (Find/SVP – UK, 12 Argyll St, London W1V 1AB)

- *International Directory of Published Market Research* (British Overseas Trade Board, 1 Victoria St, London SE1H 0ET)
  (If you wish to buy a copy, write to the BOTB directly, or write to or visit the offices of Arlington Management, the joint publishers, at 87 Jermyn St, London SW1Y 6JD.)

Research Reports Available from Companies

Unlike many other countries, companies in the UK often publish their views of their market position in detailed market reports. Contact the public or investor relations departments of the firms you are investigating to establish if they do indeed have these reports available to the public.

Research Reports Available from Stockbrokers

Many major stockbrokers provide research reports to their clients and prospective clients. For a detailed listing, reference:

- *Stockbrokers' Research and Information Services Available to Non-investor Clients* (The Oxford Centre for Management Studies)

A4.4   Databases

The following is a selection of the major vendors of on-line databases in the UK and Europe. Contact them directly for their catalogs and to learn of the many databases they carry on their systems.

- ADP Comtrend Ltd (204 Great Portland Street, London W1N 5HA)

- AGB Information Systems (16A Great Peter Street, London SW1P 2BX)

- Agdex (Edinburgh School of Agriculture, Kings Building, West Maines Road, Edinburgh EH9 3JG)

- AP/Dow Jones News Services (The Associated Press (AP/DJ), Associated Press House, 12 Norwich Street, 3rd floor, N Block, London EC4A 1BP

- Belindis, CTI-CIV (rue de Mot 30, B-1040 Brussels, Belgium)

- BIS Infomat (Information House, Cholsey, Wallingford, Oxfordshire OX10 9NA)

- Blackwell Technical Services Ltd (Beaver House, Hythe Bridge Street, Oxford OX1 2ET)

- British Telecom Enterprises (BT Centre, 98 Newgate Street, London EC1A 7AJ)

- BRS Europe (Suite 2, 73–75 Mortimer Street, London W1N 7TB)

- CMS (Cereal House, 58 Mark Lane, London EC3R 7N3)

- CNRS Pascal/Francis (Division Marketing, 26 rue Boyer, 75971 Paris – Cedex 20, France)

- Computercall Ltd (Garrett House, 24 Windmill Road, Brentford, Middlesex TW8 0QA)

- Credit Ratings Ltd (51 City Road, London EC1Y 1AY)

- DAFSA (125 Rue Montmartre, 75081 Paris – Cedex 02, France)

- DataArkiv AB (PO Box 12079, 102 22 Stockholm, Sweden)

- I/S Datacentralenaf 1959 (Retortvej 6–8, DK-2500 Valby, Denmark)

- Data Logic Ltd (Horsecroft Road, Harlow, Essex CM19 5BH)

- Datasolve Ltd (99 Staines Road West, Sunbury on Thames, Middlesex TW16 7AH)

- Data-Star (D-S Marketing Ltd, Plaza Suite, 114 Jermyn St, London SW1Y 6HJ)

- Datastream International (Monmouth House, 58–64 City Road, London EC1Y 2AL)

- Derwent Publications (Rochdale House, 128 Theobalds Rd, London WC1X 8RP)

- Dialog Information Services (PO Box 8, Abingdon, Oxford OX13 6EG)

- DIMDI (Weisshausstrasse 27, PO Box 420580, 5000 Cologne 41, West Germany)

- DRI Europe Ltd (30 Old Queen Street, St. James's Park, London SW1H 9HP)

- Dun and Bradstreet (26–32 Clifton Street, London EC2P 4LY)

- Elsevier IRCS Ltd (St. Leonard's House, St. Leonardgate, Lancaster LA1 1PF)

- Euris (Square de Meeus 5, B-1040 Brussels, Belgium)

- European Patent Office (Erhardstrasse 27, 8000 Munich 2, West Germany)

- Eurostat – Dissemination (Batiment Jean Monnet B3/86, Luxembourg, Grand Duchy of Luxembourg)

- Extel Statistical Services (37–45 Paul Street, London EC2A 4PB)

- Financial Times Business Information Ltd (Bracken House, 10 Cannon Street, London EC4P 4BY)

- Finsbury Data Services Ltd (68–74 Carter Lane, London EC4V 5EA)

- Fis-Elf (ZADI, Villichgasse 17, D-5300 Bonn 2, West Germany)

- FIZ-Karlsruhe (D-7514 Eggenstein-Leopoldshafen 12, West Germany)

- FIZ-Technik (Postfach 600547, Ostbahnforstrasse 13, D-6000 Frankfurt 60, West Germany)

- Fraser Williams (Scientific Systems) Ltd (London House, London Road South, Poynton, Cheshire SK12 1YP)

- G.CAM Serveur (Tour Maine-Montparnasse, 33 Avenue de Maine, 75755 Paris – Cedex 15, France)

- Geosystems (PO Box 1024, Westminster, London SW1)

- GSI (boulevard de L'Amiral Bruix, 75116 Paris, France)

- Harwell (UKAEA) (B329 Harwell Laboratory, Oxfordshire OX11 0RA)

- ICC Information Group Ltd (ICC House, 81 City Road, London EC1Y 1BD)

- Jordan's Information Services (Jordan and Sons Ltd, Jordan House, Brunswick Place, London N1E 6EE)

- Learned Information (Besselsleigh Road, Abingdon, Oxford OX13 6LG)

- LLR/Shipping Information Services (4 Lloyd's Avenue, London EC3N 3ED)

- NMW Computers plc (Stapeley House, London Road, Nantwich, Cheshire)

- Norsk Senter for Informatikk A/S (PO Box 350, Blindern, N-0314 0LS0, Norway)

- Pergamon Info-line Ltd (12 Vandy St., London EC2A 2DE)

- SECODIP (2 rue Francis Pedron, 78241 Chambourcy, France)

- I.P. Sharp Associates (132 Buckingham Palace Road, London SW1W 9SA)

- Sinfoni SA (129 rue Servient, Tour du Credit Lyonnais, 69431 Lyons – Cedex 3, France)

- SLIGOS (91 rue Jean-Jaures, 92807 Puteaux – Cedex, France)

- Tele Consulte SA (44 rue du Four, 75006 Paris, France)

- Telefax Data Systems Ltd. (c/o GAFTA, Baltic Exchange Chambers, 24/28 St. Mary Axe, London EC3A 8EP)

- Telekurs AG (11 Neue Hard, CH-8005 Zurich, Switzerland)

- Telesystems Questel (83–85 boulevard Vincent Auriol, 75013 Paris, France)

- Tullet & Tokyo Forex International (Futrent Ltd, Ormond House, 63 Queen Victoria Street, London EC4N 4ST)

- UAPT Infolink (Coombe Cross, 2–4 Southend, South Croyden, Surrey CR0 1DL)

- Unicorn News (72–78 Fleet Street, London EC4Y 1HY)

A4.5　Industry Data

The following is a brief selection of sources of industry information. Other sources appear in the section entitled Reference Books.

- *Industrial Performance Analysis* (7th edition, Intercompany Comparisons Ltd, 1982)

- *The A–Z of UK Market Data* (Euromonitor Publications Ltd, London)

- *MGN Marketing Manual of the UK* (annual) (Mirror Group Newspapers, London)

- *European Marketing Data and Statistics* (annual) (Euromonitor Publications Ltd, London)

A4.6　Trade Associations

Two publications provide considerable data on trade associations in the

UK and enable the researcher to target specific individuals for information requests:

- *The Directory of British Associations*

- *Trade Associations and Professional Bodies of the UK*

These publications are available from major bookstores in the UK or by mail order from:

- Parks (244 High Holborn, London WC1V 7DZ)
  Write for their catalog.

The following is a selection of trade associations and their addresses, selected to reflect the diversity of industries covered.

- Advertising Association, Abford House, 15 Wilton Road, London SW1V 1NJ

- Aluminium Foil Container Manufacturers' Association, Barclay House, Chapel Ash, Wolverhampton WV3 0TZ

- Association of the British Pharmaceutical Industry, 12 Whitehall, London SW1A 2DY

- Association of Glass Container Manufacturers, 19 Portland Place, London W1N 4BH

- Association of Manufacturers of Domestic Electric Appliances, 593 Hitchin Road, Stopsley, Luton LU2 7UN

- Association of Sanitary Protection Manufacturers, c/o Sterling Public Relations Ltd, 1 Lowther Gardens, Prince Consort Road, SW7 2AA

- Boiler and Radiator Manufacturers' Association, Fleming House, Renfrew Street, Glasgow G3 6TG

- The Brewers' Society, 42 Portman Square, London W1H 0BB

- British Aerosol Manufacturers' Association, Alembic House, 93 Albert Embankment, London SE1 7TU

- British Agricultural and Garden Machinery Association Ltd., Church Street, Rickmansworth, Hertfordshire WD3 1RQ

- British Agrochemicals Association, Alembic House, 93 Albert Embankment, London SE1 7TU

- British Baby Products Association, 60 Claremont Road, Surbiton, Surrey KT6 4RH

- British Battery Makers' Society, 15 Tooks Court, Cursitor Street, London EC4A 1LA

- British Brush Manufacturers' Association, 6A East Street, Epsom, Surrey KT17 1HH

- British Carpet Manufacturers' Association, Royalty House, 72 Dean Street, London W1V 5HB

- British Ceramic Manufacturers' Federation, Federation House, Stoke-on-Trent ST4 2SA

- British Disposable Products Association, 3 Plough Place, Fetter Lane, London EC4A 1AL

- British Footwear Manufacturers' Federation, Royalty House, 72 Dean Street, London W1V 5HB

- British Hardware and Housewares Manufacturers' Association, 35 Billing Road, Northampton NN1 5DD

- British Manmade Fibres Federation, 24 Buckingham Gate, London SW1E 6LB

- British Paper and Board Industry Federation, 3 Plough Place, Fetter Lane, London EC4A 1AL

- British Phonographic Industry, Roxburghe House, 273–287 Regent Street, London W1R 8BN

- British Photographic Association, 7–15 Lansdowne Road, Croydon CR9 2PL

- British Printing Industries Federation, 11 Bedford Row, London WC1R 4DX

- The British Radio & Electronic Equipment Manufacturers' Association, Landseer House, 19 Charing Cross Road, London WC2H 0ES

- British Toy & Hobby Manufacturers' Association, 80 Camberwell Road, London SE5 0EG

- Building Services Research and Information Association, Old Bracknell Lane West, Bracknell, Berkshire RG12 4AH

- Business Equipment Trade Association, 8 Southampton Place, London WC1A 2EF

- Cake and Biscuit Alliance Ltd. and Cocoa, Chocolate and Confectionery Alliance, 11 Green Street, London W1Y 3RS

- Catering Equipment Manufacturers' Association, 14 Pall Mall, London SW1Y 5LZ

- Coated Abrasives Manufacturers' Association, 102 Gloucester Road, Hampton on Thames, Middlesex TW12 2UJ

- Cosmetic, Toiletry and Perfumery Association Ltd., 35 Dover Street, London W1X 3RA

- Electronic Components Industry Federation, 7–8 Saville Row, London W1X 1A5

- Engineering Industries Association, 16 Dartmouth Street, London SW1

- Food and Drink Federation, 6 Catherine Street, London WC2B JSS

- Furniture Industry Research Association, Maxwell Road, Stevenage, Hertfordshire SG1 2EW

- Gin Rectifiers' and Distillers' Association and Vodka Trade Association, 37 Waterford House, 110 Kensington Park Road, London W11 2PU

- Glass Manufacturers' Federation, 19 Portland Place, London W1N 4BH

- Golf Ball Manufacturers' Conference, 7 Swallow Street, London W1R 7HD

- The Hearing Aid Industry Association, 16a The Broadway, London SW19 1RF

- High Wycombe Furniture Manufacturers' Society, Wycombe House, 9 Amersham Hill, High Wycombe, Buckinghamshire HP13 6NR

- Institute of Grocery Distribution, Letchmore Heath, Watford WD2 8DQ

- Institute of Petroleum, 61 New Cavendish Street, London W1M 8AR

- Knitting Industries Federation Ltd., 7 Gregory Boulevard, Nottingham NG7 6NB

- London and South Eastern Furniture Manufacturers' Association, 93 Great Eastern Street, London EC2

- Made-up Textiles Association Ltd., Top Floor, Park Mill, 99 Douglas Street, Dundee DD1 5AZ

- Microwave Oven Association, 16a The Broadway, London SW19 1RF

- The Motor Cycle Association of Great Britain Ltd., Starley House, Eaton Road Coventry CV1 2FH

- National Bedding Federation Ltd., 251 Brompton Road, London SW3 2EZ

- National Caravan Council Ltd., Catherine House, Victoria Road, Aldershot, Hampshire GU11 1SS

- National Council of Building Material Producers, 33 Alfred Place, London WC1E 7EN

- Paint Research Association, Waldegrave Road, Teddington TW11 8LD

- Paintmakers' Association of Great Britain Ltd., Alembic House, 93 Albert Embankment, London SE1 7TU

- Pasta Information Centre, 26 Fitzroy Square, London W1P 6BT

- Pet Food Manufacturers' Association (PFMA), 6 Catherine Street, London WC2B 5JJ

- Pianoforte Manufacturers' Association Ltd., c/o Ramsdens, 22 Beach Road, Lowestoft, Suffolk NR32 1EA

- Packaging Industry Research Association, Randalls Road, Leatherhead, Surrey KT22 7RU

- Plastic Bath Manufacturers' Association, 12th Floor, Fleming House, Renfrew Street, Glasgow G3 6TG

- Scotch Whisky Association, 17 Half Moon Street, London W1Y 7RB

- Sea Fish Industry Authority, Sea Fisheries House, 10 Young Street, Edinburgh EH2 4JQ

- Soap and Detergent Industry Association, PO Box 9, Hayes Gate House, Hayes, Middlesex UB4 0JD

- Society of British Gas Industries, 36 Holly Walk, Leamington Spa, Warwickshire CV32 4LY

- Society of Motor Manufacturers and Traders Ltd., Forbes House, Halkin Street, London SW1X 7DS

- Steel Window Association, Building Centre, 26 Store Street, London WC1E 7JR

- Tea Council, Sir John Lyon House, 5 High Timber Street, London EC4V 3NJ

- Textile Statistics Bureau, 2nd Floor, Royal Exchange, Manchester M2 7ED

- Timber Research and Development Association, Stocking Lane, Hughenden Valley, High Wycombe, Buckinghamshire HP14 4ND

- UK Petroleum Industry Association, 9 Kingsway, London WC2B 6XH

- Wallcovering Manufacturers' Association of Great Britain Ltd., Alembic House, 93 Albert Embankment, London SE1 7TU

- Wine and Spirit Association of Great Britain and Northern Ireland (Inc.), Five Kings House, Kennet Wharf Lane, Upper Thames Street, London EC4V 3BH

A4.7 Government Sources

Companies in the UK file financial and other information with the government and this can be obtained directly or through Jordan and Sons or Extel Statistical Services, listed in the database section. The government contact is:

- Companies Registration Office, Crown Way, Maindy, Cardiff, Wales CF4 3U2

or

- Companies Registration Office, 55–71 City Road, London EC1Y 1BB. Tel: 01-253-9393

A private company will also undertake relevant searches on your behalf:

- Company Searches Ltd (96 Whitchurch Road, Cardiff, Wales 49-7443)

Useful government publications include:

- *Government Statistics, A Brief Guide to Sources* (annual) (Central Statistical Office, Great George Street, London SW1P 3AQ)

- *Guide to Official Statistics* (annual) (Central Statistical Office, Great George Street, London SW1P 3AQ)

- *HMSO Books: A Guide to Publications and Services* (HMSO Publicity Department, St. Crispins, Duke St., Norwich NR3 1PD)

- *Business Monitor* (Department of Industry, Business Statistics Office, Government Buildings, Cardiff Road, Newport, Gwent NPT 1XG)

Many government departments publish statistical and other information. Contact them directly:

- Department of Employment (employment, earnings and expenditures statistics)

- Department of the Environment (housing statistics)

- Department of Trade and Industry (weekly information on retail sales, industry statistics and economic indicators)

- Department of Transport

- HM Customs and Excise (information on commodity categories being imported and exported – special computer runs will be conducted for a modest fee)

- HM Treasury (economic information)

- Ministry of Agriculture, Fisheries and Food (various statistics related to production and consumption of food products)

- Monopolies and Mergers Commission (useful company information can be obtained from reports examining anti-trust implications in specific industries)

- Economic Development Committees (examinations of specific industries)

- Office of Population Censuses and Surveys (census and population trends)

Information Services

- Statistics and Market Intelligence Library, Export House, 50 Ludgate Hill, London

- British Overseas Trade Board's Export Market Research Office, Export House, 50 Ludgate Hill, London

Appendix 5 Data Sources: Japan

- Periodical Publications

- Trade Associations

- Financial Analysts' Reports

- Government Information Sources

- Other Sources of Information

- Databases

A5.1 Periodical Publications

A listing of periodicals published in Japan is available from:

- Keizai Koho Centre, Otemachi Building, 1-6-1 Otemachi, Chiyoda-ku, Tokyo 100
  Ask for *The Japan Periodicals Guide*

The following is a selection of prominent newspapers and periodicals:

- *Asahi Evening News* (daily) (Asahi Shimbun, Tsukiji, Chuo-ku, Tokyo 104)

- *Asian Business* (monthly) (Far East Trade Press Ltd, Lockhart Centre, 15th floor, 301 Lockhart Road, Hong Kong)

- *Business Japan* (monthly) (Nihon Kogyo Shimbun, Sankei Building, 1-7-2 Otemachi, Chiyoda-ku, Tokyo 100)

- *Economic Eye* (quarterly) (Japan Institute for Social and Economic Affairs, Keizai Koho Centre, 1-6-1 Otemachi, Chiyoda-ku, Tokyo 100)

- *Focus Japan* (monthly) (Available from JETRO offices (addresses in next section))

- *Japan Echo* (quarterly) (TBR Building, 2-10-2 Nagatcho, Chiyoda-ku, Tokyo 100)

- *The Japan Economic Journal* (weekly) (Nihon Keizai Shimbun, 9-5 Otemachi, 1-chome, Chiyoda-ku, Tokyo 100)

or

The Japan Economic Journal (Nihon Keizai Shimbun, c/o OCS America Inc., Box 1654, Long Island, NY 11101. Attention: JEJ Subscription Dept.)

- *Japan Report* (monthly) (Japan Economic Institute of America, 1000 Connecticut Ave NW, Washington DC 20036)

- *The Japan Times* (daily) (4-5-4 Shibaura, Minato-ku, Tokyo 108)

- *Japan Economic Institute of America Reports* (JEI Reports – weekly) (1000 Connecticut Ave NW, Washington DC 20036)

- *Look Japan* (monthly) (2-2 chome, Kanda Ogawa-machi, Chiyoda-ku, Tokyo 100)

- *Oriental Economist* (monthly) (Toyo Keizai Shinposha Ltd, 1-4 Nihonbashi Hongokucho, Chuo-ku, Tokyo 103)

Other useful publications include:

- 'High-Tech Start-Up Ventures in Japan', *Japan Economic Journal* (9-5 Otemachi 1-chome, Chiyoda-ku, Tokyo 100)

- *Japan Company Handbook* (annual) (Toyo Keizai Shinposha Ltd, 1-4 Nihonbashi Hongokucho, Chuo-ku, Tokyo 103)

- *Kompass* (a European publication with 3 volumes for Japan) (Kompass Publishers Ltd, Windsor Court, East Grinstead House, East Grinstead, West Sussex RH19 1XB. Tel: 342-26772)

- *Moody's International Manual* (Moody's Investor Services, 99 Church St., New York NY 10007. Tel: 212-553-0300)

A5.2 Trade Associations

To identify the trade associations in your industry, reference publications available from one of the following sources:

- Ministry of International Trade and Industry (MITI) (3-1 Kasumigaseki 1-chome, Chiyoda-ku, Tokyo 100)
  Ask for the *MITI Handbook*

- The Tokyo Chamber of Commerce and Industry (Toshio Building, 2-2 Maranouchi 3-chome, Chiyoda-ku, Tokyo)
  Ask for the publication: *Economic and Industrial Organizations in Japan.*

- Your local JETRO office. In New York, this is located at the following address:

  ■ Japan External Trade Organization (JETRO), McGraw Hill Building, 44th floor, 1221 Avenue of the Americas, New York NY 10020. Tel: 212-997-0400

In Canada, there are JETRO offices in Toronto, Vancouver and Edmonton. The address in Toronto is:

  ■ Japan External Trade Organization (JETRO), 151 Bloor St. West, Suite 700, Toronto, Ontario. Tel: 416-962-5050

The head office of JETRO is at:

  ■ JETRO, 2-5 Toranomon 2-chome, Minato-ku, Tokyo 107

Trade Shows

For a listing of trade shows, contact:

- The Japan Convention Bureau, Japan National Tourist Organization, Tokyo Kotsu Kaikan Building, 10-1, Yurakucho 2-chome, Chiyoda-ku, Tokyo 100

or your local JETRO office. Addresses are noted above.

A5.3   Financial Analysts' Reports

For information on major, publicly traded Japanese firms, contact your company's stockbrokers or banks. Firms such as the following have offices in Tokyo:

- Becker Paribas Inc. (7-1 Yurakucho 1-chome, Chiyoda-ku, Tokyo 100)

- Brown Brothers Harriman (8-14 Nihonbashi 3-chome, Chuo-ku, Tokyo 103)

- Drexel Burnham Lambert (3-2-3 Maranouchi 3-chome, Chiyoda-ku, Tokyo 100)

- First Boston (S. Suite 201, Yurakucho Denki Building, 7-1 Yurakucho 1-chome, Chiyoda-ku, Tokyo 100)

- Goldman Sachs (Kasumigaseki Building, 2-1 Kasumigaseki 3-chome, Chiyoda-ku, Tokyo 100)

- Kidder Peabody (1-3 Maranouchi 1-chome, Chiyoda-ku, Tokyo 100)

- Merrill Lynch (Toranomon Mitsui Building, 8-1 Kasumigaseki 3-chome, Chiyoda-ku, Tokyo 100)

- Morgan Stanley (907 Kokusai Building, 1-1 Maranouchi 3-chome, Chiyoda-ku, Tokyo 100)

- Paine Webber (AIU Building, 1-3 Maranouchi 1-chome, Chiyoda-ku, Tokyo 100)

- Salomon Brothers (2-2 Uchsaiwai-cho 2-chome, Chiyoda-ku, Tokyo 100)

- Smith Barney, Harris Upham (Yurakucho Building, 11th floor, 1-10-1 Yurakucho 1-chome, Chiyoda-ku, Tokyo 100)

A5.4   Government Information Sources

Two sources are of particular value:

- The Prime Minister's Office (6-1 Nagato-cho 1-chome, Chiyoda-ku, Tokyo 100)

and

- The Ministry of International Trade and Industry (MITI) (3-1 Kasumigaseki 1-chome, Chiyoda-ku, Tokyo 100)

Publications available from The Prime Minister's Office include:

- *Family Income and Expenditures Survey* (annual)

- *Japan Statistical Yearbook*

- *Monthly Statistics*

- *Statistical Yearbook of Japan*

Publications available from The Ministry of International Trade and Industry (MITI) include:

- *Industrial Statistics* (monthly)

- *Statistics of Japanese Industries*

- *The MITI Organization Directory* (Names, addresses and telephone numbers of senior employees)

Establish what MITI publications are available from the department that covers your industry or areas of interest. The following are the main departments ('bureaus' or 'agencies') of MITI:

- Basic Industries

- Consumer Goods Industries

- Industrial Location and Environmental Protection

- Industrial Policy

- Industrial Science and Technology (Laboratories and Research Institutes in various industry sectors)

- International Trade Administration

- International Trade and Policy

- Machinery and Information Industries

- Natural Resources and Energy

- Patent Office

- Secretariat (Statistics)

- Small and Medium Enterprises

The central government publishing office in Japan has reports of industry statistics:

- Government Publications Service Centre, 1-2 Kasumigaseki 1-chome, Chiyoda-ku, Tokyo 100

The Japanese Ministry of Finance provides reports filed by publicly owned firms and by subsidiaries of large firms – details on sources of supply, manufacturing costs, production data, sales, earnings. Contact:

- The Ministry of Finance, Data and Statistics Office, Minister's Secretariat, 3-1 Kasumigaseki 1-chome, Chiyoda-ku, Tokyo 100

A5.5 Other Sources of Information

The following is a selection of sources that could provide you with additional industry or company information:

- American Electronics Association

    This organization opened an office in Tokyo to monitor technological and political developments. Contact: American Electronics Association,

Kioi-cho Nanbu Building, 3rd floor, 3-3 Kioi-cho, Chiyoda-ku, Tokyo 100.

- American Chamber of Commerce

  Their office in Japan keeps members informed about how to do business in Japan and relevant developments in the field. Contact: The American Chamber of Commerce, Fukide Building No. 2, 7th floor, 1-21 Toranomon 4-chome, Minato-ku, Tokyo 105.

- The US International Trade Administration

  For a listing of their published market research reports on foreign markets, contact: Office of Trade Information Services, US Department of Commerce, PO Box 14207, Washington, DC 20044. Tel: 202-377-2432.

- Japanese investment brokerage firms, such as Daiwa and Nomura.

  These provide some company and industry reports. Reports are usually not as detailed as ones provided by US brokerage companies. Contact: Daiwa Securities Research Institute, 1-2-1 Kyobashi, Chuo-ku, Tokyo 103. Nomura Securities, 9-1 Nihonbashi 1-chome, Chuo-ku, Tokyo 103.

- Japanese Banks

  Japanese banks are a major source of capital in Japan. They also hold large stock positions in many firms and are good sources of reliable information. Those not belonging to the Japanese establishment cannot usually obtain this information. For a listing of Japanese banks, contact: The Federation of Bankers Associations of Japan, 3-1 Maranouchi 1-chome, Chiyoda-ku, Tokyo 100. Ask for their publication: 'Banking System in Japan'.

- The Mitsubishi Group

  Publishes financially oriented company and industry reports. Contact: Mitsubishi International Corporation, 520 Madison Ave, New York NY 10022. Tel: 212-605-2050.

  Other trading companies are also sources of valuable information. Contact your local representatives of firms such as: C. Itoh, Marubeni, Mitsui and Sumitomo.

A5.6   Databases

In addition to Japanese company information that may be available on databases marketed by firms such as Dialog, BRS, Mead Data Central, Pergamon and others (addresses in Appendices 2 and 4), the following are companies which market Japanese databases in Japan to which you could have access. Contact them directly for more information.

- Daiwa Securities Research Institute, 1-2-1 Kyobashi, Chuo-ku, Tokyo 103

- Informatic Research Inc., Yaesu-Nagaoka Building, 8-4, Shinkawa-2, Chuo-ku, Tokyo 104

- Information Services International – Dentsu Ltd, 12-6, Tsukiji 1-chome, Chuo-ku, Tokyo 104

- The Institute of Energy Economics, 1-18-1 Toranomon, Minato-ku, Tokyo 105

- Keidanren (The Federation of Economic Organizations), 1-9-4 Otemachi, Chiyoda-ku, Tokyo 100

- Japan Computer Technology Co. Ltd, 4-3 Kanda-Surugadai, Chiyoda-ku, Tokyo 101

- The Japan Information Centre of Science and Technology, 5-2 Nagatacho 2-chome, Chiyoda-ku, Tokyo 100

- The Japan Patent Information Organization, Bansui Building, 1-5-16 Toranomon, Minato-ku, Tokyo 105

- National Diet Library, Somu-bu Denshi Keisan-ka Division, 10-1 Nagato-cho 1-chome, Chiyoda-ku, Tokyo 100

- National Institute for Educational Research, 5-22 Shimomeguro 6-chome, Meguro-ku, Tokyo

- The Nikkan Kogyo Shimbun, 8-10 Kudankita 1-chome, Chiyoda-ku, Tokyo 107

- Nippon Shuppan Hanbai Inc., 4-3 Kanda-Surugadai, Chiyoda-ku, Tokyo 101

- Nippon Telegraph and Telephone, 1-6-6 Uchisaiwai-cho, Chiyoda-ku, Tokyo 100

- Nihon Keizai Shimbun, Databank Bureau, 9-5, Otemachi 1-chome, Chiyoda-ku, Tokyo 100

- Nomura Research Institute, Edobashi Building, 1-11-1 Nihonbashi, Chuo-ku, Tokyo 103

- Science and Engineering Information Centre, 6F Cent-for Building, 12-16, Shinjuku 2-chome, Shinjuku-ku, Tokyo 160

- SDC of Japan Ltd, Nishi-Shinjuku 1-chome, Shinjuku-ku, Tokyo 160

- Tokyo Shoko Research, Shin'ichi Building, No. 9-6, Shimbashi-1, Minato-ku, Tokyo 105

Index